Character and Consequence

Character and Consequence

*Foreign Policy Decisions
of George H. W. Bush*

Robert A. Strong

LEXINGTON BOOKS
Lanham • Boulder • New York • London

Published by Lexington Books
An imprint of The Rowman & Littlefield Publishing Group, Inc.
4501 Forbes Boulevard, Suite 200, Lanham, Maryland 20706
www.rowman.com

6 Tinworth Street, London SE11 5AL

British Library Cataloguing in Publication Information Available

Library of Congress Cataloging-in-Publication Data Available

ISBN 978-1-4985-8935-2 (cloth)
ISBN 978-1-4985-8937-6 (pbk)
ISBN 978-1-4985-8936-9 (electronic)

Contents

Acknowledgements   vii

Introduction: Character Counts   1

1 Loyalty: The John Tower Confirmation Battle   7

2 Reticence: Deciding What to Say, and What Not to Say, At
       the End of the Cold War   27

3 A Gentleman's Outrage: The Tipping Point in the Decision
       to Invade Panama   49

4 Insight: German Unification Anchored in the NATO
       Alliance   69

5 Audacity: Doubling Down on Desert Shield   99

6 Compassion: The American Military Intervention in
       Somalia   123

Conclusion: Character and Consequence   143

Bibliography   149

Index   155

About the Author   163

Acknowledgements

The painting on the cover of this book is titled "Resolution" and currently hangs in the lobby of the George H. W. Bush Museum in College Station, Texas. The artist, Mark Balma, has generously granted permission for its use in the cover design.

A version of chapter 1 was previously published. The chapter includes adapted material from "Character and Consequence: The John Tower Confirmation Battle," in *41: Inside the Presidency of George H. W. Bush*, edited by Michael Nelson and Barbara A. Perry. Copyright © 2014 by Cornell University. It is used here by permission of the publisher, Cornell University Press.

Some of the material in chapter 3 was also previously published and is here republished with permission of Taylor and Francis Group LLC Books, from *Decisions and Dilemmas: Case Studies in Presidential Foreign Policy Making Since 1945*, by Robert A. Strong, second edition, 2005; permission conveyed through Copyright Clearance Center, Inc.

I wish to thank Washington and Lee University for its support of my research and writing; the Miller Center at the University of Virginia for the opportunity to participate in their Oral History Project on George H. W. Bush; the Rothermere American Institute at Oxford University; the knowledgeable, and ever helpful, staff in the Archives of the George H. W. Bush Presidential Library; and University College Dublin where, as a Fulbright Scholar, I worked on this project.

Many colleagues, friends and former students assisted me in the course of writing this book and I hope they know how much I appreciated their responses, suggestions and criticisms. Special thanks are due to my daughter Emily Strong who was a careful reader, a professional editor and a thoughtful reviewer of the manuscript in the final stages of its development.

Introduction

Character Counts

For many years I have participated in the presidential oral history interviews carried out by the Miller Center at the University of Virginia. In
these interviews, Miller Center staff and invited scholars meet with former administration officials for candid conversation about the people
and issues that were important during their public service. Transcripts of
the interviews are confidential until they are reviewed and released by
the subject of the interview. Reading the resulting documents and participating in the interviews often adds a context and texture to the other
sources—newspaper accounts, policymaker memoirs, scholarly books
and presidential library documents—that are typically used to tell the
stories of recent presidencies. This book emerged from the oral history
conversations. In the chapters that follow I review selected foreign policy
events in the presidency of George Herbert Walker Bush. I chose the
chapter topics because there was compelling evidence from the recollections of those who worked closely with President Bush or because there
was something about a particular decision that is not yet fully understood.

As the title of this book makes clear, I also paid attention to the ways
in which presidential character may help to explain some of the foreign
policy decisions and actions of the Bush administration. In the Miller
Center interviews, and in other interviews conducted for this project,
people who worked closely with George H. W. Bush often remarked on
his decency, his modesty, his sense of humor and his genuine interest in
the lives of those who worked for him. They saw how those qualities
shaped and shaded what he did in the White House. Comments like the
ones I heard are not unique to this president or to his administration.
Everyone knows that character matters. Harry Truman was decisive,
Franklin Roosevelt cagey. Jack Kennedy was witty, Lyndon Johnson
earthy. Jimmy Carter's Christian faith could make him seem self-right-
eous; Richard Nixon's insecurities led him to acts of self-destruction.
George Washington, we tell our children, never told a lie. Donald Trump
lies more often than anyone who has ever held the highest office in the
land.

No account of the presidency, or of particular presidents, is complete
without some discussion of the character traits of the central decision-

maker in the American political system. Character counts. In 1972, an influential scholar of the presidency, James David Barber, argued that careful consideration of a president's, or a candidate's, character, world-view and political style would allow scholars and citizens to classify presidents and candidates into broad categories. Those categories were fairly simple. Barber asked two questions: are presidents, or those seeking the office, active or passive in their dispositions toward political work, and positive or negative in their outlooks on the world. Those two dimensions, set into a matrix, produced four categories and the argument that the "active-positive" individuals were most likely to enjoy White House success. Barber believed that the careful examination of biographical information about sitting and prospective presidents, and the systematic classification of their backgrounds, could create a useful tool for the analysis of presidential behavior.[1] At the time of Richard Nixon's landslide reelection victory over George McGovern, Barber saw trouble ahead in Nixon's second term, believing that his character flaws would turn out to be more important to his legacy than his landslide electoral success. That prediction, and the reality that character assessments are important to voters, made Barber a frequently consulted expert during election cycles and at the routine intervals—inauguration, first 100 days, first year, mid-term elections—when evaluations of presidential performance are commonly done.

In a sympathetic and perceptive review of Barber's scholarship, Michael Nelson notes that there was real value in urging voters, and the journalists who serve their needs, to pay close attention to presidential and candidate character. But there was also widespread criticism of Barber and his four broad character types.[2] Some critics considered the categories superficial and insufficiently grounded in rigorous psychological research. Others observed that even if it were worthwhile for voters to learn about the character of White House aspirants, systemic barriers can block the acquisition of this valuable knowledge. How could citizens evaluate character if candidates constantly followed the scripts written for them by political consultants and public relations strategists? There was apparently a "new" Nixon in 1968. Where was the old one? And which Nixon was the one voters needed to know.

Problems with the evaluation of presidential character include more than campaign adviser manipulation. Partisans routinely attack each other for alleged sins of various kinds and make character assaults part of the mud slung in hotly contested elections. George H. W. Bush participated in a particularly superficial and nasty presidential campaign in 1988 in which the crimes of a furloughed Massachusetts prisoner, Willie Horton, were presented to voters as evidence of the flaws and failures of Governor Michael Dukakis.[3] In actuality, the governor had very little to do with prison furlough legislation or administration. But the claims that he was excessively liberal on criminal justice issues and indifferent to the victims of crime gained traction because they were repeated in advertisements that were emotional and racist. In the final analysis, the Willie Horton ads may tell us less about Dukakis' responses to crime, and more about George Bush's ambition and willingness to do whatever it takes to win an election. Aggressive advertising that attacks an opponent is common in presidential politics and makes sober and fair-minded candidate character assessment harder to achieve. Moreover, while there are many observations that could be made about the behavior of candidates, media commentary tends to overemphasize two kinds of stories: the ones involving sex, and the ones involving lies.[4] If a story, like the impeachment of Bill Clinton, involves both sex and lies, it is very likely to receive disproportionate attention. As James Pfiffner has observed in *The Character Factor*, there is a tendency in modern American politics to take a fairly narrow view of what constitutes meaningful evidence of presidential character.[5] And a highly partisan political culture makes the collection and evaluation of that evidence problematic.

Even when we have reliable information about a candidate's character, there is a further complication. Character needs to be evaluated in context. Veracity is laudable, but do we want presidents who always tell the complete and unvarnished truth? As Pfiffner points out, it may not have been wise for Franklin Roosevelt to give a full and fair account of how dire the national economic crisis was in 1933. It may have been better for him to offer reassurance and to say that "the only thing we have to fear is fear itself."[6] Should we admire and appreciate Ronald Reagan's optimism, even if it was sometimes based on superficial information and oversimplified analysis? In the opening chapter of this book, we will consider the role of loyalty in presidential nominations. While we can all applaud loyalty to friends and associates, particularly when those friends and associates are under attack, loyalty has its limits. Sometimes the actions of others are so egregious that unqualified support is no longer justified. The lines demarcating too much, and too little, loyalty can be hard to draw and whether high levels of loyalty constitute a virtue or a vice can be the subject of vigorous debate. The same can be said for many other character traits. George H. W. Bush was widely praised as a prudent president and politician. But he was also criticized for his prudence. Too much caution, particularly at a time of radical change and dramatic opportunity, can be a defect. When President Bush was slow to respond to the international initiatives of Mikhail Gorbachev early in his administration, commentators worried that the president was giving prudence a bad name.[7]

Making the obvious observation that presidential character counts does not answer complicated questions about which character traits are most important to a successful president or which set of circumstances may, from time to time, make virtue a vice or vice versa. Each of the chapters in this book ends with brief remarks about the ways in which a character trait or disposition on the part of George H. W. Bush may have played a role in deliberations and decisions. These are reflections not causal arguments. In this project, I make no attempt to follow James David Barber or to develop a new theory about how character contributes to foreign policy outcomes and presidential behavior. My purpose is far more modest. After reviewing the events that resulted in a speech, or an appointment, or a confrontation with Congress or an intervention abroad, I ask whether or not the president's character played some role in the foreign policy story just concluded. And if so, what that role may have been. In some cases, the evidence in support of the conclusion that character had consequence is robust; in others it is contested or incomplete. In either case, the question of what difference character may have made is worth asking.

In this project I have chosen to focus attention on the personal qualities of George H. W. Bush that were most significant to the people who worked for him. They think that you can't understand the first Bush administration unless you understand how Bush worked with the people close to him and with the large collection of friends he had made in the course of his diplomatic and political careers. They argue that his loyalty to others was solid and unshakable, to good and ill effect. They observe that his reticence to brag and boast helped him to navigate the complexities at the end of the Cold War, at the same time that it made it harder for him to earn the public appreciation he deserved. They point out that he was sentimental, polite, compassionate and old-fashioned in ways that sometimes made him appear awkward and out of step with the national politics that was emerging at the end of the twentieth century. They make the commonsense observation that character counts in the analysis of any presidency, and that it may be particularly important for understanding the presidency of George H. W. Bush.

NOTES

1. James David Barber, *Presidential Character: Predicting Performance in the White House* 4th ed. (New York: Routledge, 2017).

2. Michael Nelson, "James David Barber and the Psychological Presidency," *Virginia Quarterly Review,* 56, no. 4 (Autumn, 1980).

3. Robert A. Strong, "Ending the Cold War Without Debate: Foreign Policy and the 1988 Election," in *US Presidential Elections and Foreign Policy*, Andrew Johnstone and Andrew Priest, eds. (Lexington: University Press of Kentucky, 2017), 293–316.

4. In the 1988 presidential election, news coverage about sexual conduct played an important role in the campaign. Had Senator Gary Hart, the front-runner before controversy ended his candidacy, been Bush's opponent, the campaign would have involved much more substantive debates about defense and foreign policy.

5. James Pfiffner, *The Character Factor* (College Station: Texas A&M University Press, 2004).

6. Ibid., 4.

7. William Schneider, "Will Bush Give Caution a Bad Name," *National Journal*, June 3, 1989, 1390.

ONE

Loyalty

The John Tower Confirmation Battle

In December 1988, when George H. W. Bush announced his choice for Secretary of Defense, he was making a very conventional cabinet nomination. Like many of his other early appointments, the nominee for the Pentagon was an old friend and political ally. He was a former senator from the president-elect's home state. He had served as chairman of the Senate Armed Services Committee, as the senior member of a high-profile commission investigating the Iran-Contra scandal in the Reagan White House, as an arms control negotiator in Geneva, and was an acknowledged expert on the defense budget and national security issues. As a former member of the legislative body that would vote on his nomination, John Tower seemed likely to win an easy and early confirmation. In the history of the republic, only eight cabinet-level nominees had ever been rejected on the floor of the Senate. None had suffered that fate since 1959. No newly elected president had ever lost a Senate vote on a cabinet nomination.[1]

John Tower became the ninth cabinet nominee rejected by the Senate and the first to be denied his post at the outset of a new administration. The confirmation battle that took place in the honeymoon weeks of the Bush administration was a media circus dominated by salacious stories about the nominee's private life. Although there was truth in the observations that Tower, at various points in his career, drank alcohol and faced accusations of marital infidelity, some of the news media stories about his personal conduct were false or came from unreliable sources. Senator John McCain called the Tower confirmation a "witch trial."[2] The NBC evening news anchor, Tom Brokaw, concluded that the coverage of Tower's nomination was "unconscionable," involving the frequent airing of

7

"very damaging allegations without documentation or confirmation."[3] Despite this lack of documentation and confirmation, or perhaps because of it, the newly elected president suffered a significant defeat in his dealings with the Democratic majority in the Senate and his nominee suffered a public humiliation from which he never recovered.[4]

The Tower nomination is often studied by those who are interested in the politics of scandal, the breakdown of collegiality in Congress, and how the media should report on the personal lives of public servants.[5] But students of the Bush administration have a number of other lessons to learn from the Tower confirmation battle. In many ways, it served as a prelude to the even more controversial Supreme Court confirmation conflict involving Clarence Thomas, when once again the private behavior of the nominee, and the appropriate evidence to judge that private behavior, were critical issues. On Capitol Hill, it tested the ability of the Democratic Party to stand up to a newly elected Republican president who faced large opposition majorities in both chambers.

The fight over the John Tower nomination to be Secretary of Defense is also important for clues it gives to the character of our forty-first president.

Although Tower's rejection on the Senate floor was an unusual event, it is not unheard of for a presidential nominee to encounter difficulties in the confirmation process. When such difficulties arise, most presidents cut their losses, withdraw their nomination and move on. In 1977 Jimmy Carter abandoned Ted Sorenson as his choice for Director of the CIA. Bill Clinton, serving in the term immediately after Bush, had a series of problems with his Justice Department appointments and withdrew his support from two nominees who made mistakes in the employment of nannies and household staff.

George Bush did not withdraw his nomination of John Tower. He stuck with his nominee, even after the prospects of winning on the Senate floor were dim and even after John Tower expressed interest in calling it quits. Bush did so at some expense to his political reputation at the outset of his presidency, as well as to his relations with the Democratic Senate majority. Why did the president steadfastly support a controversial nominee when there was an easy, obvious and conventional way out? The simple answer is loyalty, but the John Tower nomination and rejection is not a simple story.

THE PRESIDENT'S CHOICE

John Tower may initially have been seen as a likely nominee for George Bush's cabinet, but earlier in his career he was a most unlikely senator. The son and the grandson of Methodist ministers, Tower was an obscure college professor and a sometime polemicist for the Texas Republican

Party when he was asked to run for the Senate in 1960. Apparently no one else could be found to stand against Lyndon Johnson, then the majority leader of the Senate and the Democratic candidate for the vice presidency. Tower garnered 41 percent of the vote, a respectable showing for a 1960 Republican in Texas. He lost the Senate race to Johnson, but because Johnson became vice president, a second election was called to fill the vacant Senate seat. Lots of Democratic hopefuls entered an open primary, and fought bitterly among themselves. In a run-off election, in which Tower faced conservative Democrat William Blakley, liberal Democrats voted for Tower as the lesser evil or stayed away from the polls completely. Tower, to nearly everyone's surprise, won a narrow victory and became the first Republican senator since Reconstruction elected from a Confederate state.

When he first went to Washington, Tower behaved as if he would only have one term in the Senate, a reasonable assumption for a southern Republican who had won his seat by a narrow margin. He enjoyed his newfound fame, was celebrated by conservative audiences across the country and became an outspoken opponent of the New Frontier and later of Johnson's Great Society legislation. Tower voted against the Civil Rights Act of 1964 and the Voting Rights Act of 1965 and supported conservative Barry Goldwater for the presidency in 1964. He also began to acquire a reputation for a liquor-lubricated social life; though to be fair, such a reputation was not distinctive in that era.

After the unlikely senator won a second term in 1966 against a still divided Texas Democratic Party, he began to moderate some of his political positions and focus more of his attention on the issues that came before the Senate committees on which he served. Over the years, Tower demonstrated that his early political success was not a fluke. He won two more terms in 1972 and 1978, despite a divorce, a second marriage and a second divorce. Always a staunch anti-communist and proponent of a strong national defense, Tower moved slightly away from the conservative movement. He took a pro-choice position on abortion and in 1976 campaigned for the moderate Gerald Ford, instead of the conservative Ronald Reagan.

In his home state, Tower remained an unusual success story. Lacking the stature of Lyndon Johnson, the wealth of Lloyd Bentsen and the flare of John Connally, Tower nevertheless led the Republican Party to a position as a consistent competitor in statewide races. Throughout these years, he was an important mentor for up-and-coming Republicans, including George Bush who was elected to the House of Representatives in Houston and tried twice to win the other Texas Senate seat. In Bush's 1970 Senate race, Tower, then the chairman of the Republican Senate Campaign Committee, provided him with almost twice as much financial support as was given to any other Republican candidate.[6] When Bush got into trouble in his Houston congressional district for a vote in favor of fair-housing legislation, Tower defended him to Texas conservatives.[7] In 1980, and again in 1988, Tower supported Bush in his campaigns for the presidency.

When Reagan, with Bush as vice president, was elected in 1980, Tower lobbied to become Secretary of Defense. It was a job he had wanted for some time, but the new president told the Texas senator that his leadership would be more important as the chair of the Armed Services Committee. From 1981 to 1984 Tower was a forceful advocate of the Reagan military buildup. As a powerful committee chair and throughout his later years in the Senate, Tower was acknowledged for his intelligence and determination to move an agenda, but he made few close friends and was thought by many to be arrogant, imperious and uncompromising. His critics would later say that he had "never seen a weapons system he did not like."[8] But he was a genuine expert on Pentagon projects and, like many other such experts, was never an enthusiastic advocate of the strategic defense initiative (the so-called "Star Wars" missile defense system). After leaving the Senate in 1985, Tower worked as a defense consultant and held two major presidential appointments as head of an arms control delegation in Geneva and as the leader of the presidential commission that investigated the Iran-Contra scandal. The *Tower Report* on Iran-Contra was highly critical of President Reagan for his loose administrative style, but placed most of the blame for the failures that took place on a few National Security Council staff members. George Bush, who publicly said that he "was out of the loop" on the decisions that led to Iran-Contra, was not seriously criticized in the *Tower Report*.

Very few knowledgeable observers were surprised by President Bush's decision to name Tower to the top Pentagon position. The president's first cabinet appointment had gone to James Baker as Secretary of State. Baker was a long-time friend from Houston, an experienced member of the Reagan administration and the campaign manager of Bush's unsuccessful run for the White House in 1980 and his successful one eight years later. Some of the other senior cabinet appointments also went to people Bush had known and trusted for many years, including Nicholas Brady as Treasury Secretary, Robert Mosbacher at Commerce and Brent Scowcroft as national security advisor.[9] The president was clearly assembling a team of advisers, particularly in the area of foreign affairs, that included friends and associates he had known for a long time. John Tower fit the profile.

Tower met with the president-elect on November 19, 1988, and outlined the case for naming a Secretary of Defense, like himself, who would not need "on-the-job training." In the talking points he prepared for this meeting, Tower argued that the administration's leading critics on defense-related issues were likely to be Democratic Senators Sam Nunn, Charles Robb and Al Gore, who had all served with Tower on the Armed Services Committee that Nunn now chaired. The president needed a secretary who knew the issues and the players on Capitol Hill and not someone from industry who would have a lot to learn about Washington and could easily be captured by Pentagon bureaucrats. Tower admitted that budgets would have to be cut and outlined his hope that cuts might be accompanied by the implementation of a two-year defense budget that would allow for more coherent planning. [10] John Sununu, who participated in some of the meetings with the prospective Secretary of Defense in the fall of 1988, reports that he was highly impressed by Tower's command of defense issues and satisfied that he had workable strategies for managing the department in austere times. "Tower really was excellent on identifying the approach that could be taken to make reductions in defense spending without severely impacting the defense readiness of the country," says Sununu. "Really was very, very impressive in his understanding of how to do this. So the President really wanted John Tower as Secretary of Defense." [11]

Although the president appears to have made up his mind about the nomination in mid-November or earlier, the announcement of the Tower choice was delayed to allow time for an extensive FBI background check. Such checks were routine, but in Tower's case would obviously include investigation of the old complaints about liquor and ladies that had circulated in Washington for nearly two decades. Those complaints may have been fueled by specific accusations emanating from the bitter divorce that had ended Tower's second marriage. While the FBI did their work, newspaper stories critical of the likely nominee appeared in the *Atlanta Constitution*, the *Los Angeles Times* and the *New York Post*. The last of these appeared on November 25 and carried the headline "TOWER FACING SEX SCANDAL." The story reported claims from the divorce proceedings that Tower had had affairs with three women in the 1980s, including a maid in Geneva when he was serving as an arms control negotiator. [12] A much more serious accusation could have been made about Tower's sexual misconduct. The *Washington Post* journalist Sally Quinn was assaulted by an inebriated Tower in the back seat of a DC cab when she was a college student. She published her account of the assault many years after the nomination controversy. When she was questioned by the FBI in 1989, she declined to discuss the incident. [13]

Questions about drinking and sexual behavior were not the only ones that kept the FBI busy. There were issues about how the former senator used his campaign war chest after he decided not to run for a fifth term in 1984 and about his work as a consultant to defense contractors in the years after his Senate career. Although it was commonplace and perfectly legal for former members of Congress to sell their expertise to corporate clients after leaving office, it was almost always difficult to prove full compliance with the complicated set of regulations that governed such activity or to avoid the appearance of improper ties and conflicts of interest for anyone returning to government service. President Bush was

broadly concerned about such issues and appointed a bipartisan commission to review the laws and ethical standards governing former and future government appointees. The president declared a National Ethics
Week shortly after his inauguration. In this climate, several members of
the new administration, including Secretary of State Baker and White
House counselor C. Boyden Gray, came under scrutiny about which of
their assets constituted possible conflicts of interest and which had to be
put into blind trusts. [14]

While the FBI was investigating Tower, some of the president's closest
advisers, reportedly including Robert Teeter, Nicholas Brady, Greg Fuller
and Boyden Gray, argued against the nomination. [15] Bush was not moved
by the objections his advisers raised or by any of the evidence that the FBI
uncovered. In mid-December, the president was briefed on what became
Tower's first FBI report. That document was based on interviews with
seventy-nine individuals and noted that one anonymous source said that
Tower abused alcohol. [16] Other witnesses reported sexual misconduct by
the nominee, but the FBI investigators could not substantiate these allegations. When the nomination was made public on December 16, the president-elect was asked about the rumors that had appeared in the press
and publicly pronounced that he was satisfied with what had been
learned in the FBI investigation and speculated that it would also satisfy
"the most inquisitive members of the Senate." [17] Senate hearings were
scheduled for January, after the holiday recess and the president's inauguration.

The initial hearings went reasonably well. Tower reassured the members of the committee, as he had earlier reassured President Bush, that he
understood the economic realities of the late 1980s. The president had
promised no new taxes and inherited a large and growing budget deficit.
In that environment, there would be pressure to reduce defense spending
and Tower was prepared to consider reforms to improve the efficiency of
the department he would lead. He answered detailed questions about his
use of residual campaign funds after leaving the Senate and about his
work as a consultant to various defense contractors. He promised to re-
cuse himself from any decisions that might involve his former clients.
Senator Ted Kennedy reflected the tone of the early proceedings and
their likely outcome when he observed that "I didn't always agree with
Senator Tower, but I respected him and am looking forward to working
with him as Secretary of Defense." [18] The Massachusetts Democrat apparently expected, as many observers did, that his former colleague would
win confirmation despite the negative news stories about his personal
life. Senator Richard Shelby of Alabama was even more dismissive of the
media accounts of Tower's private behavior when he suggested in an off-
the-record comment that he would "never trust a man who didn't drink a
little and chase a little." [19] Whatever the initial expectations of Senators
Kennedy and Shelby may have been, the dynamics of the confirmation

process changed dramatically with one of the final witnesses heard by the Armed Services Committee.

TOWER'S INFERNO

Paul Weyrich was neither a close friend nor a professional associate of John Tower.[20] He was a political activist and a fundraiser with close ties to the religious right in the Republican Party. In what *Newsweek* identified as "one of the most extraordinary moments in the history of confirmation hearings," Weyrich testified on January 31, 1989, that over many years he had seen the nominee in a condition involving a "lack of sobriety" and "with women to whom he was not married."[21] The Weyrich accusations were not much more specific than that, but because they conformed to what many members of the Senate and press corps had already heard about Tower's personal behavior, they had an immediate and powerful impact. When the committee went behind closed doors to hear more from Weyrich, and another witness who gave testimony about the prevailing rumors, a number of senators were not impressed. Senator John McCain, who earlier in his career had worked for Senator Tower, was appalled to discover that Weyrich's testimony was based on one occasion when he saw Tower "coming on" to a woman who was not his wife at the Monocle, a restaurant and bar close to the cluster of Senate office buildings. "What do you mean by 'coming on?'" McCain asked. Weyrich replied that he had seen Tower and the woman in question holding hands. According to McCain, Weyrich made "an ass of himself behind closed doors."[22] Nevertheless, his testimony was damaging. The public portion was brief and included tantalizing references to inebriation and infidelity. It played well in various media outlets that were already carrying stories about Tower's personal life. Weyrich's inability to provide any convincing corroborating detail was known only to the committee members who attended the confidential closed session.

The next day Tower returned to the witness chair to deny Weyrich's allegations. When Senator Nunn asked the nominee directly if he had a drinking problem, Tower responded, "I have none, Senator. I am a man of some discipline."[23] That direct denial did not end the issue. Though Nunn publicly predicted that his committee was likely to endorse the nominee, he postponed the committee vote that had been expected to take place immediately after the hearings. The Weyrich testimony guaranteed that there would be more FBI investigation of Tower and additional delays in any formal action taken by the Armed Services Committee.

Two days after the first round of committee hearings, Congressman Larry Combest met with Senators Nunn and John Warner. Combest had been a staff assistant to Tower before he ran for Congress and wanted to reassure his Senate colleagues that there was no serious issue about his former boss. Combest wanted to convey to the senators two conclusions from his personal observations: Tower drank more in the 1970s than he did today, and even in those earlier days his drinking had not been a serious problem. Instead and inadvertently, the congressman provided the two senior members of the Armed Services Committee with a reliable eyewitness report, by someone favorable to the nominee, that confirmed the existence of a drinking problem.

Specifically, Nunn came away from the conversation with information that Tower sometimes consumed a bottle of scotch in one evening and occasionally had to be helped to bed by an aide. Combest's later and much more detailed testimony to FBI investigators was probably more balanced and nuanced than his brief conversation with Nunn and Warner. Combest told the FBI that he had seen Tower "drink to excess" on perhaps two occasions in the mid-1970s when the senator was particularly distraught about the divorce proceedings ending his first marriage.[24] Since 1978, Combest reported, Tower had apparently given up hard liquor and Combest had not seen him consume anything stronger than a glass of wine. Combest told the FBI that he considered Tower to be a first-rate statesman, but a lousy politician. He was not a "back slapper," "a chew the fat politician" or a "bullshitter." Tower was, in reality, "a shy person, whose shyness is frequently misconstrued as 'aloofness.'"[25] The scotch he drank at the end of the day in the 1970s helped him overcome his shyness and relax with friends and staff. On the question of "womanizing" Combest speculated that this was more a matter of perception than reality. The senator dressed in expensive suits and may have cultivated a reputation as a "ladies man" to boost his ego and to demonstrate that a man of modest stature could be attractive to women. Combest reported that he never saw Tower behave "inappropriately" or in an "ungentlemanly" fashion in the presence of women.[26]

Combest's testimony, like Weyrich's, had two sides, but only the side that did damage to the nominee had real consequences. After the congressman's conversation with Nunn and Warner, the two senior senators wrote a memo arguing that the accusations involving alcohol against Tower would have to be seriously examined. Tower believes that the Combest conversation, more than the Weyrich testimony, was crucial to Sam Nunn's eventual decision to oppose the nomination, although Nunn made no public indication of how he would vote for several days after meeting with the Texas congressman.[27] Throughout this period the FBI conducted additional interviews of Combest and others whose names had come forward in connection with new accusations about Tower. Public reporting on the growing controversy made it open season for anyone who wanted to discredit the former senator. Tower remembers feeling as if he were living in a Kafkaesque world in which the cycle of investigation-allegation-investigation would never end. But if the cycle continued "enough mud would be thrown on my reputation—for whatever reason, be it malice, politics, kookiness, the vindictiveness of an ex-wife—that it would be impossible to scrape it off in a month or a year or a lifetime."[28]

Some of the accusations that were reported in this period were genuinely bizarre. In one story the senator and a former Russian ballerina danced and disrobed on top of a piano at a Texas country club. When the FBI investigated this claim, they found one Russian ballerina in Texas who had attended a fundraising event for Tower. She was seventy years old and told the FBI that the story was preposterous. She had never danced on a piano with any member of Congress, with or without clothing, and furthermore, if the story involved some other Russian émigré she was confident that she would have heard about it. It wasn't true.[29] All the same, the story was broadcast on the NBC evening news. Another accusation about a drunk driving incident involved a car that Tower had never owned. Yet another concerning sexual harassment in his Senate office came in a telephone tip from an individual who had no discernable connection to Tower. That accusation could not be corroborated by anyone with actual knowledge of the senator's staff. On February 7, a White House lawyer working on the Tower confirmation briefed the Republican Senate caucus about the failure of the FBI to find any credible evidence about either the new or old accusations. This was a preliminary report and did not reflect all of the investigations that were still underway. The final FBI report would not be completed until February 20. The fact that the Republicans received this information before it was officially delivered to the Armed Services Committee did not please Senator Nunn. He postponed the committee's official vote on the nomination until after the February congressional recess. This left more time for rumors to fly.

And fly they did. Throughout the deliberations on the Tower nomination, information from the FBI investigations was leaked to multiple media organizations. According to John McCain, "The shortest trip in Washington was the distance traveled by details from the FBI reports in committee files—no matter how salacious, absurd, or provably false—to the front pages of the nation's newspapers."[30] This was unusual in confirmation cases, since FBI files were usually treated by all who officially saw them with some sensitivity. They were often raw documents including transcripts of meetings with unreliable witnesses that included no analysis of the witnesses' veracity. If the FBI talked to someone, a summary of the conversation became part of the file. Some of those transcripts became the basis for newspaper and television stories.

It is, of course, nearly impossible to prove that a particular person was responsible for leaking FBI material to a particular news organization. Tower notes that Nunn's senior staff assistant on the Armed Services Committee, who may not have been treated well when Tower chaired the committee, was allowed to see the FBI material, something that had not happened in the past. Tower expresses his suspicions that Nunn or his staff were directly responsible for news stories based on FBI interviews.[31] As interest grew in the confirmation controversy, it is also possible that individuals who were making allegations about incidents in Tower's past to the FBI and to other government officials were also passing the same information to journalists. Several people report that Tower's second wife was the source for a number of the early press accounts of his private behavior. However they got there, the allegations made good copy and the Kafkaesque cycle that Tower feared filled the month of February.

As senators were returning from the February recess, a second FBI report was delivered to the White House and to the Armed Services Committee. The president and his staff found the report reassuring since it contained no concrete evidence that any of the various accusations about alcohol abuse or sexual misconduct were true. The report also cleared the senator of direct involvement in an ongoing investigation of contractor problems in Pentagon procurement. Despite the White House optimism about the new report, Senator Nunn and the Democrats on the Armed Services Committee read it in a different way. Although there was no convincing confirmation of recent alcohol abuse, there were plenty of allegations. "There is no smoking gun," said Senator Tim Worth, a Democrat from Colorado, "but the ground, it seems to me, is littered with a substantial number of empty cartridges."[32] In public statements by Nunn and some other Democratic members of the committee, concern was expressed about the particularly sensitive role of the Secretary of Defense in the military chain of command and the possibility that Tower's judgment might be impaired by alcohol at a time of crisis. Other Democratic senators, who did not share Nunn's concerns about alcohol or may not have wanted to publicly criticize Tower's private life, couched their reservations in comments that harkened back to old issues involving conflicts of interest and questions about Tower's behavior as a consultant.

In a straight party-line vote of 11 to 9, the Armed Services Committee recommended against the Tower nomination on February 23. Three days later the nominee appeared on a popular Sunday morning news program and pledged not to drink any form of alcohol while serving as Secretary of Defense. The "pledge," as it became known, did not help the senator's prospects for confirmation. It may actually have made matters worse, since the promise not to consume alcohol in the future suggested that the concerns about Tower's drinking in the past had some validity. Even if the pledge did some good, it was too little and too late to stem the tide of opposition to the nomination that had been growing throughout the month of February. Senator Nunn, a moderate Democrat respected for his defense expertise, was now leading the campaign to defeat the nomination and the administration had to consider whether it was wise to confront a powerful committee chair by forcing a floor vote and a likely defeat. Throughout the month of February, President Bush rejected all suggestions to withdraw the nomination, including one from the beleaguered nominee himself, and continued to privately and publicly praise John Tower.

A few Democrats, including southerners Howell Heflin and Lloyd Bentsen, broke with their party and announced that they would support the nomination. Christopher Dodd, a liberal Democrat from Connecticut, remembered that Tower was one of only five members of the Senate to support his father in a 1967 censure vote. The younger Dodd announced that he would vote for Tower's nomination. No other Democrats broke ranks.

A few days before the scheduled floor vote, the *Washington Post* ran the most damaging news story that had yet appeared concerning Tower's conduct. Bob Woodward's front-page story described incidents that allegedly occurred in the mid-1970s when Tower, as a member of the Armed Services Committee, made two visits to an Air Force base in Austin, Texas. According to a witness, retired sergeant Bob Jackson, the senator was visibly drunk during his inspection tours and fondled both a female employee and a woman among the enlisted personnel on the base. One of Woodward's sources for the story was clearly the FBI file that many senators were reviewing in preparation for the upcoming vote.[33] That night an abbreviated version of Jackson's story was included on the CBS evening news.

By the next day, the story had been largely discredited. Senator McCain, rushing to the defense of his former boss, discovered that the witness in Woodward's account had retired early from the Air Force as a result of psychological problems. According to McCain's sources, Jackson suffered from "mixed personality disorder with antisocial and hysterical features."[34] Moreover and more importantly, Jackson had not even been stationed at the Air Force base near Austin when Tower made his one, and only, official visit in 1975.[35] Air Force officers who were present when the senator toured the base uniformly reported that Tower's behavior had been professional and without incident. The *Washington Post* printed a second front-page story on March 3 with all the evidence that McCain had used on the Senate floor to undermine the original account. Years later, in a footnote in one of his books, Woodward expressed regret for publishing the Jackson story.[36]

Whatever regrets Bob Woodward may have had came far too late to help John Tower. When the Senate floor debate ended, only three Democrats—Heflin, Bentsen and Dodd—voted to support the Republican nominee. One Republican, Nancy Kassebaum of Kansas, voted with the Democratic majority. The final tally was 47 to 53, with Republicans supporting the nomination by 44–1 and Democrats opposing it by 3–52. The president had been dealt a historic defeat; John Tower's reputation had been destroyed; and new standards had been set for the evaluation of the private conduct of public officials. Those new standards were clearly higher than they had been in the past, but they were also vague about what evidence could be used to assess the behavior in question. The nation would struggle with those standards in the years ahead, up to and including the impeachment proceedings against President Clinton.

LOYALTY

George Bush quickly named Dick Cheney, another long-time friend and associate with experience in Congress, to the post of Secretary of Defense. This time the nomination was overwhelmingly approved in a matter of days. Cheney became an integral part of the administration's tightly-knit national security team and a successful Secretary of Defense during the first Gulf War. The president was no doubt pleased with Cheney's selection and performance, but he never expressed any regret about his first nominee. The president remained loyal to John Tower at every stage of the long-drawn-out confirmation ordeal and in every public comment he made about Tower for the remainder of his administration.[37]

In a diary entry on February 9, 1989, Bush recorded his frustration with the controversy that had arisen concerning his original choice for Secretary of Defense. "It's so damn ugly," he wrote. "Rumor after rumor, insinuation after insinuation, investigation after reinvestigation. And it's damned unfair."[38] Just before the Armed Services Committee vote, the president wrote a letter to a friend, Charles Bartlett, expressing his determination to stick with his nominee and complaining, "I have never seen such a campaign of innuendo, vicious rumor and gossip in my entire life."[39] On the same day the president wrote to Bartlett, he wrote in his diary: "No one has ever questioned his [Tower's] ability to run the department and his knowledge of defense matters, but he has been tested by fire and he's earned my support. And he damn sure has got it."[40] It was evidently difficult for President Bush to comment on what was happening to John Tower without using the word "damn."

The next day the president left Washington to attend the funeral of Emperor Hirohito. The news of the negative vote in the Armed Services Committee dominated his press conference in Japan and when the presidential party went on to visit Beijing, Bush spent time late at night in China calling Democratic senators back in Washington and asking them to support Tower. The president made no progress, but he refused to "knuckle down to the idea that allegations and rumors should bring down a man whose qualifications are unchallenged."[41]

On at least three occasions, John Tower considered withdrawing his name from nomination. On February 7, in a late-night conversation with Boyden Gray, he reportedly offered to withdraw.[42] Near the end of the month, after Bush returned from Asia, Tower talked to Gray again about the slim prospects for success on the Senate floor and this time made his offer to withdraw directly to the president. Bush rejected the offer without giving it serious consideration and reportedly said, "To Hell with it. Let's fight this one out."[43] Between those two conversations, Tower made another offer to drop out of the nomination process to his former staffer Fred McClure who was then working as the director of legislative affairs for the new administration. McClure reports an emotional encounter with his former boss in the Jefferson Hotel at the height of the media attacks that followed the committee hearings. Alone in the hotel room, Tower "turned to me and he said, Fred, and he had tears in his eyes, I've decided I'm going to call the President this afternoon and ask him to withdraw my name as Secretary of Defense because it's taking too much of a toll on him. It's going to affect his ability to be the leader that I'm confident that he can become and is, and I don't need to be this kind of distraction, and I'm tired of this."[44] McClure convinced Tower not to back out and to continue the fight.

And, of course, the president fought with him. President Bush spent the whole day, from 8:30 am to 6:00 pm, on February 28 talking to senators about the Tower nomination.[45] Whether he called long distance from China or talked to them in Washington, the opposition could not be moved. Democrats had, for the most part, decided to support their chairman of the Armed Services Committee, and the Democratic majority leader, George Mitchell, helped to produce a party-line vote. According to some observers, toward the end of these legislative deliberations the Tower nomination was no longer merely about the nominee. As the issue moved to the Senate floor, it became a test of partisan strength with "at least a whiff . . . of resentment over what the recent campaign had done to the character of Governor Dukakis."[46] The Democrats held their ground with just as much tenacity and determination as the president. In the end, party discipline carried more weight than the president's personal pleas on behalf of his friend from Texas.

The story of the John Tower nomination involves a complicated set of personal and partisan motives among a variety of people. In some cases, it is difficult to fully explain the behavior of principal participants. For example, it is not clear why Paul Weyrich chose to testify against the nominee with accusations about Tower's personal behavior that he could not corroborate behind closed doors. Weyrich was critical of Tower for his position on abortion and other social issues, but there were other members of the Republican Party with similar views and Weyrich had to go out of his way to get on the witness list and push the committee to public discussion of alcohol and infidelity. Exactly why he chose to do that remains unclear. There are also problems explaining the motivations of Sam Nunn. The senator from Georgia had a well-earned reputation as a moderate and studious member of the Senate. On this issue, he became the leader of a highly partisan and controversial vote against a former colleague on the Armed Services Committee. There are some reports that suggest that Nunn agonized about what to do with the mixed information his committee received about Tower's personal behavior.[47] In his public statements, Nunn said that he was worried about a Secretary of Defense who had a problem with alcohol, even if that problem was most acute in the past. The nation should not take chances with an important cabinet post. Was that the whole story? Were there incidents in Nunn's earlier committee service under Tower's chairmanship that created animosities or rivalries that came to full fruition in the nomination process? Did Nunn want the new president to appoint a less experienced Secretary of Defense so that his committee could exercise more influence over the important defense budget issues that lay ahead?[48] Questions about Nunn's decisions and actions remain. However important they may be, they are probably less important than the questions about why George H. W. Bush made the Tower nomination in the first place and why he stuck with it.

Why did President Bush insist on the selection of an individual for a sensitive senior cabinet post when the early publicity about the prospective nomination made it perfectly clear that there was likely to be some unpleasant airing of the nominee's personal behavior? Why did Bush ignore the advice of aides and counselors who warned him about the potential for controversy? And why did he continue to fully support his troubled nominee, even after Tower was ready to throw in the towel and the head counts in the Senate made it clear that the nomination was lost?

The best answer to all of these questions is the simplest one—loyalty. John Tower was George Bush's friend and political mentor and the president never gave any public or private indication that he would consider abandoning his first choice for Secretary of Defense. Gregg Fuller, a senior adviser to Bush when he was vice president, tried to convince the president not to make the Tower nomination and quickly saw the futility in his position. According to a reporter who interviewed him, "Fuller knew loyalty was a core value for Bush, and there was no budging him."[49]

There were costs associated with that loyalty and not just the obvious ones involved in the loss of an important congressional vote at the outset of the administration. The efforts of the president to make the elevation of government ethics a theme early in his administration were overwhelmed by the Tower controversy. So were many other things. The president's first major trip abroad, which included an important meeting with François Mitterrand at the Hirohito funeral and sensitive negotiations with the Japanese about the joint development of a new fighter aircraft, were hardly reported in the aftermath of the Armed Services Committee vote against Tower. The president's press conference in Japan was dominated by the news from Washington and questions about his controversial nominee. Later in his trip and when he returned to the

White House, the president devoted a significant amount of time and energy to the unsuccessful effort to win some Democratic support for his nominee, time and energy that might have been spent on other administration priorities. These costs must have been obvious to the president, but they never altered his decision about the nominee.

Bush entered the White House calling for better relations between the executive and legislative branches. The American people "didn't send us here to bicker," he told the assembled members of Congress at his inaugural address. "They ask us to rise above the merely partisan."[50] The deliberations about the president's nominee rarely rose above the partisan and were accompanied by a souring of the political atmosphere on Capitol Hill. There were many contributing factors: investigations of the Speaker of the House, Jim Wright; publicity about suspicious overdrafts allowed by a congressional credit union; and scandals involving meetings between prominent senators and a notorious savings and loan executive. In the late 1980s, a variety of ethical issues would do considerable damage to the reputations of both individual legislators and Congress as a whole. Neither the president nor the members of Congress wanted this result and even though the Tower controversy was only a small part of this larger deterioration in congressional collegiality and public esteem for legislators, it was a small part that mattered. A timely withdrawal of the Tower nomination after it was clearly in trouble would have meant one less instance of sustained national publicity damaging a public figure and the political profession.

Such a quick withdrawal would arguably have been the wise course of action for a new administration seeking better relations with Capitol Hill and would certainly have been better for Tower's personal reputation, which suffered more with each passing day in February and early March. But as the president kept insisting to anyone and everyone who urged withdrawal, that result would not have been fair. Whatever Tower's personal problems may have been, many of the published accounts of his behavior were not true and were printed and broadcast without adequate checking of facts. Reporters were no doubt able to verify that what they were reporting about Tower came from the confidential FBI file, but they could not verify whether the material in that file deserved public dissemination. Much of it did not. Tower says that the staff of the Armed Services Committee sorted accusations against the nominee into separate categories depending on the reliability of the source and the likelihood that the accusation might be substantive. One category was referred to as the X file. It contained accusations that were so bizarre and unsubstantiated that they did not deserve further investigation. Bob Woodward's damaging front-page story about alleged episodes of sexual harassment at a Texas air base, published just before the Senate vote, came from that file.[51] The treatment of John Tower was unfair. And the president of the United States did not like it and did not want to see it succeed.

Although Bush wanted to establish high ethical standards for his administration, he also understood that a cumbersome clearance and confirmation process could get in the way of finding and appointing high-quality nominees. Throughout recent administrations the confirmation process has been getting longer, increasingly intrusive, and more highly politicized. Nominees for positions that require Senate confirmation are asked to answer extensive questions about every stage of their careers and personal lives. Those who have previously served in government have to resubmit the same information for each new appointment and reopen the investigation of any questions that may have been raised in previous confirmations. Today, almost all cabinet officers, one leading scholar notes, feel that they are "innocent until nominated."[52] Once subjected to the kind of FBI investigation that has become common in the review of senior appointees, anyone would have to worry about what such a file might contain or what the readers of that file might do with the information collected. These problems would have emerged even without the Tower controversy, but his nomination clearly raised the bar on acceptable personal behavior and lowered it on what evidence could be publicly discussed regarding that behavior. There were clearly issues of fairness and even larger issues about how to structure a humane review process for prospective public servants that could have justified the president's continued support for his nominee.

Moreover, a case can be made that it was politically wise for the president to stick with his first choice apart from any considerations of personal loyalty or procedural fairness. John Sununu was convinced that staying the course would not "hurt George Bush one iota."[53] On the other hand, withdrawing a nomination quickly, on the basis of charges that were not verified by the FBI, would have been taken as a sign of weakness for a president who faced large opposition majorities in both houses of Congress. Forcing a difficult vote arguably hurt Democrats almost as much as it hurt the president. Among the senators voting against Tower there were a few whose private lives could not have withstood the kind of scrutiny Tower received. Forcing those senators to cast an unpleasant—and perhaps hypocritical—vote had to have some costs within the Democratic caucus. On the Republican side, there was genuine appreciation of the way the president stood his ground and stuck with the former Republican senator who had chaired an important committee. Some members of the party outside Congress—Paul Weyrich, Phyllis Schlafly, Pat Robertson, Kenneth Adelman and SDI advocate General Daniel Graham—openly opposed the nomination, but in the Senate, there was solid Republican support for the president's nominee. Even Nancy Kassebaum would have voted for the nomination if her vote had been decisive.[54] John McCain took particular pride in fighting this losing battle and would not have been happy with the withdrawal of a nominee he genuinely admired. This was an issue where the Republican minority in the Senate was united.

There is very little evidence to suggest that President Bush made his decision to force a Senate vote on the basis of either a principled defense of legitimate standards in the confirmation process or a political calculation that the Democrats might suffer for their action while the Republicans might benefit by standing up for one of their own. What the president recorded in his diary, what he said in lobbying for his candidate, and certainly what he said in public paints a clear and simple picture of a friend supporting a friend and of a president utterly dismissive of any advice to abandon that friend.

According to James Baker, loyalty was a "defining strength" in George Bush's character.[55] And by loyalty, Baker meant loyalty to people, not to ideas. The Tower nomination was a complicated case in which some politicians might have found their loyalties divided. If the president genuinely wanted to emphasize the highest standards for government officials in his administration, John Tower, or at least the publicity that he attracted, would not have helped his cause. If the president felt fully committed to both the idea of high ethical standards and the appointment of his friend to a cabinet post, the Tower controversy should have pulled him in opposite directions. It did not. George Bush never wavered in his support for John Tower. At one point a reportedly teary-eyed Tower told the president, "I can never thank you enough for standing at my side."[56] The president apparently gave very little consideration to doing anything else. He appears to have thought about the issue almost exclusively in terms of how it was affecting his friend. That was the loyalty that George Bush both practiced and preached.[57]

Of course, all presidents preach loyalty. They generally have in mind the faithful support they expect from those who work in the White House and in the cabinet and measure it by the absence of leaks and by a willingness to stick with the administration in controversial decisions. It goes without saying that genuine loyalty has to be reciprocal and must also involve acts of support for subordinates beyond naming them to their posts. Although that principle may go without saying, the reality is that costly acts of loyalty by senior officials on behalf of their friends and subordinates are somewhat rare. Harry Truman's decision as vice president to attend the funeral of Tom Pendergast, a notorious Missouri Democratic boss who had helped Truman in his early career and was subsequently convicted of corruption, would be one famous example. Jimmy Carter's long support for his budget director, Bert Lance, might be another. In both of those instances, the president, or future president, suffered considerable criticism and was utterly unable to bolster or rescue the reputation of his troubled associate.

Nevertheless, the test of loyalty comes in hard cases, and although it must be a two-way street, presidents obviously pay the higher price when they are called upon to travel very far along it. George Bush paid some hard-to-measure price for his loyalty to John Tower at the outset of his administration. He paid another high price at the end of his administration for a controversial decision to pardon some of the government officials involved in the Iran-Contra affair. It is significant that in both of these cases he did not appear to agonize over the decisions or regret them at a later time. Observers, even friendly observers, see this loyalty as both a strength and a weakness in the president's character. According to Robert Gates, who served as deputy national security council advisor, Bush "was at times too patient and too forgiving of the ambitions and game-playing of both foreign leaders and some of his own people. He was at times loyal to some who did not deserve it or return it."[58]

The Bush administration had an unusually talented and close-knit team of senior foreign policy advisers. They often disagreed on the policies that should be adopted, but rarely aired those disagreements in public and worked together with remarkable effectiveness during the international upheavals that accompanied the end of the Cold War and the building of a complex coalition for the conduct of the Gulf War. The level of camaraderie and collegiality that characterized the Bush foreign policy team was rare. It is often observed that these relationships were mostly a matter of fortunate circumstances. The president's team was made up of people who had known each other for many years and held positions of responsibility in both the Ford and Reagan administrations. All of this is true, but the team did not succeed merely because of these long associations or common political experiences. They succeeded, in part, because the president took positive steps to cultivate friendship and loyalty. The Tower nomination mattered to this group. A powerful demonstration of the president's loyalty at the outset of the administration made it clear to everyone in his service that they worked for a chief executive who would stand by his subordinates in hard times.

The value of that lesson, like the costs that President Bush paid in delivering it, is hard to measure.

NOTES

1. Pat Towell, "The Tower Nomination: Senate Spurns Bush's Choice in a Partisan Tug of War," *CQ Weekly*, March 11, 1989, 533.

2. John McCain, *Worth the Fighting For* (New York: Random House, 2002), 150.

3. Quoted in Larry Sabato, *Feeding Frenzy: How Attack Journalism Has Transformed American Politics* (New York: Free Press, 1991), 178.

4. Tower died in a plane crash in 1991 after writing a bitter memoir that focused on his defeat in the Senate confirmation battle.

5. See Sabato, *Feeding Frenzy;* McCain, *Worth the Fighting For;* and Suzanne Garment, *Scandal: The Culture of Mistrust in American Politics* (New York: Random House, 1991).

6. John Greene, *The Presidency of George Bush* (Lawrence: University Press of Kansas, 2000), 51.

7. Bob Woodward, *The Commanders* (New York: Simon & Schuster, 1991), 56–57.

8. William G. Phillips quoted in James D. King and James W. Riddlesperger, "The Rejection of a Cabinet Nomination: The Senate and John Tower," in Meena Bose and Rosanna Perotti, eds., *From Cold War to New World Order* (Greenwood, CT: Greenwood Press, 2002), 380.

9. The president admits that Scowcroft would have preferred to be Secretary of Defense, "but I needed him at my side in the White House." George H. W. Bush, *All the Best* (New York: Scribner, 1998), 426. There was press speculation about other candidates for the post including Sam Nunn, Don Rumsfeld or corporate CEOs Paul O'Neil and Norman Augustine. See Fred Barnes, "Tottering Tower," *The New Republic,* December 19, 1988, 8.

10. "Suggested Talking Points for Tower-Bush Meeting," John C. Tower Collection, Southwestern University Library NA 59–4.

11. John Sununu Interview, November 9, 2000, George H. W. Bush Oral History Project, Miller Center, University of Virginia.

12. For a summary of the *New York Post* stories and others that appeared at the time see, Mark Hosenball and Michael Isikoff, "Psst: Inside Washington's Rumor Mill," *The New Republic,* January 2, 1989.

13. Sally Quinn, "The Secret That Didn't Reach Washington's Lips," *Washington Post,* June 3, 2005.

14. Maureen Dowd, "Conflict Over Ethics Divides 2 of Bush's Closest Advisers," *New York Times,* February 15, 1989.

15. Greene, *The Presidency of George Bush,* 53. Bob Woodward, *Shadow* (New York: Touchstone, 1999), 176.

16. John Tower, *Consequences* (Boston: Little, Brown, 1991), 46–47. Of course Tower may not be the best source for this conclusion.

17. Ibid., 50.

18. Quoted in Suzanne Garment, "The Tower Precedent," *Commentary* (May 1989): 43.

19. Quoted in Tower, *Consequences,* 7.

20. "Towering Inferno," a reference to a popular disaster movie of 1974, was the headline used for an article by Martin Schram in the May 1989 *Washingtonian* magazine. It was also the title for a William Safire column in the *New York Times,* February 13, 1989.

21. "Tower's Troubles," *Newsweek,* March 6, 1989, 20.

22. McCain, *Worth the Fighting For,* 139.

23. Alyson Pytte, "Questions of Conduct Delay Vote on Tower," *CQ Weekly,* February 4, 1989, 222.

24. U.S. Federal Bureau of Investigation, "Report on John Goodwin Tower," February 13, 1989, John G. Tower Collection, Southwestern University Library, Vertical File, 28–32.

25. Ibid., 28.

26. Ibid., 34.

27. Tower, *Consequences,* 182. A *New York Times* story on February 7, four days after Nunn spoke to Combest, quoted Senator Exon saying that Nunn would vote no on the nomination.

28. Tower, *Consequences,* 196.

29. Tower reports that the story is not true. Ibid., 296. The same conclusion was reached by various media organizations after they finally saw the redacted FBI files on Tower. See John Elvin, "Investigators Couldn't Catch Tower With Pants Down," *Insight,* March 27, 1995.

30. McCain, *Worth the Fighting For*, 149.

31. Tower, *Consequences*, 90–91.

32. Pat Towell, "Senate Panel Deals Bush His First Big Defeat," *CQ Weekly*, February 25, 1989, 397.

33. Bob Woodward, "Incidents at Defense Base Cited; Drunkenness, Harassment of Women Alleged," *The Washington Post*, March 2, 1989.

34. Dan Balz and Bob Woodward, "Senate's Debate Over Tower Becomes Partisan Free-for-All; Allegations About Visit to Base Challenged," *The Washington Post*, March 3, 1989.

35. McCain, *Worth the Fighting For*, 154.

36. Bob Woodward, *Shadow: Five Presidents and the Legacy of Watergate* (New York: Simon & Schuster, 1999), 545.

37. George H. W. Bush, "Statement on Death of John Tower," April 5, 1991. There are multiple sources for accessing full texts of President Bush's speeches and public statements. They can be found in print in the series titled *Public Papers of the Presidents of the United States* published by the Government Printing Office. For George H. W. Bush, they are also available online from the George Bush Presidential Library and Museum, at https://bush41library.tamu.edu/archives/public-papers/. Hereafter, Bush's presidential speeches and public statements will be cited by title and date.

38. Herbert S. Parmet, *George Bush: The Life and Times of a Lone Star Yankee* (New York: Scribner, 1997), 371–375.

39. Bush, *All the Best*, 414.

40. Parmet, *George Bush*, 374.

41. Quoting the president's diary, Ibid., 375.

42. Woodward, *The Commanders*, 57–58.

43. Tower, *Consequences*, 317.

44. Frederick McClure Interview, September 20, 2001, George H. W. Bush Oral History Project, Miller Center, University of Virginia.

45. Greene, *The Presidency of George Bush*, 57.

46. Parmet, *George Bush*, 375. A similar view was expressed by Jack Germond and Jules Witcover, "Memories of Harsh '88 Race Haunt Bush," *National Journal*, March 11, 1989.

47. Joe Klein, "The Least and the Dullest," *New York Magazine*, March 27, 1989, 16.

48. Ibid.

49. Woodward, *The Commanders*, 57.

50. George H. W. Bush, "Inaugural Address," January 20, 1989.

51. Tower, *Consequences*, 335–336.

52. Paul Light, "Late for Their Appointments," *New York Times*, November 16, 2004.

53. John Sununu Interview, November 9, 2000.

54. Towell, "The Tower Nomination: Senate Spurns Bush's Choice in a Partisan Tug of War," 530–34.

55. Quoted in Greene, *The Presidency of George Bush*, 144.

56. Parmet, *George Bush*, 373. See also Barbara Bush, *A Memoir* (New York: Scribner, 2003), 268.

57. The president in his memoir admits that Tower was not perfect. He "had short-comings, but none so glaring that he did not deserve my loyalty, my standing by him when the going got downright tough." George Bush and Brent Scowcroft, *A World Transformed* (New York: Knopf, 1998), 22.

58. Robert Gates, *From the Shadows* (New York: Simon & Schuster, 1996), 454.

TWO

Reticence

Deciding What to Say, and What Not to Say,
At the End of the Cold War

On May 12, 1989, the president of the United States gave the commencement address for the graduating class at Texas A&M University. He announced to the "Aggies" in College Station, Texas that the United States was moving "beyond containment" in its dealings with the Soviet Union. The president also told his Texas audience that he planned to revive an old Eisenhower arms control proposal called "Open Skies." The president's speech was not particularly successful. The Eisenhower idea of facilitating mutual aerial inspection of military activities on both sides of the Iron Curtain eventually became a treaty, but not a terribly important one. As for "beyond containment," it was a catchphrase that never quite caught on.[1]

The little-remembered commencement address at Texas A&M was part of a larger rhetorical strategy in an administration that was frequently accused of not having one.[2] It was the second of four major foreign policy speeches that the president delivered in various locations across the country following a formal review of the international issues facing the new administration. The speeches were intended to set the stage for important presidential trips to Western and Eastern Europe.

The president and his senior national security advisor arrived in the White House convinced that the Reagan administration had been too harsh in its criticisms of the Soviet Union in its first term and too adventurous in its embrace of Mikhail Gorbachev in its second.[3] Their first decision about East-West relations was to call for a careful review of foreign policy.[4] While that review process was coming to an end, the

administration prepared a series of public statements about its international agenda for Europe, arms control negotiations, and relations with
the Soviet Union. At Hamtramck, Michigan in mid-April Bush spoke
about the remarkable developments in Eastern Europe. The Solidarity
movement was negotiating with the communist government of Poland
over rules that would be used in the first free elections that country had
seen since the Second World War. On May 21, the president received an
honorary degree from Boston University, along with François Mitterrand, and talked about developments in Western Europe. Among our
NATO allies there was considerable unease about the changes taking
place in the East, the prospects for further European integration and the
important Western alliance defense decisions that would involve continued modernization of NATO nuclear forces. Later that month at the
Coast Guard Academy in New London, Connecticut Bush announced
some of his plans for strategic nuclear deployments, arms control proposals and European security negotiations.

The *New York Times* was not impressed. Its editors called the last
speech in the series, the one delivered to the graduates of the Coast
Guard Academy, the president's "fourth, final, flat and flimsy speech on
East-West relations."[5] According to the editorial writers at the *Times*,
President Bush and his key foreign policy advisers were missing important opportunities to join Gorbachev in bringing about dramatic international change. The problem was their moderation: "For most situations,
that's a virtue. But in the present circumstances, seeing different sides to
every argument has become stifling. Their very moderation tends to
blind them to the vast changes unfolding around the world, and to the
power of language and bold goals."[6] The senior White House observer
for the *National Journal* delivered a harsh judgment, complaining about
the president's "penchant for 'prudence' in the face of Soviet diplomatic
vigor."[7] Another commentator feared that Bush gave caution a bad
name.[8]

The second "flat and flimsy speech" was delivered in the president's
home state at the university that would later host his presidential library.
It was not a casual speaking engagement. The speech was carefully
crafted over a six-week period in which the White House staff produced
at least ten different versions of what the president should say. In the key
passage, he declared that the policy of containment had succeeded and
that we were now in a new era in which American relations with the
Soviet Union were no longer dominated by the goal of blocking Soviet
expansion.[9] Our new goal was to integrate the Soviet Union into the
global community of nations. Beyond proposing a conditional liberalization of US-Soviet trade and providing a list of additional concessions that
Gorbachev should make, the speech did not offer analysis about how this
integration would take place. Nor was there much in the way of ringing
rhetoric. Moving "beyond containment" was an important step in the

development of US-Soviet relations, but by itself it was not a particularly ambitious one. Like the hyphenated "post-Cold War," the phrase "beyond containment" was a reference to the past rather than a description of the future. It looked back and declared the success of an old and established policy that was no longer needed. As to what might come next in US-Soviet relations, the language used by the president in College Station, Texas was cautious and qualified.

Though "vision" was notoriously a thing that the Bush presidency lacked, preparing foreign policy speeches in the spring of 1989 involved serious internal debates about American relations with its primary rival and about the future of international politics. Those debates took place in the midst of growing criticisms that the new administration was excessively moderate and likely to miss opportunities that Mikhail Gorbachev's dynamic leadership was generating. The speech drafts were written for a president who was often uncomfortable talking about himself or the big ideas his administration was promoting. Carefully reviewing the preparation of the speech for Texas A&M by closely reading the multiple drafts from the speechwriter files in the Bush Presidential Library may help us judge whether the criticisms of the president and his administration have merit. It may also help us understand the motives behind the moderation and reticence that seemed to come so naturally to this chief executive.

COLD WAR LEGACIES

The reexamination of US-Soviet relations that George Bush called for shortly after his inauguration was not well received by foreign policy elites in the United States and Europe. Very few observers saw the need to pause and study Soviet behavior when so many changes taking place in that country were so obviously positive. The thing to do was to get on the Gorbachev bandwagon, not step back and try to figure out where it might be going. Gorbachev was reforming the political institutions and economic practices of his nation while allowing freer speech than any previous Soviet leader. He was withdrawing forces from Afghanistan and talking about reducing Soviet deployments in Eastern Europe. His speeches in Moscow, in Europe and at the United Nations involved provocative language and policy initiatives that were celebrated around the world. For the first time since the late 1940s serious policymakers in Washington began to think that the Cold War might be coming to an end. For decades, the "unthinkable" end to that conflict had always been a reference to all-out nuclear war. Ironically, a peaceful end to the Cold War was almost as hard to think about as the unleashing of apocalyptic violence.

The potential for that apocalyptic violence was one of the foundations of Cold War foreign policy. For decades, both the United States and the Soviet Union built nuclear weapons in vast numbers with plans to deliver them in a variety of bombs, missile warheads, artillery shells, grenade launchers and land mines. The horror they would produce was, of course, intentional and so extreme that its mere contemplation would, hopefully, prevent war from ever occurring. But deterrence depended on a willingness and an ability to unleash devastating destruction should it ever fail. Early in the Cold War, Winston Churchill gave this strategy its most eloquent description and defense. We have by a "process of sublime irony," the prime minister said, "reached a stage in this story where safety will be the sturdy child of terror, and survival the twin brother of annihilation."[10] Nowhere in the world was the irony of the nuclear age more palpable than on the continent of Europe. For most of the Cold War, nuclear weapons were considered essential to defend Western Europe from the large and heavily equipped Soviet and Warsaw Pact conventional forces. A conventional imbalance in Europe meant that NATO nations had to be prepared to use nuclear weapons to keep from being overrun if an invasion ever took place.

Though nuclear weapons were considered critical to NATO strategy, they were also controversial. No one wanted to think about what an actual nuclear war in Central Europe would be like; and while West Germany and other continental nations wanted the security of an American nuclear guarantee, they dreaded the possibility that such a guarantee would ever have to be exercised on their soil or anywhere near it. As a result, maintaining and modernizing nuclear weapons in Europe were frequent sources of friction between allies. In the 1970s and 1980s painful political decisions about introducing new nuclear warheads and missiles into the European theatre led to public protests, government instability and new attempts to negotiate arms control agreements. The protests in the early 1980s against American deployments of new intermediate range missiles in Western Europe were some of the largest in the history of the continent. The successful initiation of those deployments had been one of Ronald Reagan's major foreign policy accomplishments, but within a few years, he threw that accomplishment away in a reversal of policy that may have marked the beginning of the end of the Cold War.

In 1987, Gorbachev and Reagan signed a ground-breaking treaty eliminating medium-range nuclear-armed missiles. This was not arms control of the traditional variety that capped deployments of nuclear armaments at specified numbers. This agreement got rid of one group of highly effective missiles based arbitrarily on their range. And it involved another important innovation. The INF agreement was asymmetrical. In order to get to zero, the Soviet Union had to remove four nuclear warheads from Central Europe for every one that the US gave up. When it was fully implemented, both superpowers would have no medium-range missiles armed with nuclear warheads. Earlier in Reykjavik, Reagan and Gorbachev talked briefly, but seriously, about the possibility of eliminating nuclear weapons altogether in a series of surprising and confusing conversations that shocked traditional cold warriors on both sides. In 1989, no one was sure whether the INF agreement was some sort of anomaly that had been possible because the initial deployments were so controversial in the West and because both sides had so many nuclear weapons that they could easily do without one category of them. For the NATO alliance, the agreement exacerbated deliberations about the fate of the remaining nuclear armaments committed to alliance defense. The large and aging arsenal of short-range nuclear forces in Europe had never been talked about in any arms control negotiations and parts of that arsenal would need to be replaced or removed at some time in the not too distant future. Would the alliance have to go through another round of controversial modernization? Or if more nuclear weapons were eliminated would the conventional imbalance between NATO and the Warsaw Pact become more dangerous? These were questions alliance members did not particularly wish to confront and they were related to still larger questions about the political future of the continent.

In the same year that the INF treaty was signed, Gorbachev called for the creation of a "common European home."[11] It was not entirely clear what this new phrase meant though it vaguely suggested the possibility of a resolution of the fundamental issues that had divided Europe into East and West. Gorbachev was already carrying out a liberalization of the Soviet Union. After 1987, he appeared to be inviting reform in Eastern Europe as well—a part of the world where his predecessors had repeatedly used military force to crush political independence and economic change. Perhaps the Brezhnev Doctrine, justifying Soviet domination of Eastern Europe, would soon be repealed. Perhaps the Cold War, as we knew it, would come to an end. In 1988, some prominent political leaders were already saying that it was over.[12]

Of course, the Cold War was not literally a war, so there would be no surrender, no ceasefire, no armistice, no peace treaty to let everyone know that it had reached its conclusion. The war, such as it was, began for the United States with an internal government memo written by George Kennan, a famous speech delivered on a college campus by Winston Churchill and a presidential doctrine announced to the Congress by Harry Truman. Perhaps the Cold War would end with similar pieces of paper and public statements.

Perhaps some of those public statements had already been delivered. In December of 1988, about a month after the American presidential election, Gorbachev told a UN audience that he was prepared to unilaterally reduce Soviet military personnel by 500,000 and deployments in Eastern Europe by 50,000 soldiers and 5,000 tanks.[13] These were large round numbers, and even if the Soviets retired or withdrew surplus forces and old equipment without radically changing the balance of military power on the European continent, the fact that they were making these changes unilaterally without ruling out further reductions made the initiative dramatic. The *New York Times* compared Gorbachev's UN speech to Woodrow Wilson's Fourteen Points and to the Atlantic Charter announced by Franklin Roosevelt and Winston Churchill.[14] Everywhere Gorbachev traveled outside the Soviet Union in the late 1980s he garnered massive media coverage and seemed to regularly surprise his Western observers with new ideas and proposals. According to the British foreign secretary, Gorbachev had "a well-stocked hat full of well-armed rabbits," and there would be no early end to the surprises he might pull out during his meetings with Western leaders.[15] When Secretary of State Baker met the Soviet leader in Moscow in the spring of 1989, Gorbachev once again captured the headlines with a last-minute, though modest, unilateral reduction in the controversial short-range nuclear weapons which were so troubling to West Germany and other NATO nations. There would have to be an American response to Gorbachev's UN speech, to his enticing language about a new European home and to his latest offer to reduce the huge number of short-range nuclear weapons in Central Europe.

At the beginning of the Bush administration, more important issues were in play between the United States and the Soviet Union than at any time since the allied conferences at the end of the Second World War. No wonder the Bush team wanted some time to think about what they would do next. But time was in short supply. Throughout the spring of 1989, pressure was building for an American response to the gush of Gorbachev initiatives. When the Soviet leader visited London early in April, he publicly complained about the absence of serious American discussion of his UN speech.[16] When the president was asked at a press conference about the delay in the developments in East-West relations, he responded in an uncharacteristically curt manner. "We're making a prudent review," he said, "and I will be ready to discuss that with the Soviets when we are ready."[17] Two weeks later he was asked more or less the same question in connection with an evaluation of his administration's early accomplishments. "I don't feel a need for some precipitous and dramatic initiative in order to salve the consciences of those who are saying you've got to do something in 100 days."[18] Publicly the president was prepared to wait. Privately he and senior members of his administration were expressing their own frustrations with Gorbachev's ability to garner favorable media coverage for his ambiguous proposals and pronouncements while the American bureaucracies ground out good reasons for not moving quickly on the global agenda that Gorbachev appeared to dominate. Secretary of State Baker remembers the emerging review documents in the spring of 1989 as little more than "mush."[19] Brent Scowcroft was equally dissatisfied and called in Condoleezza Rice and Robert Blackwill late in March to give them rather broad marching orders. "This is going nowhere," he said, referring to the review process. "See if you can write something that has some bite."[20]

CRAFTING A MESSAGE

A White House meeting was held on April 6 to begin planning the speech for the forthcoming Texas A&M graduation.[21] It was known at that point that the speech would be part of a series of public statements on foreign policy planned for the spring and that the Texas topic would be US-Soviet relations. The phrase "beyond containment" had already been used by Rice and Blackwill in a memo to Scowcroft on thinking boldly about US-Soviet relations.[22] Handwritten notes from the April 6 meeting have the word "containment" followed by an arrow pointing to a blank line bracketed in quotation marks. Filling in the blank was the rhetorical challenge for those who worked on the subsequent drafts.

The April 6 meeting did not produce a new name for the relationship between the superpowers or for American policy toward the Soviet Union. Instead, the jotted notes experiment with an explicit acknowledgment that the period following containment did not yet have a label. We are "poised at the end of one era" and at the beginning of another, writes the note taker, Mark Davis of the speechwriting staff.[23] We are in a "transition period," in "the quiet time between the end of one age and the beginning of another." "Transition" may well have been the right word to describe what followed containment; "quiet time" was probably less apt. Neither phrase was the stuff from which memorable quotes are made.

At this early stage, there was more agreement about what *not* to say. The speech should not endorse "peaceful coexistence" — the old Khrushchev slogan used to describe improved relations between East and West. That phrase, later associated with détente, suggested that the two political and economic systems could live together without either open military conflict or resolution of the underlying differences between communism and capitalism. Peaceful coexistence may have had its day, but in 1989 that day had passed. By the first year of the Bush presidency it was clear that one side was winning the ideological contest at the heart of the Cold War. What was taking place, the April note taker suggested, was "peaceful conquest" — an interesting and provocative rephrasing of the Khrushchev language that never appeared in the subsequent drafts.[24] The notes from the April 6 meeting say that in addition to avoiding the phrase "peaceful coexistence," the speech should avoid the word "convergence." There could be no mutual movement by East and West to some center ground. "We are not meeting in the ideological middle."

What has happened in the Soviet Union is the result of a "failure of policies."[25]

In the spring of 1989, the Soviet economy was in crisis, partly as a result of the long stagnant period of communist rule and partly as a result of the disruptive reforms that Gorbachev set in motion. The full dimensions and consequences of the crisis were hard to perceive and predict, but they clearly put Gorbachev in a precarious position. Problems in the Soviet Union and the growing restlessness of the people in Eastern Europe could easily lead, as it eventually did, to Gorbachev's fall from power. Or it could lead, as it also did, to an end to the Cold War and to the collapse of communism. No one in the April 6 meeting, it can reasonably be assumed, suggested those possibilities as likely or proposed that the president should make those possibilities the theme for his upcoming speech. But any serious discussion about what would follow containment had to involve speculation about how far Gorbachev's domestic reforms and international initiatives would go and whether or not a decisive Western victory in the Cold War was in the offing. Deliberations in the senior foreign policy counsels of the Bush administration over the Texas A&M speech were essentially deliberations about how far to go with such speculations in formal public pronouncements. The decision they made was to not go very far. But along the way they experimented with some language that tells us something about how much further they might have gone.

Every draft of the Texas A&M speech observed that actions are more important than words. Gorbachev had promised troop and nuclear weapon reductions in Eastern Europe, but those reductions had not yet taken place. The Cold War had seen earlier promises of this kind that had not been kept. "Soviet foreign policy has been almost seasonal," the final version of the speech would remind the audience, "warmth before cold, thaw before freeze." What we want now is a "friendship that knows no season of suspicion, no chill of distrust."[26] Gorbachev would have to deliver on the promises he had already made and then take further actions recommended by the president of the United States. Every version of the speech contained a list of steps that Gorbachev should take. Many of the items on that list were predictable objectives in US-Soviet foreign relations: further arms reductions, self-determination in Eastern Europe, respect for human rights and the resolution of regional disputes around the world. In addition, the list also called for superpower cooperation in addressing new global problems like drugs and the environment. The first full draft of the speech, dated May 5, went further. It said that "the Soviets must step forward from the darkness of a failed ideology into the daylight of the modern world."[27] The Soviets must "renounce the principle that class conflict is an inevitable source of international tension."[28]

At the bottom of the page that contains the class conflict renunciation there is a marginal note which says to add somewhere a "bold step on ideology" and the phrase "new world."[29] The "new world" would come later. The bold step on ideology was already in the speech in the odd suggestion that Gorbachev should renounce the role of class conflict in international politics. One has to wonder how many new graduates in the Texas audience would have studied Marxism with sufficient care to fully recognize the revolutionary nature of the statement that class struggle is not the cause of conflict around the world.

Why should the president of the United States ask the leader of the Soviet Union for such a renunciation? Condoleezza Rice may have been the author of this language and it certainly fits with her analysis of how significant and sweeping were the changes in Soviet thinking.[30] The list of concessions was mostly a set of tests or markers that the administration was setting for Gorbachev. Reduce arms, loosen the Soviet grip on Eastern Europe, pull back from overseas adventures in Africa and Latin America, continue the political and economic liberalization in the Soviet Union. The class conflict concession was the only one that involved words and not deeds. It basically asked Gorbachev to say that Marxist ideology no longer governed Soviet foreign policy. Intellectuals and serious students of Soviet affairs, like Rice, might have appreciated such a declaration, but her boss, Brent Scowcroft, had reservations. The copy of the speech in the speechwriters file that has his comments includes a large question mark next to the class conflict paragraph.[31] That item was dropped from the emerging list of new steps that Gorbachev should take.[32]

In all likelihood no great rhetorical opportunity or memorable sound bite was lost when the class conflict passage was cut. Still, it is curious that it ever made it into a draft. Early in 1989, there was considerable speculation about how far Gorbachev's reforms of the Soviet system would go and whether the Soviet Union would tolerate a genuine loosening of their control in Eastern Europe. Gorbachev saw himself as the Mark Anthony of international communism. He wanted to praise Marxism and reform it, not bury it. But how much reform could communism endure before it ceased to be communism? Would Gorbachev knowingly and willingly preside over the end of an ideology he saw himself saving? Asking him to renounce a fundamental Marxist idea may have been a tentative way of exploring whether he understood just how radical his own policies were. Of course, if Gorbachev did not realize how radical his own ideas were, or where they might lead, or how close communism might be to its demise, it was questionable whether the United States would have been wise to remind him of these things.

Even after the reference to class conflict was cut, the Texas A&M speech drafts still contained some rather remarkable language about an American, or Western, ideological victory at the end of the Cold War. Some of that language involved an experiment with the possibility of declaring a Bush doctrine and calling it the doctrine of "reconciliation."

That word—reconciliation—more than any other, was the closest the speechwriters ever came to filling in the blank for what would follow containment. The seventh version of the speech includes a clear and simple account of what this doctrine would have entailed. It would have been a very one-sided reconciliation. "But understand this," says the key paragraph, "the Soviet Union is changing its values. We are not. The Soviet Union has stood apart from and in opposition to the world. We have not. It is the Soviet Union which must reconcile itself to free values and free nations. If they do, we will welcome them with enthusiasm. In this way, the doctrine of reconciliation can succeed where the Spirit of Geneva and Détente failed."[33]

In the drafting process the phrase "reconciliation of the Soviet Union with the west," eventually became the much milder "integration of the Soviet Union into the community of nations." All references to the doctrine of reconciliation were eventually dropped and all that remained was the acknowledgement that we were moving "beyond containment."[34] Again, Brent Scowcroft played a leading role in the changes that toned down the Texas A&M speech. Among other things, he argued that it was unseemly to announce your own foreign policy doctrine. The existence of a new doctrine was something appropriately declared by the press, by commentators and by scholars, not by policymakers. Moreover, and more importantly, caution was the correct course of action in speaking publicly about the dramatic developments in Gorbachev's Soviet Union. A major Soviet reconciliation with the West might well be taking place and it could clearly involve a continuing series of painful concessions from the Soviet side. The Texas A&M speech, in all its drafts, listed what some of those concessions might be. Of course, the hope that those concessions would be made ran up against the realization that too much talk about an ideological victory and a communist failure would not have helped Gorbachev take the steps we wished him to take.

The central foreign policy problem for the Bush administration in the spring of 1989 was developing a strategy for dealing with the unbelievable, and perhaps uncontrollable, changes in the Soviet Union and in Eastern Europe. Where would those changes lead? Would they succeed? And what would success really mean for the Soviet Union and for the United States? Did Gorbachev know what he was doing? And if he did not know, would it serve our interests to tell him? Administration voices were heard on these questions throughout the early months of the year, but they were not always consistent. Secretary of Defense Dick Cheney speculated in a television interview at the end of April that Gorbachev would fail in his reform endeavors and would most likely be replaced by a more hard-line Soviet leader.[35] Such a prediction was certainly plausible and was no doubt talked about in the senior counsels of the administration. Even the Soviet ambassador to the United States wondered whether or not Gorbachev would survive.[36]

Wondering it was one thing, talking about it on national television was another. White House officials distanced themselves from Cheney's public remarks at the same time that they were toning down rhetorical reflections on the possibility of a Western ideological victory and a collapse of communism. On the delicate subjects of Gorbachev's political prospects, the degree to which the Soviet leader was consciously contradicting Marxist principles, and the possibility that the Cold War was ending with a clear Western victory, the better part of wisdom was silence or cautiously phrased language that amounted to the same thing.

This may have been a time when silence on sensitive subjects made sense, but that silence did not make it easy for speechwriters to create memorable language about the momentous events that were underway. Once the doctrine of reconciliation, the end of class conflict and statements about an unambiguous Western victory in the Cold War were deleted or toned down, there wasn't much left for the president to say in College Station, Texas. Containment was declared to be at an end and Gorbachev was given a list of new concessions he should make to longstanding Western positions. The United States was not offering any new initiatives of its own or much in the way of rewards for the good deeds that Gorbachev was doing. The president did promise at the end of the speech to temporarily waive the Jackson-Vanik amendment—a law which restricted trade between the United States and the Soviet Union unless and until the Soviets changed their emigration policies. As a result, in order to earn even a temporary waiver in trade restrictions the Soviets would have to make yet another concession. They would have to liberalize their emigration laws, particularly for Jewish dissidents, and then implement the new liberalized arrangements by actually allowing significant numbers to leave the country. This American offer was a watered-down version of a more generous proposal to "repeal" the Jackson-Vanik amendment which was discussed on April 6 and tentatively included in the first draft of the speech.[37] The Soviet leader was being told to keep his promises, to make additional concessions to the West, to revise and implement new Soviet immigration policies and then the United States would temporarily waive trade restrictions.

The emerging speech needed something more. At least that is what the president thought when he read the fifth draft. In the only documentary evidence of his direct participation in the speechwriting process, the president typed some notes for his staff on the typewriter he kept behind his Oval Office desk.[38] "We need a Noonansm [sic] or two more," he observed with his less than perfect typing skills. The invented word, "Noonanism," however it might be spelled, was a reference to the memorable phrases that Peggy Noonan had often written for Ronald Reagan and occasionally for George Bush. The president does not say what those phrases should be, only that the speech needs more of them. His note goes on to suggest that the speech include a tribute to Soviet patriotism and courage in the Second World War, something that was standard form in presidential speeches about the Soviet Union in the era of dé-tente, and a personal observation about a recent trip his son and grand-son took to the city of Yerevan in Armenia where international relief efforts were helping that community recover from a devastating earth-quake. The speechwriters never used the World War II language, but they did incorporate the story about the president's son and grandson being moved to tears by scenes they witnessed in Armenia.

The call for more Noonanisms brought forth at least one possible candidate with a riff on Gorbachev's desire to create a "common Euro-pean home." In a reminder that the Berlin Wall was still in place and restrictions on movement in most of Eastern Europe were still being en-forced, the speechwriters suggested a line in which the president would say that if there really were a "common European home," the people living in that home should be "free to move from room to room."[39] That phrase did not make it into the Texas A&M speech, but it was used effectively shortly thereafter in a speech the president delivered after the NATO summit in the summer of 1989. With or without new Noonan-isms, the toned-down speech still needed something.

That something turned out to be a recycled arms control proposal from an earlier Republican president who had been Senator Prescott Bush's most famous golfing partner. At the beginning of the drafting process, the speechwriters were reminded to look at what Eisenhower had said about the Soviet Union during his first year in office.[40] Follow-ing the death of Stalin, there had been genuine hope that the worst of the Cold War might be over. New Soviet leaders might be willing to change Stalin's foreign policies and engage in serious arms control negotiations. Eisenhower had, in fact, given two major speeches in 1953, one called the "Chance for Peace" in which he urged a worldwide reduction in expendi-tures on armaments and another called "Atoms for Peace" in which he suggested a modest plan to divert nuclear material from the making of bombs to the generating of electricity.[41] The speeches were very well received, but did not lead to any major breakthroughs in the superpower conflict. In 1955, Eisenhower tried again when he finally met the new post-Stalin Soviet leaders at a summit in Geneva.

In the mid-1950s both the United States and the Soviet Union had tabled grand designs for controlling nuclear weapons and reducing mili-tary forces in Central Europe. But in all of the international forums where these ideas were under review, there was no agreement about how to verify the proposals being made. In general, the Soviets insisted that not much verification was necessary and the United States rejected any agreements that did not contain clear provisions for observing and cer-tifying compliance. At the Geneva meetings, Eisenhower casually in-serted a proposal into his formal opening remarks that he hoped would jump-start the deadlocked arms control process.[42] He called the proposal

"Open Skies" and promised to allow Soviet planes to fly freely over American military facilities and take whatever pictures they wanted if the Soviets reciprocated by opening their airspace to similar inspection flights by American aircraft. This was just before the initiation of regular U-2 flights and well before satellite photography would accomplish the same objective. Open Skies would have legitimized the aerial spying that was about to begin and, in addition, would serve as a way of testing Soviet seriousness about exchanging information and reducing tensions. Khrushchev, who was just emerging as the new Soviet leader, rejected the idea at the Geneva summit. In subsequent negotiations, Soviet officials made it clear that the proposal was just another dead document in the pile of arms control ideas that littered Cold War conferences.

Thirty-five years later it came back to life. According to Scowcroft, the idea of reviving Open Skies originated with Brian Mulroney, the Conservative Prime Minister of Canada who called Bush to suggest it shortly after he had a brief visit with Gorbachev.[43] It also appeared on lists of what the US might consider in its review of East-West relations and would have been found by the speechwriters looking back at things that were said by Ike when hopes ran high for a new relationship between the United States and the Soviet Union. Wherever it came from, the idea became part of the Texas A&M speech in the fourth draft, dated May 7, and stayed in all the subsequent drafts.

Scowcroft thought the Open Skies idea "smacked of gimmickry" and should be dropped.[44] This time he lost the argument. Advocates for the idea had a few compelling points. As good as satellite photography was, the ability to fly below cloud cover and take pictures from airplanes instead of space-based platforms could provide a faster, more reliable and possibly cheaper way to collect information about military exercises and the movement of forces and equipment. If Gorbachev was really going to pull back troops and tanks from Central Europe, as he promised in his December UN speech, there would be a new premium on timely information regarding any redeployment of manpower and equipment that might subsequently take place. In addition, there was probably some small symbolic value in reviving an old idea that had died in an earlier Cold War thaw and using it as a measure of Soviet seriousness this time around. The concessions Gorbachev was asked to make in all the drafts of the Texas A&M speech were substantial and mostly one-sided. Opening airspace to photography involved reciprocal obligations.

The Open Skies revival had an origin that was independent of the early preparations for the Texas A&M commencement address,[45] but after May 7, it was firmly imbedded in the "Beyond Containment" draft. There was an obvious flaw in this rhetorical strategy. Going beyond containment by going back to a modest arms control proposal from the 1950s was not likely to win much national or international praise for vision or boldness. Responding to Gorbachev's announcement of significant uni-

lateral military reductions in Eastern Europe and the Soviet Union by
calling for new, or old, forms of verification rather than matching reductions on the western side would almost certainly be seen as small-minded
and ungenerous. The criticisms of the Texas speech, and the whole series
of foreign policy speeches that were delivered in April and May, should
not have been hard to predict. In fact, while those speeches were being
prepared the president was urging his staff to think more boldly. Unfor-
tunately, those bolder ideas were not ready for public dissemination until
the president was on his way to Brussels and his first NATO summit.

MAKING A POLICY

In the early months of the new administration, two sets of commitments
were made to the president's calendar in order to force foreign policy
deliberations and decisions: the commencement addresses that he would
give in Texas, Massachusetts and Connecticut; and two trips he would
take to Western Europe to celebrate the 40th anniversary of the NATO
alliance and to see firsthand the dramatic developments in Poland and
Hungary. The first set of commitments produced the speeches that failed
to impress the editors of the *New York Times*. The second set produced
much better results.

At a meeting in Maine after the Texas A&M speech and just before
President Mitterrand arrived for a personal visit, the president told his
senior advisers that he was not satisfied with the pace of foreign policy
development or the consequences of the policy review process.[46] He
wanted to take serious proposals to the NATO meeting in Brussels at the
end of May. "I want this thing done," he said.[47] The "thing" the president
wanted done was a specific Western response to Gorbachev's European
unilateral arms reduction proposals. Scowcroft had been lobbying for a
major conventional force reduction in Europe. Gorbachev's proposals,
and the INF precedent of asymmetrical reductions, suggested that meaningful agreements might be possible in this area. Independent observers
seemed to agree. General Andrew Goodpaster, Eisenhower's White
House staff assistant when the Open Skies proposal was developed, and
later commander of NATO forces, publicly called for a 50 percent reduction in the number of US troops in Europe.[48] In Kennebunkport, Bush
suggested that American NATO deployments might be cut by 25 percent,
a figure that alarmed Admiral William Crowe and the other members of
the Joint Chiefs of Staff. They countered with a much more modest 10
percent reduction. No one was carefully analyzing what the optimal level
of troop deployments in Central Europe would be on either side of the
Iron Curtain. Instead there was a general proposition that the West
needed to show its interest in Gorbachev's proposals and some imagina-

tion about how large a change might be coming and how quickly it might be implemented.

The final package that Bush proposed to our NATO allies involved significant and asymmetric cuts to a common cap of 275,000 troops for the United States and the Soviet Union in Central Europe with an early deadline for achieving agreement and actual force reductions. The proposed number was a compromise between the president's 25 percent cut and the Defense Department's 10 percent alternative, but because it would be a common cap, the Soviets would have to make a much larger reduction than the United States. On the subject of tactical nuclear weapons, the president proposed new negotiations on their future and a temporary postponement of any replacement of the aging short-range missiles in West Germany. The new negotiations would aim to reduce, but not necessarily eliminate, tactical nuclear weapons in Central Europe. None of these proposals were promises for unilateral American or NATO action, except perhaps the postponement of short-range missile modernization. They were invitations to get serious in the ongoing negotiations about conventional force reductions in Europe and to begin new talks about the remaining tactical nuclear weapons on the continent. Like the language of the Texas A&M speech, the NATO proposals asked for significant concessions from Gorbachev. But because the president was now introducing his own numbers into the public discourse and because those numbers involved large cuts in US NATO deployments and some hope that the most controversial weapons on the continent might be reduced, the package met with diplomatic, public and media endorsement.[49] The NATO allies in Brussels approved the president's plans, though some, particularly Margaret Thatcher, were privately worried about the dangers of precipitous negotiation processes that might weaken the West's nuclear deterrent. The news coverage of the president prior to his trip to Europe for NATO consultations involved widespread criticism of the commencement speeches. The summit turned things around and news organizations declared the new arms control proposals and the president's trip to Europe a great success.

In Mainz, Germany, after the formal NATO meetings, the president delivered his best speech to date on the developments in Europe and the changing relationship between the United States and the Soviet Union. The speech repeated the phrase "beyond containment" and mentioned the Open Skies idea, but it coupled them with a summary of the new NATO proposals and put all of these ideas into the wider context of transformations taking place across the continent of Europe. This time the writers used the phrase about allowing Europeans to move more freely from room to room in their common home. Along the border between Hungary and Austria that freer movement was already beginning to take place. In another Noonanism, the president called for the creation of a Europe that would be "whole and free" without artificial dividing lines or political subjugation. The Mainz speech took seriously the possibility that the Cold War might be ending and said clearly that if it did end, it would do so in the place where it began, in the nations of Central Europe. At the end of May in 1989, no one knew or could have predicted how quickly and how decisively that end would come.

The Mainz speech, the best in the series of foreign policy addresses that President Bush gave in the spring of 1989, was partially the product of a careless error. Mark Davis, the speechwriter traveling with the president, accidentally deleted the speech and all of its earlier drafts from the only computer that had copies of the president's proposed remarks. Davis remembers reporting his mistake to David Demarest, the White House communications director, who calmly suggested drinks and dinner before assembling selected staff to recreate the speech from their collective memory. They did their work in one long and productive night.[50] It is possible that the compressed time and pressure that accompanied the final drafting session may have produced a more elegant and coherent speech than the usual process of circulating multiple drafts throughout the foreign policy bureaucracy. It also helped that the Mainz speech was given at the end of the spring and early summer policymaking deliberations and that it was the occasion to summarize and tie together what the president had proposed to our NATO allies and to the audiences that had heard his earlier statements about East-West relations in Hamtramck, Boston, New London and College Station, Texas.

This time the president's words were well received. The editorial writers at the *New York Times* put their comments under the headline "Mr. Bush Takes the Lead," and news articles had even flashier titles like Tom Friedman's "How Bush Finally Got Foreign Policy Pizazz."[51] On Air Force One on the way back to the United States, the president soaked in the new praise for his foreign policy success and told reporters that he was not like Rodney Dangerfield. He had all the respect he needed.[52]

MEDIA, MODERATION AND RETICENCE

Of the two very different media portraits of George Bush just before and just after the NATO summit, the earlier one involving caution, moderation and a lack of vision was by far the more powerful and the more persistent portrait of his presidency. At the end of his first year in office, following the dramatic and favorable events in Eastern Europe as well as the invasion of Panama, the president was still seen as excessively cautious. *U.S. News and World Report* called his first year in office "The Year of Living Timorously."[53] Academic commentators described a Bush administration foreign policy that was characterized by "tactical mastery" and "strategic indirection."[54] David Broder assessed the Bush presidency as "minimalist"; George Will called it "empty."[55]

Where did the president's reputation for excessive moderation come from? In presidential reputation, making first impressions counts and there was certainly a cautious delay in developing new policies for East-West relations in the early months of the administration. The presidential foreign policy speeches in the spring of 1989 did lack luster and intentionally avoided declaring an end to the Cold War or an immanent Western victory. Both of those declarations would have been premature in April and May, even if they looked rather obvious six months later. The president was fully aware of the caution he was exercising and the criticism that caution brought forth. Behind the scenes, he was trying to push his own administration and his allies to bolder policies but he was not much interested in bolder pronouncements. He succeeded on the policy agenda and then gave a well-received speech in Mainz, Germany.[56] Why didn't those successes change the president's reputation?

It was, of course, hard to keep pace with the international events of 1989. And everything the president said and did in response to those events was moderated by a number of factors—some structural, some rhetorical and some personal. Structurally, the administration was constrained by a deep deficit and divided government. Bush was the first vice president to succeed his predecessor since Martin Van Buren, but the only president to win the White House while his party simultaneously lost seats in both the House and Senate. There were no coattails in the 1988 election; there was barely any coat. The promise made, and made emphatically, during the campaign that there would be no new taxes further constrained the president. Whenever there was talk of providing significant amounts of aid to Poland and Hungary to encourage their steps toward democracy or aid to the Soviet Union to support and shore up Gorbachev's reforms, the talk ended with the recognition that there was very little money for these important objectives. Controversial legislative proposals, like repealing Jackson-Vanik instead of just waiving it, would have cost the president dearly in a Congress where he faced serious opposition—opposition that was willing, as we have seen, to reject one of his senior cabinet nominees. Part of the president's reluctance to make bold statements in 1989 came from a realistic recognition of his relatively weak political position. He inherited Ronald Reagan's revolution including its monumental deficits, he promised no new taxes and he faced a disciplined partisan opposition on Capitol Hill. He found himself without much room in which to maneuver.

George Bush did not have Ronald Reagan's rhetorical skills. The president occasionally gave an effective speech, as he did in Mainz, but more often than not he received poor reviews for his public presentations. Richard Haass, who often worked on foreign policy speeches related to Middle East issues, told a group of scholars in 2004 that "Bush does not like Reagan-like rhetorical flourishes." If you are writing for President Bush you need to "keep it straight, not fancy, sentences short, very direct kind of speeches."[57] Richard Ben Cramer, a perceptive reporter on the 1988 election, records a painful description of George Bush speaking on the campaign trail during his first run for statewide office in Texas. Bush would "get cranked up, dive into a twisty river of a sentence, no noun, a couple or three verbs in a row, and you wouldn't know where he was headed." When he emerged on the other side of the sentence "red in the face, pleased as hell with himself, spluttering out the predicate, or maybe the indirect object of that second-last verb, and a couple more random words that had occurred to him in the meantime," you could easily tell that he cared about what he was saying, even if you still didn't know what it was.[58] Decades later he was a better public speaker, but never as committed or attentive to speechwriting and speechwriters as his predecessor. According to Noonan, speechwriters were simply not important in the new administration. "They're just above the people who clean up after Millie [the White House dog]," she said to a reporter doing a story on the fact that the speechwriting staff had lost their White House mess privileges early in the Bush presidency.[59]

Bush provided input to the writing of his speeches and paid particular attention to the acknowledgements at the beginning of his remarks where he introduced friends in the audience.[60] At Texas A&M, he made sure to mention Fred McClure, his director of legislative affairs, and Lieutenant Colonel Dan Barr, the pilot of Air Force One, who both earned degrees on the College Station campus. The president liked humor in his speeches and got a good laugh when he made a reference to Senator Phil Gramm's "humility" in offering instruction on economics to the rest of the Senate. Towards the end of the drafting for Texas A&M, a little levity was added just after a complicated paragraph on the Jackson-Vanik waiver. "It had to happen," the president told the seniors in Texas. "Your last day in college had to end with yet another political science lecture."[61] These personal touches were generally well-received by audiences, but rarely helped garner serious attention from media or foreign policy elites. The fact that the president sometimes stumbled over key passages, or left them out, when he delivered a speech did not help.[62] This was not a president who particularly enjoyed using bold phrases or dramatic public statements and he had to know that no matter how hard he tried to deliver an effective speech, he would always face unflattering comparisons to his remarkably accomplished predecessor.

In the spring of 1989, George Bush was much more concerned about the substance of his policy decisions than about their presentation. He was not pleased with the foreign policy review documents he had asked for; and though he was attributed with the caution those reports contained, he was actually prodding his staff to come up with more in the way of bold policy initiatives. In doing so he encountered considerable restraint from bureaucrats, particularly in the Pentagon, who were skeptical about Gorbachev's motives and the likelihood that he would remain in office. In Europe, he encountered allies who had a complicated set of responses to Gorbachev. Helmut Kohl was anxious to move on the possibility of transforming relations between the two Germanys and wanted to avoid another public debate about nuclear weapon modernization. Margaret Thatcher was willing to work with Gorbachev, but was passionately committed to maintaining a viable NATO nuclear deterrent. François Mitterrand was worried about the possibility that changes in Eastern Europe would result in a reunited Germany or a weakened NATO alliance. Successfully weaving one's way through these positions was bound to produce moderate policy outcomes and reticent public pronouncements.

Moreover, there was an obvious set of dilemmas in dealing with Mikhail Gorbachev. Getting what we wanted from him required being very careful about what was said about his programs and prospects. Reminding the Soviet leader, or reminding the world, that he was moving away from communism might make him stop. Reminding him, or reminding the world, that the Cold War looked like it was ending with the West triumphant might have made Gorbachev's enemies bolder and more willing to wreck that triumph just as it was being achieved. Throughout the Bush administration the president would be criticized for not sufficiently celebrating the events associated with the end of the Cold War— for failing to dance on the Berlin Wall as the metaphor makers would have it. These may have been failures, but they were also conscious choices made in a calculation about what strategy would get the most out of the opportunities that Gorbachev was creating. Those choices gave the administration a justified reputation for moderation and reticence.

But moderation and reticence also came naturally to George Bush. He was taught as a child never to boast and repeatedly told his speechwriters to reduce the "I" quotient in speech drafts.[63] A politician who does not want to talk about himself is a rare member of that profession, but Bush had a highly unusual political career. He had more of a parliamentary than a presidential background. He rose to the top of American politics by taking a variety of appointed jobs, not by winning elections or building electoral coalitions. He was known for the competent accomplishment of challenging assignments rather than the passionate pursuit of political causes. On some of the hot-button issues of his day—race and reproductive rights—he held complicated, evolving and seemingly contradictory positions. He was usually identified with the center of the Republican Party; he was less liberal than his father and less conservative than his son. In his association with Ronald Reagan, he loyally served a more ideological president who almost certainly held international and domestic views that his vice president did not fully share. As president in his own right, he genuinely wanted a "kinder and gentler" version of the Reagan Revolution. But kindness and gentility do not lend themselves to the creation of memorable rhetoric.

George Bush's first year in office was not a good year for moderates who were reluctant to talk about dramatic change. It turned out to be a year with more revolutionary events than almost anyone expected. The president sat in the center of those events without regret or apology for his moderate and reticent inclinations.

NOTES

1. The phrase was repeated in a number of speeches that Bush gave after the one at Texas A&M and was widely used by senior administration officials in background briefings. Don Oberdorfer, "Bush Finds Theme of Foreign Policy: 'Beyond Containment,'" *Washington Post*, May 28, 1989.
2. For a review of Bush administration rhetoric see, *The Rhetorical Presidency of George H. W. Bush*, Martin J. Medhurst, ed. (College Station: Texas A&M University Press, 2006).
3. Don Oberdorfer, *The Turn*, (New York: Poseidon Press, 1991), 329.
4. Robert Hutchings, *American Diplomacy and the End of the Cold War* (Baltimore: Johns Hopkins University Press, 1997), 21–27.
5. "What East-West Policy?" *The New York Times*, May 25, 1989.
6. Ibid.
7. Burt Solomon, "Being a Good Manager Isn't Enough If You Can't Deliver a Good Speech," *National Journal*, May 27, 1989, 1316–17.
8. William Schneider, "Will Bush Give Caution a Bad Name," *National Journal*, June 3, 1989, 1390.
9. "Remarks at the Texas A&M University Commencement Ceremony in College Station," May 12, 1989. Hereafter referred to as "Remarks at Texas A&M." In addition to *Public Papers of the Presidents of the United States* and the Bush Library website noted in chapter 1, note 37, which provide access to the full text of the presidential speech, an edited version is published in George H. W. Bush, *Speaking of Freedom: The Collected Speeches* (New York: Scribner, 2009), 33–38.
10. Winston Churchill, Speech to the House of Commons, March 1, 1955.
11. Gorbachev used this phrase on a number of occasions, but his 1987 speech in Prague contained his fullest account of what it might mean. Mikhail Gorbachev, *Memoirs* (New York: Doubleday, 1995), 430–33.
12. In 1988 both the British Prime Minister Margaret Thatcher and the outgoing American Secretary of State, George Shultz, said that the Cold War was indeed coming to an end.
13. Michael Dobbs, "Gorbachev Announces Troop Cut of 500,000," *Washington Post*, December 8, 1988. The total number of tanks in the reductions would be 10,000 covering both Eastern Europe and the European portions of the Soviet Union.
14. Editorial, *New York Times*, December 8, 1988, 34.
15. Howe quoted in James Baker, *The Politics of Diplomacy* (New York: G.P. Putnam, 1995), 70.
16. "Gorbachev Criticizes Lack of U.S. Policy," *Washington Post*, April 7, 1989, A14.
17. George H. W. Bush, "The President's News Conference, April 7, 1989."
18. Ibid., 452.
19. Baker, *The Politics of Diplomacy*, 68.
20. Philip Zelikow and Condoleezza Rice, *Germany Unified and Europe Transformed* (Cambridge, MA: Harvard University Press, 1995), 26.
21. The commentary and quotations that follow are from a handwritten document titled "NSC April 6, '89 10:15," in Bush Presidential Library Speechwriting, Speech File Backup, Chron File 1989-1993, OA/IO 13667, Box #13, "Texas A&M 5/12/89," OA 8489 [2].
22. Zelikow and Rice, *Germany Unified and Europe Transformed*, 26.

23. Interview with Mark Davis, September 9, 2005.

24. "NSC April 6, '89 10:15," in Bush Presidential Library Speechwriting. In the handwritten notes the word conquest is in brackets suggesting that it may be a problematic term to apply. It is followed by the word "ideas," which is underlined four times.

25. Ibid.

26. "Remarks at Texas A&M."

27. Version One, 4. All versions of the speech are located in Bush Presidential Library Speechwriting, Speech File Backup, Chron File 1989-1993, OA/IO 13667, Box #13, "Texas A&M 5/12/89," OA 8489. In the notes below, different versions (or drafts) of the speech are identified by their Version number which appears in the heading of each document.

28. Version One, 5.

29. Ibid.

30. Zelikow and Rice, *Germany Unified and Europe Transformed*, 26–27.

31. Version Five, 6.

32. It came back several months later in the official policy document that emerged from the spring deliberations and was signed by the president on September 22, 1989. NSC-23 has a list of Gorbachev concessions that runs parallel to the Texas speech drafts and includes "renunciation of the principle of class conflict." Declassified copy of NSC-23 on the Bush Library website.

33. Version Seven, 3. This version of the speech in the speechwriters file has a handwritten notation on the top of page one that says "Reconciliation"—out.

34. In the first four drafts, the speech is titled the "Texas A&M Commencement Address." Thereafter, the president's remarks bear the additional title "Beyond Containment." The final version of the speech does contain one line about a Western ideological victory, but like the phrase "beyond containment" it is backwards looking with references to language Truman had used at the outset of the Cold War. The speech says, "We are approaching the conclusion of an historic postwar struggle between two visions: one of tyranny and conflict and one of democracy and freedom."

35. Cheney did this on CNN's *Evans & Novak* program. See, Molly Moore, "Cheney Predicts Gorbachev Will Fail, Be Replaced," *Washington Post*, April 29, 1989.

36. Baker, *The Politics of Diplomacy*, 63.

37. Version One of the speech has alternative language in which the president either calls for the repeal of the Jackson-Vanik and the Stevenson amendments to the Trade Act of 1974 or promises to waive both. Version One, 8. Thereafter the drafts call for a one-year or a temporary waiver of Jackson-Vanik. The promise to repeal or waive the Stevenson amendment is dropped between versions seven and eight.

38. Undated typed note with handwritten notations, Bush Presidential Library, Speechwriting White House Office, Speech File Backup, Chron File 1989-93, OA/ID 13667, Box #13, "Texas A&M 5/12/89," OA 8489 [1].

39. This suggested line is pencilled in at the bottom of the president's undated note to the speechwriters and it is written in the margins of Version Seven of the "Beyond Containment" draft. It was later used in the president's remarks to the people of Mainz, Germany just after the NATO summit. "Remarks to the Citizens in Mainz, Federal Republic of Germany, May 31, 1989," in Bush, *Speaking of Freedom*, 51–58.

40. "NSC April 6, '89 10:15," in Bush Presidential Library Speechwriting.

41. See, Ira Chernus, *Eisenhower's Atoms for Peace*, (College Station: Texas A&M Press, 2002).

42. The president's language was in fact carefully prepared and seriously debated among the president's advisers. See, W. W. Rostow, *Open Skies: Eisenhower's Proposal of July 21, 1954* (Austin: University of Texas Press, 1983).

43. Bush and Scowcroft, *A World Transformed*, 54. Speechwriter Mark Davis credits Robert Blackwill for introducing Open Skies into the Texas A&M speech. Interview of Mark Davis, September 2, 2005.

44. Ibid.

45. The Open Skies language first appears in Version Four of the speech dated May 7, 1989; but the speechwriters file also contains a loose undated page titled "Open Skies paragraphs for a Presidential speech" which was apparently drafted before it was decided which speech would use it.

46. Bernard Weinraub, "How a Frustrated Bush Moved to Out-Gorbachev Gorbachev on Weapons," *New York Times*, May 30, 1989.

47. Herbert Parmet, *George Bush: The Life of a Lone Star Yankee* (New York: Scribner, 1997), 388.

48. Don Oberdorfer, "An Old Warrior Rocks NATO's Boat," *Washington Post*, April 30, 1989. See also Andrew J. Goodpaster, "New Priorities for U.S. Security: Military Needs and Tasks in a Time of Change," occasional paper, The Atlantic Council of the United States, June 1991.

49. According to Philip Zelikow, the preparation of the May 1989 NATO proposals became the model for how to achieve successful national security policy development. The National Security Council Project, Oral History Roundtables, "The Bush Administration National Security Council," April 29, 1999, Ivo H. Daalder and I. M. Destler, Moderators, The Brookings Institution, Washington, DC, 6.

50. Interview with Mark Davis, September 2, 2005.

51. "Mr. Bush Takes the Lead," *New York Times*, May 31, 1989; Tom Friedman, "How Bush Finally Got Foreign Policy Pizazz," *New York Times*, June, 4, 1989.

52. Ann Devoy, "Bush Vows to Seize Opportunity in Europe: President Returns Home Amid Wide Praise," *Washington Post*, June 3, 1989.

53. Quoted in Larry Berman and Bruce Jentleson, "Bush and the Post-Cold War World," in Colin Campbell and Bert A. Rockman, eds., *The Bush Presidency: First Appraisals* (Chatham, NJ: Chatham House, 1991), 94.

54. Terry L. Deibel, "Bush's Foreign Policy: Mastery and Inaction," *Foreign Policy*, no. 84 (Autumn, 1991): 3.

55. Quoted in Ibid., 18.

56. Mark Davis, one of Bush's speechwriters, reports that years later he still hears praise for the Mainz speech when he talks to Germans. Email to author May 9, 2005.

57. Richard Haass Interview, May 27, 2004, George H. W. Bush Oral History Project, Miller Center, University of Virginia.

58. Richard Ben Cramer, *Being Poppy* (New York: Simon & Schuster, 1992), 96–97.

59. Quoted in Bernard Weinraub, "How the President Lost His Tongue, or the Bush Speechwriters Leave a Mess," *New York Times*, April 7, 1989.

60. Michael Duffy and Dan Goodgame, *Marching in Place: The Status Quo Presidency of George Bush* (New York: Simon & Schuster, 1992), 47.

61. "Remarks at Texas A&M."

62. Duffy and Goodgame, *Marching in Place*, 47.

63. Interview with Mark Davis, September 2, 2005.

THREE

A Gentleman's Outrage

The Tipping Point in the Decision to Invade Panama

On December 16, 1989, Panamanian military forces shot an off-duty American marine officer, First Lieutenant Robert Paz, when he and his companions drove away from a roadblock in Panama City. Another American officer, Navy Lieutenant Adam Curtis, and his wife Bonnie witnessed the shooting. The Curtis couple were blindfolded and taken away from the scene by Panamanian officials. Before they were released, Lt. Curtis was badly beaten and his wife was pushed against a wall, groped, taunted and threatened with sexual assault before she collapsed.[1]

Four days later the augmented American armed forces still stationed in Panama to protect the canal moved quickly in the middle of the night to disarm the Panama Defense Forces (PDF) and capture Manuel Noriega, the head of the PDF and the recently declared "maximum leader" of the nation. The invasion of Panama brought to an end a long and convoluted struggle between the United States and the indicted drug dealer and dictator who had become a major irritant to the Reagan administration. There were many reasons why President Bush decided to use force to resolve America's problems with Panama, and there was a long train of events that led to the brief, lopsided military engagement. There were many reasons for the United States to overthrow the government of Manuel Noriega. Nevertheless, questions remain about precisely why the invasion took place, when it did and what factors led George H. W. Bush to issue orders for military action against the Noriega regime.

According to many who have written about these events, the decision to remove Noriega was made well in advance of the killing of Robert Paz and the brutal interrogation of Lt. and Mrs. Curtis. Scholars and commentators often say that the invasion involved issues other than the ones that were stated at the time. John Greene points out that the president, well before the threats to American personnel in Panama, was "obsessed" with getting rid of Noriega.[2] Contemporary news articles based on interviews of senior administration officials concluded that the decision to use military force had been almost inevitable after an October 1989 coup attempt against Noriega failed.[3] According to the sources for a story by Maureen Dowd, the decision was not merely a response to the assaults on Americans in mid-December and was taken "largely on the basis of Mr. Bush's visceral feelings about the Panamanian leader."[4] Later Robert Tucker and David Hendrickson noted that while the stated reasons for the invasion were the protection of the Panama Canal and the American nationals working near it, the actual reason was to remove "a dictator who had defied Washington once too often."[5] In even blunter language, Steven Hurst concludes that the Bush administration invaded Panama "in order to save face rather than American lives."[6]

Why, exactly, did the United States decide to invade Panama and remove Noriega from power? Even those who were there when the decision was made can be hard-pressed to know for sure what was decisive in the mind of the president they served. It is harder still for those who consider these matters at some distance to do so. Nevertheless, it is worth trying. Presidents are tested and measured by difficult decisions and those involving the commitment of armed forces into combat are among the hardest decisions that presidents make. Why did George Bush order the invasion of Panama on the eve of the Christmas holidays in 1989? The answer to that question begins with another leader who, like the American president, led an intelligence agency before he led his nation.

NORIEGA'S RISE TO POWER

Manuel Antonio Noriega's father was an alcoholic civil servant, his mother was the family maid. He became an orphan when his mother disappeared sometime before his fifth birthday and grew up in urban poverty. Unusually short and severely pockmarked, he earned the nickname *cara de pina*, "pineapple face." Poor, small, disfigured with an older half-brother who was openly homosexual, Noriega seemed an unlikely candidate for success in Latin American military or political circles.[7] His rapid rise in the ranks of his nation's military service was the result of cunning, hard work and a penchant for double-dealing.

Noriega began his military training by simultaneously working for both Panama and the United States. Reportedly recruited by the CIA as a young cadet, Noriega filed reports about the students and instructors in his military training who had discernable leftist leanings. First placed on the CIA payroll around 1960, Noriega would remain in the service of the

American intelligence community, off and on, for the next quarter century.[8]

Throughout his adult life he worked in the Panamanian National Guard, later renamed the Panama Defense Forces (PDF). In a small nation without hostile neighbors and plenty of American troops to defend the Panama Canal, there was little need for a large professional military. Nevertheless, during the decades after the Second World War the Panamanian military grew in size and power and emerged as Panama's most important institution. By the time of the Omar Torrijos coup in 1968, the National Guard was the nation's army, navy, air force, coast guard, CIA, FBI, secret service, border patrol, police force and drug enforcement administration all rolled into one. Torrijos permitted the election of civilian politicians and plebiscites on various issues, including the Panama Canal treaties, but he ruled for more than a decade from his position as senior military commander.

Noriega was a participant in the coup that put Torrijos in power and took his side again in the following year when a counter-coup tried to unseat him. As a result, Noriega was promoted from commander of a provincial military district to head of the nation's military intelligence. From that vantage point he was able to keep tabs on every aspect of the Torrijos regime. From the beginning of his rule, Torrijos worked to negotiate a revision of the 1903 treaty with the United States. He was often openly anti-American and reestablished relations with Castro's Cuba in order, in part, to goad his American counterparts in the treaty negotiations. In Panama, he instituted mildly socialist reforms of agriculture, health care and education and liberalized banking laws, making the nation a haven for shady business transactions. During the 1970s Torrijos tripled the membership of the armed forces and vastly expanded the nation's civil service. Government became more important in Panamanian society, and of course the military remained the most important part of the nation's government. Meanwhile, drugs and drug money flowed ever more freely, and American officials who wanted to simultaneously maintain good relations with Panama and stop the flow of illegal drugs were presented with a dilemma.

During the Carter administration, Noriega was temporarily removed from the CIA payroll because of his links with drug trafficking and other questionable activities, but he continued to provide occasional services for the American government.[9] His intelligence agents captured a number of Colombian drug dealers and arranged for their extradition to the United States. This won Noriega credit in Washington and also made it easier for him to demand substantial bribes from other drug dealers who were set free.[10] Throughout this period, problems in Panama involving drugs and corruption were overshadowed by larger questions. For the Carter administration, the probable involvement of Panamanian officials in illegal activities was less important than the resolution of the strategic issues surrounding the future of the canal.

When Noriega replaced Torrijos as the head of Panama's military, his actions became harder to ignore. Noriega had none of Torrijos' charisma or charm and no ambitions for major accomplishments in foreign or domestic affairs. As his nation's leading intelligence officer, he had been a shadowy figure little-known to the outside world; but as Panama's acknowledged ruler, Noriega became the focus of national and international attention. Throughout his career, Noriega was accused of scandalous behavior. From time to time he drank heavily, womanized frequently, kept a number of mistresses, was accused of rape, accumulated a substantial personal fortune from a modest officer's salary and reportedly participated in acts of torture against his enemies. Insecure and fearful of his personal safety, Noriega at the end of his rule kept an erratic schedule, organized phony motorcades, used tape-recorded phone conversations to disguise his whereabouts to electronic eavesdroppers and slept in a variety of locations. Fascinated by religion and the occult, he maintained an eclectic set of spiritual beliefs and superstitious practices. According to one of his hired psychic consultants, Noriega was "a Christian, a Rosicrucian, a Freemason, a Buddhist, a Taoist, a man protected by God and the Son of God."[11] In Panama and in his international travels, Noriega sought out mediums, astrologers, mentalists, witch doctors and tarot card readers. When his homes and offices were raided during the American invasion, soldiers found objects suggesting he was an active practitioner of voodoo and may have cast spells on Ronald Reagan, George Bush and the entire United States Congress.[12] These religious beliefs and practices were not unusual in Central America, but they often made it difficult for American officials to understand Noriega's erratic personal behavior. It was easier to understand his ruthless pursuit of power.

A self-trained expert on psychological warfare, Noriega was extremely adept at manipulating those around him. Domestically he foiled repeated coup attempts, restricted freedom of expression, staged phony elections, ordered the torture and murder of his most serious political enemies and organized a group of street thugs, called the "dignity battalions," to carry out special tasks that he did not want associated directly with the PDF. Internationally, he managed in the early years of his dictatorship to maintain good relations with the United States despite mounting evidence of his drug connections and corruption. He did so by continuing to provide information and arrests for the American drug enforcement agencies, whose administrators regularly praised his "cooperation" in the war on drugs, and by making himself useful to the Reagan administration.

Noriega sold arms to the Sandinistas earlier in his career, but in the Reagan era he joined the Contra cause and provided assistance to the forces fighting communism in Central America. According to documents filed in connection with the trial of Oliver North, Noriega personally made a $100,000 contribution to the Contras in July of 1984.[13] At the same time he was helping the White House fight communism in Nicaragua, he was improving Panamanian relations with Cuba, assisting a Marxist revolutionary group in Colombia, opening new ties with Libya and enjoying his resumed payments from the CIA—reported in the early 1980s to be between $100,000 and $200,000 a year.[14] Throughout his career Noriega skillfully played communist against anti-communist, Castro against the CIA, Colombian drug dealers against US drug investigators and foreign interests against those of Panama. Panama under Noriega became a haven for all sorts of unsavory characters and transactions. The whole nation, observed an American who worked with Noriega in the 1980s, was "a brothel for intelligence agencies, arms merchants, drug dealers, and soldiers of fortune."[15] Getting rid of Noriega would not be easy.

DEPOSING THE DICTATOR

The Panamanian elections of 1984 were controlled by the PDF and the results were the predictable product of fraud. Popular Panamanian nationalist and former president Arnulfo Arias was defeated by the candidate Noriega and his lieutenants chose for the presidency, Nicholas Barletta.[16] According to the journalist and author of a book on Noriega, John Dinges, the slogan in Panama was always "It's not who wins that counts; it's who counts that wins."[17] In the aftermath of the elections, Noriega's and the PDF's control over the country tightened and the repression of dissident forces became more frequent and more deadly. The popular opposition leader Hugo Spadafora was captured, tortured and killed; his headless body stuffed in a mailbag was deposited in Costa Rica just across the border. When President Barletta announced plans to appoint an independent commission to investigate the Spadafora murder, Noriega forced his resignation.

The U.S. government raised no serious objections to these actions, in part, because of Noriega's willingness to help the Reagan administration in Central America. Vice president George Bush traveled to Panama in 1983 for talks with Noriega. The two had met once before in 1976 when they were each in charge of their respective national intelligence agencies. In 1983, they reportedly discussed Panamanian support for Reagan policies in El Salvador and Nicaragua.[18] There was apparently no discussion of Noriega's involvement with drugs and drug money, though the subject of money laundering in Panama was on the agenda.[19] The Bush visit may have been the high point in good relations between Panama and the United States in the early years of the Reagan presidency. In Reagan's second term, things changed.

In June of 1986, front-page stories in the *New York Times* by investigative journalist Seymour Hersh revealed Noriega's connections to the Spadafora murder and to other illegal activities.[20] Anti-drug legislation passed in 1986 suspended half the annual foreign aid to twenty-four countries, including Panama, unless the president certified that the named countries were cooperating with US anti-drug efforts. When Reagan provided that certification for Panama in March of 1987, Senators Jesse Helms and John Kerry, in one of their rare collaborations, joined forces to suspend all aid to Panama. Their legislative initiative nearly succeeded.

In the summer of 1987, public revelations by a former Noriega associate, Diaz Herrera, about the rigged elections of 1984 and the corrupt practices of the PDF led to riots and demonstrations in Panama. As a kind of "fruity effigy," pineapples were hung from telephone poles in Panamanian cities.[21] Some observers of the Panamanian protests in 1987 thought they were similar to the kind of public outcry that had toppled Ferdinand Marcos in the Philippines during the previous year. Instead, on July 10, a date known as "Black Friday" in Panama, Noriega cracked down even harder against his opposition. Fifteen hundred protesters were arrested and hundreds more were injured by riot police using live ammunition. Herrera's home was stormed and he was arrested.

The Reagan administration could no longer tolerate Noriega's behavior. In 1987 his annual CIA payments were suspended and diplomatic protests were lodged publicly and privately against his violations of human rights and disrespect for democratic processes.[22] American economic and military assistance programs were suspended, and in January of 1988 Assistant Secretary of Defense Richard Armitage went to Panama to urge Noriega to step down.[23] He refused. Shortly thereafter, he was indicted by two district attorneys in Florida.

Independent criminal investigations, one in Miami and one in Tampa, produced convincing evidence that Noriega was directly involved with the Colombian Medellin cartel in the trafficking of narcotics and the laundering of drug profits. In February of 1988 grand juries in both Florida cities issued their unusual indictments against a foreign leader. Three weeks later, Eric Delvalle, the Panamanian president who had replaced Barletta, fired Noriega as commander of the PDF. His courageous action had no effect. Noriega ignored the decision, forced Delvalle into hiding, and replaced him with a more compliant president. The Delvalle decision did, however, manage to produce considerable confusion about who legally ruled in Panama. When the State Department announced that the United States considered Delvalle to be Panama's legitimate head of state, lawyers in the US representing opposition groups in Panama went to court to take control of Panamanian assets in American banks and prevent their use without Delvalle's permission. Even before the United States officially imposed sanctions against Noriega, private attorneys using the American legal system produced a major banking crisis in Panama. On March 11, 1988, the Reagan administration added to Noriega's troubles by announcing that all payments due to Panama for use of the canal would be held in escrow until the Delvalle government was fully restored. In April, after another failed coup attempt against Noriega, Reagan declared a state of emergency in US-Panamanian relations and imposed further economic sanctions against Panama.

Throughout the spring and summer of 1988, members of the Reagan administration debated additional steps against Noriega. Secretary of State George Shultz and his assistant for Latin American policy, Elliott Abrams, urged military action. Pentagon officials, including the general in charge of American forces on the scene, objected because they were worried about the safety of the canal and our ability to protect the many Americans still living and working in Panama. President Reagan instead approved a plan to bargain for Noriega's departure in exchange for dropping the Florida indictments. George Bush, caught between his obligations as a loyal vice president and the demands of his campaign for the 1988 Republican presidential nomination, publicly broke with the president and criticized the proposed deal. It failed.[24] With no diplomatic end to the Noriega regime, the president turned to covert action and approved a CIA plan to sponsor another Panamanian coup. The new coup planning involved the possibility of Noriega's death and the possible violation of a prohibition against American participation in assassination plots. Shortly after it was reviewed by members of Congress, in accordance with established procedures, a detailed description of the plan appeared in the *Washington Post*.[25] The Reagan administration and the Senate Select Committee on Intelligence publicly argued about who was responsible for the leak, and the bold covert action plans were shelved. When George Bush won the 1988 presidential election, America's problems with Panama were unresolved.

BUSH AND THE DECISION TO INVADE

For the first eleven months of 1989 the Bush administration tried various tactics for addressing the Noriega problem. The sanctions imposed by President Reagan remained in effect and over time did considerable damage to the relatively weak Panamanian economy. But because Noriega's financial strength came from illegitimate dealings that continued during the period of sanctions, and because Noriega was able to replace American aid with assistance from Cuba, Libya, and other nations, Noriega remained in power. The CIA installed a radio transmitter to broadcast opposition news and information in Panama, but its location was discovered by the PDF and CIA agent Kurt Muse was captured and imprisoned.

In May of 1989, new elections in Panama offered a unique opportunity to remove Noriega in a peaceful fashion, or at least focus international attention on his dictatorship. Preoccupied with more pressing problems in the early months of a new presidency and busy making appointments to key foreign policy positions, the members of the Bush administration initially gave little attention to the upcoming elections in Panama. But after some congressional pressure, led by Senator Richard Lugar who had been the senior American observer in the crucial 1986 elections in the Philippines, the White House arranged for a team of American observers to monitor the polling in Panama.[26] Other teams sponsored by international organizations and independent groups, including one led by former president Jimmy Carter, also went to Panama for the May voting. The Senate and House Intelligence committees reportedly approved $10 million in covert support for candidates and organizations campaigning against Noriega.[27] On May 2, Bush spoke to the Council of the Americas and emphasized the importance of elections scheduled that year in El Salvador, Nicaragua and Panama. Recycling a line he had used in his inaugural address, the president told leaders from Latin America that "the day of the dictator is over" and that "the people's right to democracy must not be denied."[28]

In Panama, it was denied. Fraud, violence and intimidation were practiced on a scale that was obvious to everyone. The exit polls indicated that opposition candidate Guillermo Endara was the decisive winner despite the official vote counts announced by the government.[29] Jimmy Carter, whose support for the canal treaties had won him many Panamanian friends, took a leading role in denouncing the elections and the Noriega regime. Television cameras captured the essence of evil in Panama. They showed an opposition candidate for the vice presidency being beaten by Noriega's street thugs. The televised footage and newspaper photographs of his bloody face became the powerful visual images of Panama's dictatorship. The May elections did not end Noriega's rule, but they weakened his standing in world opinion and decisively demonstrated that he governed without popular support. After the May elections, President Bush ordered additional troops to be deployed to Panama and dependents of US personnel to come home. He publicly encouraged a coup in Panama that would overthrow Noriega and put the rightfully elected president in power.[30]

In July the commander of US armed forces in Panama, General Frederick Woerner, who had consistently cautioned against the use of American military power in the fight against Noriega, was replaced by General Maxwell Thurman, nicknamed "Mad Max." Thurman was instructed to begin updating existing plans for an American military mission to remove Noriega.[31] The decision to carry out such a mission had not been made, but Noriega's outrages were such that contingency planning and precautionary steps were clearly necessary. More of the dependents of American military personnel stationed in Panama were sent home; the number of US troops in Panama was increased from ten thousand to twelve thousand; base personnel were put on a higher state of alert; and military exercises, on and off the bases, took on a greater significance.

The contingency plans for an operation against Noriega fell roughly into three categories.[32] At the lowest level, a commando raid could have been used to capture Noriega, bring him to one of the American bases and fly him to Florida to face drug charges. There were a number of problems with this option. Noriega's extreme care in disguising his whereabouts meant that a small-scale raid could not be carried out successfully without excellent intelligence on Noriega's location. That information was very hard to come by. US intelligence about Noriega was rarely as good as Noriega's sources about American activities. Moreover, a simple plan to remove Noriega did nothing to change the structural problems in Panama. The PDF would still have remained the nation's most powerful institution, and the new leader of the country would most likely have been one of Noriega's cronies, rather than Presidents Delvalle or Endara. The other two options were aimed against the PDF, rather than Noriega alone, and involved either moderate or major invasions of the country. The moderate invasion would have used the American forces already in Panama to neutralize PDF units in and near the nation's major cities, making it impossible for Noriega to get any military protection and difficult for him to escape capture. This option would, however, have left some provincial PDF forces intact and raised the danger that the invasion would be followed by guerrilla fighting in Panamanian jungles and possible attacks against the canal by renegade forces. The third option was the invasion that would actually take place at the end of the year. It involved nearly twice as many troops as the moderate plan, but gave the best prospects for neutralizing the PDF completely and creating an opportunity to dramatically change the politics of Panama. Planning for that option took place throughout the fall.

As tensions between the United States and Panama rose, a final coup attempt almost ended Noriega's dictatorship without the need for any American military operations. President Bush had publicly called for a coup against Noriega after the May elections. At a May 11 press conference, the president announced new sanctions against Panama and clearly stated that the United States could continue to work with the PDF if Noriega was removed from power.[33]

In the fall of 1989, Major Moises Giroldi, Chief of Security at PDF headquarters and one of the few people allowed to carry weapons in Noriega's presence, began plotting a coup. Giroldi's plan was simple: he would choose a time when he was in a small group with Noriega and together with a few friends capture the dictator and force him to resign. Catching Noriega off guard would be relatively easy for someone with the kind of access Giroldi enjoyed, but in order to keep the dictator in captivity, it was crucial that loyal units of the PDF be prevented from coming to his rescue. Before the coup, Giroldi instructed his wife to approach American officials in Panama and request that US troops block various roads and bridges by which PDF forces might come to Noriega's assistance. Mrs. Giroldi also asked for sanctuary for members of their family on whatever day the coup might take place.

Coups and rumored coups in Panama were fairly common in 1988 and 1989 and American intelligence officers had relatively little information about Giroldi, beyond the fact that he was one of Noriega's trusted officers. Limited American support for his plan was, however, authorized at senior levels of the Bush administration where there was not much confidence or expectation of success. When confusion arose regarding the timing of Noriega's capture and when American troops failed to take any action beyond blocking the designated routes for Noriega's possible rescue, Giroldi's prospects for success significantly diminished. In what James Baker would later call "a comic-opera coup," Giroldi and his co-conspirators did manage to hold Noriega prisoner for a number of hours, but they chose not to kill him or quickly turn him over to US authorities.[34] Amazingly, Noriega was allowed to make phone calls and alert some of his loyal supporters to the fact that he was being held. General Thurman, newly at his post in Panama, and Colin Powell, on only the second day of his service as Chairman of the Joint Chiefs of Staff, agreed that not enough was known about the coup plotters to risk a large-scale American involvement.[35] Thurman was afraid that the whole endeavor might be a Noriega plot to catch the United States in the act of supporting a coup that was being staged only for that purpose. In the end, Thurman's fears were misplaced. Giroldi's coup was the genuine article, but his hesitancy about what to do once Noriega was under his control, as well as the American failure to take him more seriously, saved Noriega. The dictator was rescued by loyal troops who entered Panama City without using the US-blocked routes. Giroldi was tortured and killed.[36]

The response of commentators and members of Congress to the news from Panama was blistering. George Will, never a fan of Ronald Reagan's vice president and successor, wrote a column labeling the new administration "an unserious presidency." Jesse Helms compared the Bush team to the "Keystone Kops," while others called the failed coup "a total fiasco" and an "amateur hour" performance.[37] Members of the administration accepted the validity of some of the criticisms they received and made changes to the way they would handle international crisis situations in the future. After October 1989, the deputies committee of the National Security Council, chaired by Robert Gates, took responsibility for coordinating rapidly developing situations like the coup attempt in Panama City.[38] Even if that committee had been in charge of the events in

October, lack of knowledge about Giroldi's motives and the reservations expressed by General Thurman, a trusted commander on the scene, might well have led to a similar result.

After the failed coup, according to many of those who have reviewed Bush administration policy on Panama, the likelihood of a large-scale American invasion to remove Noriega was heightened. For some it was nearly inevitable. Even before the October coup, Admiral William J. Crowe, Powell's immediate predecessor as Chairman of the JCS, told Thurman to be prepared to invade. "Pretty soon," Crowe reportedly told Thurman, "Noriega is going to do something stupid." [39] In December that is exactly what he did.

On Friday, December 15, Noriega promoted himself, declaring that he would henceforth be known as Panama's "maximum leader," with new powers that ended the last illusions of constitutional government in Panama. These added powers were necessary, according to the maximum leader, to control domestic resistance and respond to the "state of war" which now existed with the United States. Initial public responses by junior members of the Bush administration to Noriega's "declaration of war" were dismissive. On the next day, a Panamanian holiday commemorating Noriega's assumption of power in 1983, Lt. Paz and three friends who had gone to dinner at a restaurant in Panama City got lost on their way back to the base and had their fateful encounter with a roadblock near PDF headquarters. The Americans were ordered to stop and get out of the vehicle at the same time that an angry crowd surrounded their car. Instead of following those commands, the driver gunned the engine and drove away. It was then that PDF guards opened fire. There had been earlier incidents of harassment of Americans at roadblocks in the weeks following the Giroldi coup, but this was the first that involved the use of lethal force. Paz was pronounced dead fifteen minutes after the car arrived at a hospital; one of the other passengers was injured. News about the incident got to Washington fairly quickly, but the details were not clear in the earliest reports and the fate of the Curtis couple, taken away after they witnessed the roadblock shooting, took longer to reach the nation's capital.

Once the story was known, the senior members of the Bush administration rapidly reached the same conclusion: the time had come to execute the plans for an invasion of Panama. Powell, with long experience in the upper levels of foreign policy decision making, but newly appointed to the JCS, had a succession of meetings with Secretary Cheney and the other chiefs in which he argued for execution of the large-scale invasion. Powell was the first JCS chairman to serve under the changed responsibilities legislated in the Goldwater-Nichols Act. Unlike his predecessors who represented the service chiefs, Powell was expected to give independent military advice to the president along with a report on the opinions of his service colleagues. He was pleased, in this his first crisis, when there was unanimity in favor of invasion from all the officers in charge of the service branches. His conversations with Cheney were brief, professional and clearly indicated that the Secretary of Defense had made up his mind to support an invasion even before their conversations took place.[40] Thurman, who was visiting the Pentagon on the weekend before the Christmas holidays, immediately flew back to Panama and began preparations for what might lie ahead.

On Sunday, December 17, there was a meeting in the White House with the president, the secretaries of state and defense, the national security advisor, his assistant, the vice president, chief of staff John Sununu and press secretary Marlin Fitzwater.[41] The president was dressed informally with seasonal socks that said "Merry" and "Christmas" on his left and right ankles.[42] Powell and his assistant, Lt. General Tom Kelly, summarized the facts about the Paz and Curtis incidents, and some other encounters between Americans and PDF forces that occurred throughout the weekend.[43] Powell made the case for the large-scale invasion and when questioned by the president about the possibility of a smaller operation to capture Noriega responded that Noriega would be hard to find and that such a mission, even if successful, would leave the PDF intact. As long as the PDF ruled Panama, none of the fundamental problems would be resolved. First the president, then his national security advisor, pressed the chairman about casualties, both for Americans and for Panamanians. No definitive answers could be given to questions about how many people might be killed. Powell tried to honestly explain that there would certainly be casualties and there were risks that PDF resistance would be substantial in some locations. When the hour-and-a-half meeting was nearing its conclusion and when Powell feared that it might end—as many meetings in the Reagan administration had ended—without a clear resolution about what would happen next, the president made a few decisive statements. His words are reported in slightly different language by different sources, but all amount to the same thing. "Let's do it," he is quoted as saying, "the Hell with it."[44] "This is just going to go on and on."[45] "This guy is not going to lay off. It will only get worse."[46]

Two days later, just after midnight, the invasion began with a successful Special Forces operation to rescue Kurt Muse, the captured CIA agent, from a Panamanian prison. Over 20,000 US troops moved quickly to major PDF strongholds throughout the country and either negotiated their surrender or engaged them in combat. As Powell predicted, PDF resistance varied. The fighting was heaviest, and most destructive to civilian lives and property, in some urban areas where attacks on PDF facilities produced explosions and fires in nearby homes. Controversy arose about whether the newest stealth aircraft used in the operation were necessary or effective. Some Americans were killed by friendly fire. Noriega, reportedly hiding in a brothel, was not immediately captured, though the American forces successfully destroyed boats and airplanes he might have used to escape Panama City.[47]

The next morning the president went on television to explain why he had ordered the military operations that were still underway. He said that the goals of the invasion were to "safeguard the lives of Americans, to defend democracy in Panama, to combat drug trafficking, and to protect the integrity of the Panama Canal treaty."[48] The first two objectives were identical to the objectives he had stated seven months earlier when new sanctions were imposed on Noriega after the fraudulent elections.[49] "I'm worried about the lives of American citizens," the president had said in May, "and I will do what is necessary to protect the lives of American citizens."[50] Protection of Americans was on both occasions the first, and arguably most important, objective. In a diary entry on the night of December 17, Bush said that "we cannot let a military officer be killed, and certainly not a lietenant and his wife brutalized."[51] When the president spoke to the American people on December 20, he briefly reviewed what had transpired over the previous two years and then reported the most recent incidents. "Last Friday, Noriega declared his military dictatorship to be in a state of war with the United States and publicly threatened the lives of Americans in Panama. The very next day, forces under his command shot and killed an unarmed American serviceman; wounded another; arrested and brutally beat a third American serviceman; and then brutally interrogated his wife, threatening her with sexual abuse. That was enough."[52]

In the days following the invasion, there was considerable concern that Noriega might escape capture, but he was unable to leave Panama City and eventually sought sanctuary in the Vatican embassy. Once his whereabouts were known, negotiations began for his surrender to the US authorities surrounding the building. While awaiting the outcome of these negotiations, Noriega reportedly heard news coverage of the collapse of communism in Romania and the killing of Nicolae Ceaușescu.[53] Panamanian crowds gathered to demand his surrender, and in what was described as an act of psychological warfare, the American troops guarding the embassy blared rock music toward the windows of Noriega's guestroom: "Voodoo Child," "You're No Good," "Nowhere to Run, Nowhere to Hide," and "I Fought the Law and the Law Won."[54] On January 3, 1990, Noriega surrendered to American forces and was flown to Florida to stand trial.

Endara's inauguration as Panama's properly elected president and Noriega's conviction on drug charges made the mission a success to most Americans. Bush's standings in the polls went up at the end of his first year in the White House and media references to him as a "wimp," an unkind label that had dogged him since the 1988 campaign, declined. The invasion was condemned at the Organization of American States and the United Nations but those reactions did not appear to bother the

American people or their president.[55] Rioting and looting which added to the disruption and destruction in Panama's cities following the invasion was probably predictable given the broad role played by the PDF in domestic security. US forces were slow to stop it, and Congress was slow to authorize funds for the rebuilding of damaged property. Panama clearly demonstrated that the Bush administration was willing to use force when it was deemed necessary and that a president could do so largely on his own authority.

DISSECTING THE DECISION

By most standards, the invasion was a success, and gets relatively less attention from students of the Bush presidency than the later, and larger, military operations in the Persian Gulf. Among those who do write about Panama, questions linger about when and why the president decided to use force. The straightforward answers to those questions are that he made his decision at a meeting with his senior advisers on Sunday, December 17, and did so for the reasons he shared with the American people in his television broadcast three days later. He was protecting American citizens, standing up for democracy and against drugs, and he was ensuring the security of the Panama Canal.

Of course, it may be more complicated than that. James Baker reports that the meeting on December 17 was anticlimactic. The Secretary of State knew, before the meeting began, that the president would order military action.[56] Powell, new to the national security team, was not so sure. Cheney, if he heard what the president wanted to do before the senior advisers gathered on the 17th, did not share that information with Powell.[57] Was the crucial policy choice already made before the president's advisers met? Robert Gates notes that President Bush rarely made important decisions in formal meetings of foreign policy advisers like the one that took place that Sunday. Instead, the president's style was to have constant conversation with a small circle of close associates and with a much larger group of people, inside the government and out. He sought ideas and alternatives from all of these people. Somewhere in the midst of those conversations and consultations the most consequential presidential decisions got made.[58] Our access to those decision points depends crucially on what the president reports himself and what his closest foreign policy adviser, Brent Scowcroft, may have to say. In their joint memoir, neither comments about the Panama decision, except to compare some features of that situation to the later events in the Persian Gulf.[59]

In an oral history interview, Scowcroft gives more attention to Panama. He observes that "at the outset of the administration, Panama was not on my list of concerns, Nicaragua was, Panama was not."[60] Two key events put Panama high on the NSC agenda. First was the stolen election that isolated Noriega from any remaining international or regional support he may have had. The fact that multiple election watchers all agreed that there had been widespread fraud made it easier to contemplate future action against Noriega. The vivid pictures of a bloodied vice-presidential candidate gave those elections a powerful image that everyone remembered. The second key event was the failed coup attempt in the fall of 1989. Scowcroft is convinced that there would never have been major American support for Giroldi. The Bush administration simply knew too little about who Giroldi was, or what he was planning, to take risky steps on his behalf.[61] But the public and congressional response in the aftermath of the failed coup, portraying the administration as inept, is what mattered. It elevated the importance of the next incident involving Panama and guaranteed that it would be taken seriously. The May elections isolated Noriega, making it easier to take action against him; the October coup elevated interest in Panama, ensuring that senior members of the administration would pay close attention the next time Panama became an immediate concern. That said, even Scowcroft was surprised at the modest nature of the actual grounds that triggered the president's decision to order a large-scale military operation.[62]

The weakness of the immediate provocation has led some commentators at the time and since to speculate that a decision to depose Noriega was made shortly after the failed October coup and merely awaited an excuse to proceed. This is one possibility, but there is another. Some of the reports about the December 17 deliberations suggest that the president may have been responding to the immediate provocations rather than giving a pre-determined order to go. Bob Woodward tells us that General Kelly, the principal briefer at the December meeting, noticed that the people in the room were more disturbed when hearing the details concerning Bonnie Curtis than they were about the killing of Lt. Paz.[63] Perhaps, that was because the detailed information about the interrogation, beating and harassment of Lt. and Mrs. Curtis was newer than the reports about the roadblock shooting.[64] Or perhaps it was something else.

Another participant in the December 17 meeting, Robert Gates, saw the same thing that Kelly saw and thinks the president was affected more by what happened to Mrs. Custis than by any other news that came out of Panama. "My recollection," Gates reports, "is that the assault on the American officer and his wife absolutely drove Bush around the bend. That was the last straw as far as he was concerned."[65] Elsewhere, Gates writes that throughout his years of association with George H. W. Bush, the president was always "a gentleman in an age when not much premium is placed on that quality."[66] Everyone involved in the Panama deliberations was offended by the PDF abuse of an innocent woman whose only offense was to witness one of their crimes. Perhaps the presi-

dent was more offended than others. Maybe the December 17 meeting
was the rare occasion when this president made a major decision at a
formal gathering of his senior advisers.[67]

The US invasion of Panama is a classic case of an over-determined
event. There were multiple reasons for the decision to execute military
operations against Noriega's regime. By the beginning of the Bush administration, the Panamanian dictator had made himself a major problem
for a powerful nation that had a long history of domination in Central
America. The old excuses for tolerating Noriega—the Cold War of the
1980s and the negotiation of new treaties for the future of the canal in the
1970s—no longer protected him. Drugs and drug trafficking were becoming important issues on the national security agenda and, after the Florida indictments, Noriega's ties to the drug trade were impossible to ignore. In an age when democracy was spreading in Latin America, behind
the Iron Curtain and even in the streets of China's capital city, Noriega's
flagrant disregard for elections marked him and his regime as anachron-
istic. And of course, the special interests and history that the United
States had in connection with the Panama Canal made Noriega a substantial threat to the timely implementation of plans to transfer control of the
canal to Panamanians. There were lots of reasons for getting rid of Noriega. And by the fall of 1989, nearly everything in the arsenal of foreign
policymaking tools—condemnations, sanctions, monitored elections,
negotiations, bribes, coups and covert operations—had been tried. Everything had failed. The sentiment that Admiral Crowe expressed to General
Thurman, that something was bound to happen to provoke an American
use of force in Panama, was an understandable sentiment held by others.[68]

Ultimately, Manuel Noriega was responsible for taking things too far
and making the likely American invasion a certainty. He did so when he
issued a declaration of war against the United States and allowed, or
ordered, the PDF to ratchet up the harassment of Americans. Whether he
was directly involved in any of the orders that led to the shooting of Lt.
Paz or the harsh treatment of Lt. and Mrs. Curtis is not known. But the
tipping point in the mind of the president may well have been the things
that happened to a young serviceman's wife pressed against a wall in a
Panamanian interrogation room. The old-fashioned gentleman, who now
lived in the White House, had had enough.

NOTES

1. For general descriptions of events in Panama see Richard Ben Cramer, *What It
Takes* (New York: Random House, 1992), 1042–43; Timothy Naftali, *George H. W. Bush*
(New York: Times Books, 2007), 88–89; and Robert A. Strong, *Decisions and Dilemmas*
(New York: M. E. Sharpe, 2005), 184–85. Detailed official incident reports can be found

at George H. W. Bush Presidential Records, National Security Council, Pryce, William T., Files, Subject Files, Folder CF00732-013.

2. John Robert Greene, *The Presidency of George Bush* (Lawrence: University Press of Kansas, 2000), 101. See also, R. W. Apple Jr., "Bush's Obsession," *New York Times*, December 26, 1989, A11.

3. See for example, Joe Pichirallo and Patrick E. Tyler, "Long Road to the Invasion of Panama," *Washington Post*, January 14, 1990.

4. Maureen Dowd, "A Sense of Inevitability in Bush's Decision to Act," *New York Times*, December 24, 1989.

5. Robert W. Tucker and David C. Hendrickson, *The Imperial Temptation: The New World Order and America's Purpose* (New York: Council on Foreign Relations, 1992), 46. See also, *Encyclopedia of U.S. Foreign Relations*, Vol. III, Bruce Jentleson and Thomas Paterson, eds., (Oxford: Oxford University Press, 1997).

6. Steven Hurst, *The Foreign Policy of the Bush Administration: In Search of a New World Order* (London: Cassell, 1999), 56.

7. Two books describe Noriega's life and associations with the United States: Frederick Kempe, *Divorcing the Dictator* (New York: Putnam's, 1990); and John Dinges, *Our Man in Panama* (New York: Random House, 1990). Dinges gives a slightly different account of Noriega's parents than the one summarized above, Ibid., 31.

8. Dinges, *Our Man in Panama*, 45–46. Documents prepared for Noriega's trial provide detailed information on the payments he received from the Department of Defense and from the CIA. See "Substitution Documents on Noriega Payments," in George H. W. Bush Presidential Records, National Security Council, Pryce, William T., Files, Folder CF00732-020.

9. Stansfield Turner, *Burn Before Reading: Presidents, CIA Directors, and Secret Intelligence* (New York: Hyperion, 2006), 211–12.

10. Kempe, *Divorcing the Dictator*, 90–95.

11. Quoted in Kempe, *Divorcing the Dictator*, 2.

12. William Branigin, "Army Reveals Details of Noriega's Lair of Magic," *Washington Post*, December 26, 1989.

13. Stipulated in the Oliver North trial documents as reported by Kempe, *Divorcing the Dictator*, 165.

14. Dinges, *Our Man in Panama*, 51; Kempe, *Divorcing the Dictator*, 162. See also Seymour Hersh, "Our Man in Panama," *Life*, March 1990.

15. Joel McCleary quoted in Kempe, *Divorcing the Dictator*, 173.

16. The State Department acknowledged in its annual report on human rights that the 1984 elections had been rigged. "Country Reports on Human Rights Practices For 1985," *Report Submitted to the Committee on Foreign Affairs House of Representatives and the Committee on Foreign Relations U.S. Senate by the Department of State* (February 1986), 640.

17. Dinges, *Our Man in Panama*, 41.

18. Kevin Buckley, *Panama: The Whole Story* (New York: Simon & Schuster, 1991), 229–31.

19. Ibid. See also, Murray Waas, "Cocaine and the White House Connection," *L.A. Weekly*, September 30–October 6, 1986.

20. Articles by Hersh appeared in the *New York Times* on June 12, 13, and 22, 1986. The first on June 12 was particularly embarrassing to Noriega because it was published while he was visiting the United States on official business.

21. Kempe, *Divorcing the Dictator*, 255.

22. Ibid., 223.

23. Steve C. Ropp, "Panama's Defiant Noriega," *Current History* (December 1988): 417–18.

24. David Hoffman, "Bush Splits with Reagan on Handling of Noriega," *Washington Post*, May 19, 1988.

25. "Covert Action on Noriega Is Cleared," *Washington Post*, July 29, 1988.

26. "Lugar Urges Crackdown on Noriega," *Washington Post*, April 22, 1989, A8. See also Juan Sosa, *In Defiance* (Washington, DC: The Francis Press, 1999), 79.

27. "Taking Aim at Noriega," *U.S. News and World Report*, May 1, 1989, 40–41.

28. President George H.W. Bush, "Remarks to the Council of the Americas," May 2, 1989.

29. In some accounts, Endara won by a three-to-one margin. Eytan Gilboa, "The Panama Invasion Revisited," *Political Science Quarterly*, 110, no. 4 (Winter 1995–1996): 553.

30. Linda Robinson, "Dwindling Options in Panama," *Foreign Affairs* 68, no. 5 (Winter 1989).

31. Pichirallo and Tyler, "Long Road to the Invasion of Panama."

32. Kempe, *Divorcing the Dictator*, 11.

33. George H. W. Bush, "Remarks and A Question-and-Answer Session With Reporters on the Situation in Panama," May 11, 1989.

34. James Baker, *The Politics of Diplomacy* (New York: G. P. Putnam's, 1995), 186.

35. Colin Powell, *My American Journey* (New York: Random House, 1995), 405.

36. Buckley, *Panama*, 193–208.

37. R. W. Apple Jr., "Prudent Meets Timid," *New York Times*, October 14, 1989.

38. Robert Gates, *From the Shadows*, (New York: Simon & Shuster, 1997), 459.

39. Pichirallo and Tyler, "Long Road to the Invasion of Panama."

40. Powell, *My American Journey*, 409.

41. Buckley, *Panama*, 229–231. Powell says that Sununu was not present. Powell, *My American Journey*, 410.

42. Bob Woodward, *The Commanders* (New York: Simon & Schuster, 1991), 168; and Powell, *My American Journey*, 410.

43. Some American soldiers had been detained at the Panamanian airport where their weapons were confiscated. On Sunday morning a US officer shot a PDF policeman when he thought the Panamanian was reaching for a gun. Gilboa, "The Panama Invasion Revisited," 558.

44. Powell, *My American Journey*, 412. In Woodward the same quote is given as "Okay let's go. We're going to go." Woodward, *The Commanders*, 171.

45. Baker, *The Politics of Diplomacy*, 189.

46. Woodward, *The Commanders*, 171.

47. "Inside the Invasion," *Newsweek*, June 25, 1990, 30.

48. George H. W. Bush, "Address to the Nation Announcing United States Military Action in Panama," December 20, 1989.

49. George H. W. Bush, "Remarks and a Question-and-Answer Session With Reporters on the Situation in Panama," May 11, 1989.

50. Ibid.

51. Diary quoted in Jon Meacham, *Destiny and Power: The American Odyssey of George Herbert Walker Bush* (New York: Random House, 2015), 388.

52. Bush, "Address to the Nation Announcing United States Military Action in Panama."

53. Kempe, *Divorcing the Dictator*, 411.

54. Some sources describe the music as psychological warfare, others say it was used to prevent reporters from hearing the discussions that were underway about Noriega's surrender. Gordon Rottman, *Panama 1989–1990*, Elite Series 37 (London: Osprey Publishing, 1991), 56.

55. Scowcroft points out that Bush helped to ensure a relatively mild OAS condemnation by taking time to talk to Latin American leaders about the Noriega problem throughout the fall of 1989. "My guess is that he talked to every Latin American leader a minimum of half a dozen times about Panama." Brent Scowcroft Interview, November 12–13, 1999, George H. W. Bush Oral History Project, Miller Center, University of Virginia.

56. Baker, *Politics of Diplomacy*, 189

57. Powell, *My American Journey*, 409.

58. Gates, *From the Shadows*, 454.

59. George Bush and Brent Scowcroft, *A World Transformed* (New York: Knopf, 1998), 463 and 489.

60. Brent Scowcroft Interview, November 12–13, 1999.

61. Ibid.

62. Ibid.

63. Woodward, *The Commanders*, 168.

64. The "Situation Room Note" in the White House Files for December 17, 1989 describes only the facts surrounding the shooting of Lt. Paz. The note from the following day titled "Panama Update" describes both the Paz killing and the incidents involving a "US Naval officer and his wife." George H. W. Bush Presidential Records, National Security Council, Rostow, Nicholas, Files, Panama Files, Folder CF00741-017.

65. Robert Gates Interview, July 23–24, 2000, George H. W. Bush Oral History Project, Miller Center, University of Virginia.

66. Gates, *From the Shadows*, 455. Powell also describes Bush as a "well bred gentleman" in his character sketch of his former boss. Powell, *My American Journey*, 568.

67. John Sununu, who attended the December 17 meeting, disagrees with this assessment and reports his impression that the president had made up his mind before the meeting had begun, John Sununu, *The Quiet Man: The Indispensable Presidency of George H. W. Bush* (New York: Broadside Books, 2015), 323.

68. Baker reports that from his first day as Secretary of State he was worried that a military solution might be needed. Baker, *The Politics of Diplomacy*, 177.

FOUR

Insight

German Unification Anchored in the NATO Alliance

At the end of the president's trip to Eastern Europe in the summer of 1989, George Bush was convinced that the time had come to meet with Mikhail Gorbachev and directly address the dramatic changes taking place in Europe and the Soviet Union.[1] This was, of course, something he had been urged to do by commentators and critics throughout the early months of the administration. On the flight back to the United States, the president drafted a personal letter to Gorbachev that led to a meeting in Malta in December of 1989 and a formal summit in Washington, DC six months later.

The Washington Summit produced one of the most remarkable conversations in the history of Cold War diplomacy. The president of the United States asked Gorbachev if he accepted a principle in the Helsinki Accords: the sovereign nations of Europe have the right to make their own decisions about alliance affiliations. Though framed as an abstract question about a document signed in the era of détente, Bush's question was neither abstract nor historical. He was asking, as everyone present fully understood, whether or not a soon-to-be reunited Germany could choose to remain a member of the North Atlantic Treaty Organization (NATO).[2] To the amazement of everyone in the room, Gorbachev said yes. An NSC staff member quickly passed a note to President Bush asking him to get Gorbachev to repeat the incredible thing that had just been said. After Gorbachev had some private conversations with some of his advisers in a corner of the room and returned to the table, Bush reiterated the proposition that European nations have the right to choose their own alliance partners, this time observing how pleased he was that both the

United States and the Soviet Union accepted this idea. Again, Gorbachev agreed.

Other discussions with Gorbachev at the Washington Summit, and before, had not been as simple or straightforward. Gorbachev sometimes expressed a desire to postpone any final decisions about NATO and a united Germany, arguing that European-wide security issues had to be settled first. At one point, he offered the observation that a reunited German state might simultaneously be a member of NATO and a member of the Warsaw Pact (the alliance of East European communist regimes), an odd idea that he and other Soviet officials had mentioned on previous occasions. At another point, Gorbachev suggested that the Soviet Union might apply to become a member of NATO.[3] These inconclusive comments were superseded by the surprising acknowledgment that national sovereignty matters. That idea was consistent with Gorbachev's commitment to new political thinking, to his wish to end a long era of Soviet domination in Eastern Europe and his encouragement of change and reform in the Warsaw Pact nations. It was consistent with his efforts to reduce confrontation with the West in order to facilitate military budget savings and reform at home.

It was not, however, consistent with then established Soviet policy on the future of a reunited Germany. Earlier in the spring, both Gorbachev and his foreign minister, Eduard Shevardnadze, had publicly accepted the reality that the two German states—the German Democratic Republic (GDR) in the East and the Federal Republic of Germany (FRG) in the West—would soon be one. There had been no public acceptance of the idea that a reunited Germany could remain a partner in the Western alliance that had opposed the Soviet Union and its Eastern European empire for decades. The planning document prepared by the Central Committee of the Communist Party of the Soviet Union for the Washington Summit, and for a preliminary Moscow meeting with Secretary Baker, clearly stated that "it would be politically and psychologically unacceptable for us to see a united Germany in NATO. We cannot agree to the destruction of the balance of power and stability that would result from this step."[4]

The surprise in the US delegation at Gorbachev's acceptance of the Helsinki principle was genuine. So was the confusion it caused on the Soviet side of the table. Though there were some efforts to get Gorbachev to back off, the Soviet delegation did not formally object when President Bush included a description of Gorbachev's commitment in his public statement at the end of the summit deliberations. The world was still months away from any final agreements about German unification and a statement in a summit conversation was not a legally binding commitment.[5] But the Washington Summit exchange between Bush and Gorbachev was a breakthrough that strongly suggested that German reunification might be concluded in short order and on terms that met the

American preference for Germany to remain a full member of the NATO alliance.

For Brent Scowcroft, the president's national security advisor, the Soviet and American agreement on this issue was the moment when the Cold War ended.[6] When asked about that judgment in a later interview, Scowcroft—not an individual prone to grandiose pronouncement—said this:

> The Summit meeting, and the discussion that took place at the Summit meeting in early June of 1990, was a turning point in world history. For months, the President's speechwriters had included a phrase in speeches saying "the Cold War is over." And I routinely crossed it out and crossed it out and crossed it out. After this meeting, I came to the conclusion that this time I could leave it in the President's speeches.[7]

From the beginning of the administration, Scowcroft had been cautious about allowing Bush to say that the Cold War was over. He recognized that the president would only be able to make such a statement once, and he wanted that opportunity to be used to good effect.[8] Moreover, a presidential pronouncement that the Cold War was history carried with it the risk that a change of government in Moscow or a change in policy by Gorbachev would revive old animosities and anxieties. A mistimed presidential pronouncement would open the president to serious criticism. There was, of course, a risk on the other side of Scowcroft's calculations. Waiting too long to acknowledge the obvious changes in the Soviet Union and in Eastern Europe opened the president to a different kind of critique. In general, Scowcroft's caution early in the Bush administration carried the day. For Scowcroft, the time for setting that caution aside came at the Washington Summit.

In the twelve months between the president's letter to Gorbachev in the summer of 1989 and their remarkable conversation in the summer of 1990, a major transformation took place in the political landscape of the European continent. It was a transformation as large and consequential as those that accompanied the end of the twentieth century's two world wars. When the president wrote his letter to Gorbachev inviting direct communication, it was almost unthinkable that there could be a rapid, peaceful and successful reunification of Germany with uninterrupted and unimpeded German participation in the NATO alliance. It was harder still to believe that the Soviet Union would accept such developments. A little over a year later, it all happened. George Bush was way ahead of both public and expert opinion when he began to talk seriously about German unification with continued NATO membership. He and his Secretary of State pursued those objectives in an impressive and intensive application of personal and professional diplomacy. They were supported by extraordinary staff work across the foreign policy institutions and organizations of the Bush administration.

In the catalogue of Bush administration foreign policy achievements, this one sits at or near the top of the list. It provides a vivid example of American foreign policy leadership in action, even though much of what Bush did on this issue was done behind the scenes and with minimal fanfare. The president should be given credit for both perceiving that a reunited Germany anchored in an American-led alliance was possible and for the persistent pursuit of what appeared, at the outset, to be a highly unlikely outcome.

BUSH'S EARLY ACCEPTANCE OF GERMAN REUNIFICATION

For decades before the 1990 Washington Summit, the working assumption of diplomats and international observers was that the division of Germany at the end of the Second World War was unlikely to change. The division began as a temporary arrangement after hostilities ceased and before a peace treaty could be signed. But the breakdown in relations between the Soviet Union and the Western allies precluded the negotiation of a formal treaty ending the war, and the allied sectors became two separate states. The Federal Republic of Germany was comprised of the sectors administered by France, Britain and the United States; the smaller Soviet sector became the German Democratic Republic. The city of Berlin was also divided, and each of the German states had alliance commitments on their side of the ideological division in Europe.

In the West, this arrangement was never officially accepted. The constitution of West Germany included provisions anticipating reunification that would take place at some unknown point in the future. All the NATO allies agreed that the restoration of a united Germany should be sought. But that was an easy commitment to make so long as it did not actually occur, or was unlikely to occur anytime soon. For France, Great Britain and other European nations, the division of Germany and the subsequent anchoring of the FDR within the NATO alliance, and within the trade and economic agreements that became the European Community (EC), were welcome developments. A divided Germany mitigated historic concerns about German power in the center of Europe; and among European diplomats, there was little discussion or interest in a rapid or radical change to the post-war map. A frequently repeated joke captured a common attitude toward German reunification. The French, it was said in the aftermath of World War II, came to love the German nation. And loved it so much they hoped there would always be two of them.[9]

In the East, the division of Germany was seen as an important strategic accomplishment for the Soviet Union. The USSR was the nation that suffered the largest allied losses in the Second World War, and the Soviet Union had reason to be apprehensive about any possible reemergence of

German military power or territorial ambition. The Kremlin maintained close ties to East Germany, the crown jewel of their East European empire. They kept over three hundred thousand troops within its borders, provided subsidies to its economy and engaged in extensive trade. The Soviet Union fully accepted the post-war status quo of a divided Germany.

The Soviet troops, tanks and missiles in East Germany, and elsewhere in Eastern Europe, were supposed to defend the Warsaw Pact against Western aggression. In fact, Soviet military forces in Eastern Europe never fought NATO. Instead, they were used to suppress reform movements in East Germany, Poland, Hungary and Czechoslovakia. In 1989, far more sweeping reforms than those contemplated in the 1950s or 1960s were taking place in Eastern Europe. And the Soviet Union, for the first time since the beginning of the Cold War, was allowing those reforms to move forward and encouraging the leaders who were implementing them.

During the early months of 1989, the Bush administration focused on the political changes in Poland and Hungary, the two nations Bush visited on his trip to Eastern Europe, and the nations he talked about during his speech at Hamtramck, Michigan. As Brent Scowcroft recalled, "At the outset of the administration, I was very careful on German unification. My sense was that it wasn't an active issue. . . . Nobody was talking about it. We had ritual incantations about German unification, but it was not an issue for anybody."[10] In March of 1989 a report drafted by a senior State Department official restated the conventional wisdom about German re-unification: "There is no more inflammatory and divisive issue [in Europe], and it serves no US interest for us to take the initiative to raise it."[11] In April a draft memo to the president from Brent Scowcroft on "Dealing with the Germans" contained the commonly believed conclusion that "for most Germans, the reunification of Germany is seen as a desirable but unattainable goal."[12]

It started to become attainable when elections in Poland produced a new government with a solid Solidarity majority that Gorbachev accepted and when reforms in Hungary introduced relaxed security measures on the border between Hungary and Austria. Erich Honecker, the long-serving East German leader, opposed the political and economic liberalizations in Warsaw and Budapest, but events in neighboring nations put pressure on his government. The Polish example generated demands for free multi-party elections in East Germany. And the border policies in Hungary made it possible for East Germans to "vacation" in Hungary, cross into Austria, and make their way to West Germany. Initially, the Hungarians respected agreements with the GDR that prohibited East Germans from using the newly liberalized border crossings, but some vacationers got through and others went to Western embassies in Hungary, and later in Czechoslovakia, seeking asylum and relocation to the West. The numbers of asylum seekers in West German embassies ballooned in the fall of 1989 and led to negotiations to allow some of them to officially migrate to West Germany. This was a stopgap measure that temporarily reduced congestion in embassy compounds but did little to reduce the number of East Germans attempting to get to the West.

When the Hungarian government stopped officially restricting the movement of East Germans at their borders in September of 1989, the number of emigrants grew dramatically. The exodus of East Germans into the West—the problem that had led to the construction of the Berlin Wall in the early 1960s—was back more than a quarter of a century later and on a scale that could not be ignored. Throughout the fall of 1989, Helmut Kohl, the West German chancellor, kept Bush informed about emigration from East to West. Each time Kohl mentioned the subject, the numbers got larger.[13] In the month of November 1989 alone, there were 130,000 East Germans who left the country, nearly 1 percent of the population.[14] No one knew how many East Germans would leave if given the chance to do so, but one Hungarian official estimated a number measured in the millions.[15] When Baker talked to the Soviet foreign minister in September, Shevardnadze guessed that the exodus of East Germans from the GDR might well involve a seven-figure number.[16] Those who were choosing to leave were disproportionately young and well educated and their departure would have significant consequences for an already weak East German economy.

Throughout the fall of 1989 and well into 1990, the movement of East Germans to the West put constant pressure on both German states. It was an embarrassment to the leaders of the GDR that so many of their citizens wanted to leave; and it was a growing burden in the FRG, where the new arrivals needed to be housed, employed and welcomed without causing a backlash from the GDR. Moreover, it was a constant reminder that some form of reunification, or closer association or, at a minimum, resolution of migration issues would be necessary. Earlier in European history, German territorial boundaries and jurisdictions had been altered by war. Now there was a demand to fundamentally alter relations between East and West Germany coming from courageous individuals. This was revolution by the suitcase, not the sword.

Other East Germans—those who were not packing up to leave—were organizing demonstrations. Throughout the fall of 1989, there were large gatherings in East German cities and protests against the hated state secret police. In the city of Leipzig, demonstrations took place on nearly every Monday that fall, and the number of people participating grew over time. When Gorbachev visited East Germany early in October of 1989 to celebrate the 40th anniversary of the GDR, he was greeted by huge crowds chanting, "Gorby help us! Gorby save us!"[17] These were crowds presumably arranged or approved by the East German government. Their chants were genuine cries for change. During his visit, Gor-

bachev urged Honecker to initiate reforms. Later Gorbachev gave orders
to Soviet troops stationed in East Germany to stay in their barracks during protests that were taking place across the country. Selective East German crackdowns on the protesters were never enough to stop their momentum. A physically ailing and politically weakened Honecker was
forced to step down shortly after Gorbachev's October visit. His succes-
sors, Egon Krentz and Hans Modrow, promised to introduce reforms,
including new policies for freer movement across borders. As East Germany's new leaders worked to develop these reforms, events in the
streets of Berlin got ahead of them.

An erroneous public statement about forthcoming policies to allow
freer movement between East and West Germany inadvertently implied
that the borders were already open. The people of Berlin made that error
into a reality with spontaneous crossings at checkpoints followed by the
joyful destruction of the wall. Because the boisterous crowds in Berlin
took matters into their own hands, the post-Honecker East German
government never got credit for genuine, though belated, efforts to liberalize travel restrictions. Instead, the collapse of the Berlin Wall, and the
demonstrations that accompanied it, left the impression that no one was
really in charge on the eastern side of the old barrier and that additional
dramatic changes in East Germany might be forthcoming. In November
of 1989, the issue of German reunification that Scowcroft had earlier ignored, and that the State Department had labeled as inflammatory and
divisive, became an urgent matter for everyone living in Europe and for
those watching from around the world.

George Bush reacted to the dramatic events in Berlin with the prudence that became the catchphrase attached to his presidency. Asked at
an impromptu news conference shortly after crowds in Berlin began freely moving back and forth across the previously armed checkpoints, the
president said he was very pleased by the events in Berlin. Asked why he
was not more excited by these dramatic and historic developments he
famously told the assembled reporters, "I am not an emotional kind of
guy." [18] George Bush was, in fact, a very emotional person and the pos-
tured prudence—or what might be called his irrational lack of exuber-
ance—was scripted. The president was delivering a carefully calibrated
response to remarkable international events. He intentionally tempered
his response in the weeks that followed because he had decided to forego
taking credit or making headlines about the events in Berlin. He wanted
to avoid anything that would complicate East German or Soviet acquiescence to the surprising and positive things that were taking place in
Germany. This was not just a matter of rhetorical moderation. It was a
deliberate decision to be careful in all of the American responses to the
events in Berlin. Secretary Baker, in appearances on US television the day
after the wall fell, used language similarly designed to avoid any unnecessary agitation. For a time, Baker even refrained from using the word

reunification in connection to prospective developments in Germany and instead talked about *reconciliation*.[19] The president would later, and frequently, describe his decisions not to go to Berlin, not to immediately give a dramatic speech about the end of the Cold War and not to "dance on the Berlin Wall" as important contributions to the successful cultivation of Soviet acceptance to developments in Germany. Gorbachev acknowledged his appreciation of the president's rhetorical restraint at their meeting in Malta.[20]

The president's prudence did not mean that he was completely caught off guard by what was happening in Germany or that he had not given thought to what might transpire as a result of the Gorbachev-inspired liberalizations in Eastern Europe. Well before the collapse of the wall, Bush was thinking seriously about the possibility of a forthcoming German reunification. The president raised the subject in Kennebunkport when he met with Mitterrand before their joint appearance at the MIT commencement in May of 1989. He was pleased when the French leader said, "If the German people wished it, I would not oppose it."[21] Mitterrand went on to express the conventional wisdom on the subject of German reunification: it was unlikely in the near future because the Soviets would not accept it and Europe was not ready for it. But Bush, unlike his guest at Kennebunkport and most of the foreign policy experts in his administration, did believe that German reunification was worth considering. In the months before the collapse of the Berlin Wall, Bush was thinking about reunification and was ready for it.

Earlier in the month of May when asked by a reporter what he thought about German unification, Bush had given a positive response. "I'd love to see Germany reunited," he said. "If you can get unification on a proper basis, fine."[22] At the end of the month, in his speech at Mainz, he emphasized the need for close cooperation between West Germany and America as "partners in leadership" in responding to the recent developments in Eastern Europe. He described the history of post-war Europe as a time that had resolved the long-term conflict between France and Germany, just as an earlier period of European history had resolved the conflict between Britain and France. "The NATO alliance did nothing less than provide a way for Western Europe to heal centuries-old rivalries, to begin an era of reconciliation and restoration . . . a second Renaissance of Europe."[23]

The laudatory language in the Mainz speech reflected Bush's personal conviction that Germany, or at least West Germany, was no longer a threat to European peace and stability. NATO membership, European economic cooperation and decades of successful democratic governance in the Federal Republic of Germany had transformed the Germans on the western side of the Iron Curtain. The dramatic changes taking place in Eastern Europe during his presidency would clearly involve enormous challenges, but Bush never believed that those challenges included a reversal of the political progress that West Germany had made after World War II. If German unification could take place without destruction of the alliances and economic institutions that had emerged in Western Europe, it would pose no threat to America or to America's European allies. To the contrary, that version of reunification would guarantee continued participation by the United States in European security—a crucial factor in the restoration, reconciliation and renaissance Bush had praised in Mainz.

President Bush was confident that "the German question"—the question about German power and territorial ambition in Central Europe; the question that had arguably led to two twentieth-century wars—was now resolved. That confidence made him unique among international leaders in 1989. Margaret Thatcher, François Mitterrand and Mikhail Gorbachev all held, to varying degrees, lingering suspicions about German nationalism that made them urge caution and delay in the immediate aftermath of the collapse of the Berlin Wall.[24] A few months before the dramatic events at the wall, Margaret Thatcher was willing to tell Gorbachev in a private conversation that no one in Europe really wanted to see German reunification.[25]

Commentators writing about Germany in 1989, often and openly, speculated about security dangers associated with German reunification. These observations were sometimes framed as problems of public opinion in the European countries where older citizens clearly remembered the horrors of World War II. Even if Germany had changed, public attitudes toward Germany may not have. Those attitudes would matter in democracies. Other commentators were less concerned about public reactions and made their observations within the context of traditional realist theories of international politics. They warned that the distribution of power among states, not political institutions, or recent histories, or public attitudes would determine state behavior and generate systemic security problems. If a larger Germany, combining the wealth and power of the FDR with the additional territory and population of the GDR, were suddenly created in the center of Europe, it was bound to change the balance-of-power on the continent.

Bush rejected the caution of allied leaders and the power calculations of realist commentators. He was not unaware of public concerns or international relations theories that raised questions about a reunited Germany, but he was not persuaded by them. He demonstrated his own ability to move beyond World War II attitudes and animosities when he attended the funeral of the Japanese emperor early in his presidency. If a pilot shot down in the Pacific could respectfully honor the leader of the nation that attacked Pearl Harbor, surely others could move beyond old ideas about Germany.

George Bush was sure that German reunification could be safely contemplated and, if it was done without weakening NATO or Germany's

other regional and international associations, it could be safely and swift-
ly implemented.[26] Bush reached this important insight ahead of his advisers and well ahead of his allied partners in Western Europe. He never
abandoned it. He stated his convictions in these matters publicly in September of 1989, nearly two months before the fall of the Berlin Wall.
Asked by a reporter on a visit to Helena, Montana to comment on the fact
that the recent exodus of East Germans to the West was getting lots of
people thinking about reunification, Bush said this:

> I would think it's a matter for the Germans to decide. But put it this
> way: If that was worked out between the Germanys, I do not think we
> should view that as bad for Western interests. I think there's been a
> dramatic change in post-World War II Germany. And so, I don't fear
> it. . . . But I think there is in some quarters a feeling — well, a reunified
> Germany would be detrimental to the peace of Europe, of Western
> Europe, some way; and I don't accept that at all, simply don't.[27]

In Montana, the president said that the reunification of the two Germanys was a legitimate goal. That was something other Cold War presidents
had said on multiple occasions. But Bush went further and shared an
important observation. He said that the emerging concerns about German reunification as something dangerous to European security or to
Western interests were unwarranted. The president was not afraid of a
Germany that combined the territory and populations of the FRG and the
GDR. He welcomed it.

Bob Gates, the deputy director of the NSC who was traveling with the
president on the trip to Helena, remembers immediately calling Brent
Scowcroft. "Brent, we now have a policy on German reunification," Gates
told his boss. And Scowcroft responded, "'What is it?' I said, 'We're for
it.' He said, 'Who says so?' I said, 'The President.' He said, 'Oh, shit.'"[28]

THE COMPLEXITIES AND COMPLICATIONS
OF GERMAN REUNIFICATION

Scowcroft's expletive was probably not a reflection of reservations about
German reunification, though he may have had more such reservations
than the president.[29] It was probably related to his exasperation with the
pace of events in Eastern Europe during the fall of 1989 and his recognition of the difficulties that a decisive presidential commitment to German
reunification could create. But in the final months of 1989, neither the
president nor his national security advisor, nor Gorbachev and other
Soviet leaders, had much control over the pace of developments in Eastern Europe. Scowcroft's expletive was a fact of life.

After the fall of the Berlin Wall in November of 1989, American intelligence analysts, State Department officials and NSC staffers rather quickly
reached a common assessment: East Germany would soon collapse from

its long-term economic weakness and from the growing public demands for change. Reunification could occur soon. The East German leaders after Honecker were trying to introduce reforms, but they could not keep pace with public expectations or growing domestic problems. They were unable to stop the movement of their citizens to West Germany. They could not fix an economy that was heavily in debt, short on foreign currency, and obviously lagging far behind the vibrant success that was evident in the West. Nor could they depend on new Soviet help to prop up their faltering regime. Both before and after the resignation of Honecker, East German leaders contemplated using large-scale force against the continuing demonstrations and protests. Some talked about a "Chinese option," in a reference to the crackdown on demonstrators in Tiananmen Square in the summer of 1989. But East German leaders never had Gorbachev's support for that course of action, and never agreed among themselves to bear the risks it would entail.

Shortly after the fall of the Berlin Wall, and just before Bush met with Gorbachev in Malta, Kohl gave a major speech to the Bundestag outlining steps that could be taken in a gradual but dramatic transformation of relations between East and West Germany. Read today, Kohl's ten-point plan seems modest in its scope and timeline, but for a West German leader in November of 1989 to make serious public pronouncements about movement toward reunification was a bold step on its own. Kohl took it without any prior notice to his American or European allies and without consulting his domestic coalition partners. It was Kohl acting alone on the basis of his conviction that the opportunity for reunification, or at least for a radical change in the relations between the two Germanys, was clearly at hand. In the days after the fall of the Berlin Wall events moved quickly in Europe.[30] In Washington, Bush and Baker were caught off guard by Kohl's speech; in London and Paris there were signs of real resistance to the changes that Kohl saw on the horizon.

The United States responded to Kohl's proposals relatively quickly. Just before the Malta meeting early in December, Secretary Baker speaking to the press outlined four principles that should be followed in any movement toward German reunification. It should occur only on the basis of self-determination with mechanisms that allowed the German people to express their wishes. It should be gradual and peaceful. Long-standing commitments to maintain the integrity of European borders should be honored. And reunification should not come at the expense of existing relationships with NATO or the European Community. The day after Malta, the president endorsed Baker's principles.[31]

Most of the ideas in the four principles were not controversial. Self-determination was axiomatic for democracies and a principle that Gorbachev had endorsed on a number of occasions. The Helsinki accords had settled the European boundaries drawn at the end of the Second World War—boundaries that included the Oder-Neisse line, the controversial demarcation of territory between Poland and East Germany. No one in Europe wanted a German reunification that was sudden or violent, though the pace of change in Central Europe was on the cusp of an acceleration that would make the Baker commitment to gradual change irrelevant. The biggest sticking point in the four principles, at least the sticking point in relations between the United States and the Soviet Union, would be a reunited Germany that remained a member of the NATO alliance. This was not one of Kohl's proposals in his ten-point plan, but it was central to the shorter list of principles prepared by Baker and endorsed by Bush. Once NATO membership for a united Germany became US public policy, everything depended on getting the Soviet Union to accept it.

Any negotiations that could produce a reunited Germany would not be simple. Agreements would have to be reached between the two Germanys about a complex set of economic, political and policy issues. There would have to be negotiations about currency, property, social services and financial commitments. Two different legal systems would have to be reconciled and rules regarding retirement, health care and a wide range of government services would have to be made comparable for all Germans. Huge price tags were connected to getting these matters resolved. And even if those domestic issues could be settled, there would have to be a separate set of agreements with the United States, the Soviet Union, Britain and France. Soviet and American troops were stationed on German territory and the two superpowers, along with the French and the British, had international legal responsibilities for German security left over from World War II. Though Helsinki had involved commitments to maintain existing borders in Central Europe, there were special sensitivities about the border between Poland and a reunited Germany.

And who would make the important decisions, internal and external, that would guide and govern a possible reunification? How long would the decision-making process take? Would there be temporary or intermediary steps along the way? Early on, the Bush administration was convinced that the victorious allies from World War II could not hold meetings and dictate the fate of the two Germanys. The German people were no longer the defeated and destitute population that existed after the collapse of the Nazi regime. There could be no new Yalta or Versailles where allied leaders held private discussions about the future of the European continent. The Bush administration was equally sure that while German reunification raised concerns in many European capitals, there could be no successful deliberations about those concerns in the Conference on Security and Cooperation in Europe (CSCE), or in some other continent-wide forum. If too many nations were involved, the chances for delay and disarray, in what were inherently complicated questions in the first place, would multiply. Moreover, there was a concern that those calling for an active and growing role for CSCE in European security deliberations were actually interested in a Europe that would have less dependence on the United States and its NATO leadership.

To simplify and speed up the negotiations, State Department officials, working closely with Secretary of State Baker, proposed a formula that came to be called "Two-Plus-Four." The two German states would work out their own arrangements for reunification including the myriad of questions about melding two different economic and political systems. This would be followed by meetings of the four major World War II allied powers to resolve security issues. Negotiations between the FRG and the GDR would come first, and because the West Germans had vastly more economic strength and stability than their East German counterparts, the FRG would dominate those negotiations. The European security issues including German alliance participation, endorsement of existing European borders, ending the special status provisions governing Berlin, the future of foreign troop deployments on German territory and the role of nuclear weapons in European security were full of pitfalls and challenges. In the two-plus-four scheme, those European issues would be taken up only after the two Germanys already had a plan for becoming one and after the process of reunification was well underway. Putting the two ahead of the four was a formula for weakening the ability of the Soviet Union to stop or slow down the early steps in reunification and a way to create momentum for the final ones.

The West German constitution provided for the possibility of a future reunification that would take place in one of two ways. One section of the constitution envisioned a confederation between the two German states. The other left the basic institutions and policies of the FRG unchanged and simply added eastern districts as new jurisdictions with the same levels of local autonomy and responsibility that were practiced by existing German districts in the west. The first step, in either case, was the election of a new government for East Germany that would be empowered to make decisions regarding unification. Those elections, originally scheduled for May 1990, were moved forward to March, to facilitate the early initiation of serious German negotiations and a more rapid response to the desperate economic problems that were multiplying in East Germany.

The broader diplomatic forum involving the two German states and the four wartime allies was bound to be difficult. In planning for it, the Bush administration had interconnected problems. The French and British governments would have to be persuaded to accept the rapid emergence of a fully sovereign reunited Germany. There would be even more resistance from the Soviet Union. Getting Soviet acquiescence to a reunited Germany would be difficult even without the insistence that a united Germany would be free to choose its own allies. With that insistence, something that Bush made a priority and something that would help the

French and British accept German unification, it would be even harder for the Soviets to say yes.

Though the two-plus-four proposal would facilitate the separation of the domestic and the international questions related to German reunification, everyone understood that a rapid resolution of the issues would be problematic for the wartime allies who, except for the United States, wanted a slow and cautious reunification process. West Germany, the nation that would take a leading role in the resolution of the domestic issues, would have to eventually deal with the European powers, particularly the Soviet Union, that had well-known reservations about a unified German state. Ultimately, whatever negotiations took place between the two Germanys or among the four allied powers from World War Two, there would almost certainly be important negotiations between West Germany and the Soviet Union. The FRG was likely to lead and speed up the deliberation of the two Germanys; and the Soviets were expected to drag their feet in the discussions of the four wartime powers. Some resolution between Bonn's urgency and Moscow's reluctance would ultimately be necessary for a final settlement of the reunification issues.

For members of the Bush administration there was always a fear that the Soviets might say yes to a united Germany, but no to a Germany in the NATO alliance. And if they could not block a German reunification on Western terms, they might try to slow things down by throwing a wrench into the motor moving in that direction. In a reflective memo written for the president at the end of January 1990, Scowcroft warned that the Soviets would try to say "Nyet," while the Germans would be tempted to give away a great deal in order to achieve the dream of reunification.[32] German unification, Scowcroft observed, was too important to be left to the Europeans; American leadership was needed. The biggest threat involved what would happen if the West Germans, soon to be the Germans, were at some point offered a tempting agreement with the Soviet Union. That agreement might have involved German neutrality or disarmament or some other fundamental compromise of Germany's participation in Western military, political and economic organizations. Such a demand from the Soviet Union was easy to imagine and would have been hard for Kohl to resist if it was the only remaining obstacle in the path to reunification. That prize held such enormous value in German politics, society and national psychology that American policymakers could easily imagine the pressures that would fall on Kohl if he were ever given a stark choice between the achievement of reunification and the continuation of his existing commitments to his Western allies.[33]

But, of course, it was those commitments that helped to alleviate fears in Western Europe about the restoration of German power and concerns in America about our status in European security forums. A Germany in NATO and a Germany in the European Community[34] reassured France and Britain, and kept the United States fully engaged in the security of a continent that had generated two world wars. Those continued affiliations, so important to the United States and to Western European nations, also made it harder for the Soviet Union to accept reunification.

If Germany elected to weaken its Western ties in order to placate a likely Soviet offer, such a decision would introduce new questions about the future of Europe. If a newly reunited Germany were not tethered to NATO and the EC, what organizations would it join? What commitments would it make? Would it stand alone in the center of the continent? Would a reunited Germany isolated from allies on either side of the old Cold War divide feel the need to build nuclear weapons to provide for its own defense? What consequences would that have? A German reunification that followed the anticipated Soviet preference for some kind of neutrality could lead to a catalog of questions about the future of European security that had no readily discernable answers. A neutral Germany making its own defense decisions independently of others on the continent and in North America was a Pandora's Box. Once it was opened it was not clear what would come out. For the Soviet Union, maybe a Germany that remained in NATO and the EC was the better choice, or the lesser evil, in the circumstances at hand. This was certainly the argument that Secretary Baker made to Gorbachev on several occasions.[35] In Gorbachev's memoirs, he recalls a Baker warning in February of 1990 that a "neutral Germany does not necessarily mean a demilitarized Germany."[36] It might mean just the opposite.

The core security questions in German reunification were complex and controversial by themselves. But there were additional layers of complexity in the political landscape in which those questions arose. In Germany, Kohl led a coalition government. His foreign minister, Hans-Dietrich Genscher, was the head of a small party that was critical to, and sometimes critical of, Kohl's leadership. Genscher and Kohl did not always speak with one voice, or to each other. At one time or another, each of them gave important speeches about reunification that had not been shared with, or cleared by, coalition partners. Moreover, the sudden arrival of German reunification as a real and pressing matter arose at a time when elections in the FDR were forthcoming and clearly on the mind of the policymakers in multiple German parties. Before the issue of reunification became a serious concern, Kohl's government was not in a position to assume that reelection would be easy. Conservatives who were part of Kohl's coalition had to be kept in line and could be difficult partners on some of the issues that would arise in reunification deliberations. It was complicated. One member of the Bush team reports that the White House sometimes knew more about the differences between the parties in Germany than German leaders did.[37]

In the Soviet Union, Gorbachev and Shevardnadze expressed some willingness to accept the reality that a reunified Germany was forthcoming, even as they balked at a reunited Germany in NATO.[38] But their conclusion that the Soviet Union had to accept new realities in Central Europe was not a conclusion shared by others in the Soviet government and military establishment. Strong opposition to German reunification within the Soviet Union was widespread and Gorbachev and Shevardnadze sometimes had to say things to placate their domestic critics. In Washington, there was a constant concern that those domestic critics would, at some point, force a change in policy or a change in government that would derail any hope for Soviet acceptance of German reunification with or without its Western ties intact. In December of 1989, Gorbachev told François Mitterrand that "on the day Germany unified a Soviet marshal will be sitting in my chair."[39]

Gorbachev, throughout the discussions about a possible German reunification, was facing intense domestic pressure on other issues. The Soviet economy was weak and slow to respond to the reforms he had initiated. The country still had an antiquated political system. In the middle of the two-plus-four discussions, and just after his visit to Washington for the summit with Bush, Gorbachev had to manage a major meeting of the Communist Party that took up new and dramatic political reforms. Shevardnadze gave a speech at about that time that renounced the idea of a reunited Germany with membership in NATO. His speech sounded like a formal withdrawal of Gorbachev's summit commitment, but it was more likely a rhetorical tactic in ongoing struggles with domestic opposition.[40]

And, of course, events surrounding German reunification were not the only ones garnering attention in a period of revolutionary political developments. The changes in Poland, Hungary and East Germany were followed by huge demonstrations in Czechoslovakia that forced the resignation of Communist Party leaders and made possible the selection of Vaclav Havel—a poet, novelist and dissident—as the new president. In Romania, the change of regime was just as sudden but more violent and was accompanied by the summary executions of Nicolae Ceaușescu and his wife.

In the Baltic republics, political leaders who saw what was happening in Eastern Europe–led movements to declare independence from Moscow. In December of 1989, Lithuania issued a declaration of independence. That declaration brought East European–style revolutionary activity inside the borders of the Soviet Union. Gorbachev's refusal to accept the independence of the Baltic republics and his blockade of fuel deliveries to Lithuania generated enormous problems for the Bush administration. The United States had never accepted the incorporation of the Baltic republics into Stalin's Soviet Union, and well-organized emigrant groups from Estonia, Latvia and Lithuania had prominent political connections in Washington. Bush, like every president from Franklin Roosevelt on, supported the independence of the Baltic republics, but had to consider his response to developments within the Soviet Union at the same time he was calculating the best way to induce Soviet acceptance of a reunited Germany in NATO. Observations that the administration gave priority to German reunification, in part, at the expense of the Baltics, probably have some merit, even though the administration clearly wanted progress in both areas.[41]

The road to German reunification was paved with complicated and sometimes contradictory interests and intentions. But the centerline of that road was carefully walked by Helmut Kohl and George H. W. Bush. Both leaders wanted a rapid and peaceful reunification. The Bush administration, which famously began with a "pause" in US-Soviet relations, shifted gears at the end of 1989. The pace of high-stakes and high-level negotiations and deliberations on German reunification in the first nine months of 1990 have few, if any, precedents in American diplomatic history.

Throughout these negotiations, Bush and Kohl were in constant communication. The Kohl speech immediately after the fall of the Berlin Wall caught the Bush team off guard. Thereafter, the two governments and their two leaders coordinated policy at nearly every important milestone. For the US, the movement toward German reunification began in earnest at Malta. Though billed as an informal get-acquainted session without the usual pomp and circumstance of a full-fledged summit, Malta actually turned out to be more substantive than many observers had expected. Bush came to the talks with extensive prepared remarks. Among other things, he reminded Gorbachev of the care he had taken to frame his remarks about the Berlin Wall in "ways not to complicate your life."[42] Both Gorbachev and Bush observed that Kohl's pre-Malta speech about a possible path to reunification could be related to his pending election calculations, but Bush added that the subject of reunification and the fall of the Berlin Wall were emotional topics for the German people and that it was understandable that Kohl would speak about them. The president promised continued rhetorical caution, while Gorbachev stated vaguely that history had created two German states and "history will decide what will happen."[43]

That may have been true, but history needed some help. In February, Kohl made an important trip to Moscow to discuss reunification with Gorbachev. Before he left, he received a letter from President Bush wishing him well and stating the president's full support for Kohl's endeavors. The German leader has called this letter "one of the great documents in German-American history."[44] In Moscow, Kohl won Gorbachev's support for the proposition that the two Germanys could resolve their own domestic arrangements in forthcoming negotiations, the key first step to any formula for reunification.

While Kohl was in Moscow European foreign ministers gathered in Ottawa to discuss the "Open Skies" proposal Bush had made in his speech at Texas A&M. Because the senior diplomats were together in one place, Baker used the meeting as an opportunity to push the allies to accept the two-plus-four scheme for addressing German unification issues, even though that strategy had not yet been fully studied and approved by all the key players in the American national security establishment or by America's allies. One NSC staffer called Ottawa "a three-ring circus." Baker was apparently an effective ringmaster. He got all of the foreign ministers involved in the two-plus-four process, and some of the nervous European states left out of that process, to agree to the basic procedures that would be followed in subsequent negotiations.[45]

At the end of the month, Kohl met with Bush at Camp David. He was the first West German chancellor invited to the presidential retreat. The discussions between the two leaders were unusually frank. Kohl predicted a rapid collapse of East Germany and a likely acceleration of the timetables for reunification. In confirmation of the internal fears of the Bush administration, Kohl suggested that Germany might consider a special status in the NATO alliance along the lines of one adopted by the French under Charles de Gaulle. Bush pushed back, observing that one France in NATO was more than enough and asked the German leader to make new public commitments about the continuity of Central European borders. Kohl promised that the border with Poland would remain unchanged, but wanted the formal commitment on that question to come in the form of a treaty negotiated and signed after Germany was reunited. Bush trusted Kohl's promises in this regard, though the delay in a final resolution of the issue would cause problems for Britain, France and, of course, Poland.[46] The president offered personal assurances to Polish leaders that a treaty with Germany completely settling the border questions would come later in the reunification process. The Poles were not happy about this delay, but accepted Bush's promises on this important subject.

In the middle of March, mid-level diplomats met for the first two-plus-four session in Bonn. At the same time, the Third Soviet Congress of People's Deputies convened in Moscow to repeal the monopoly of political power held by the Communist Party and to elect Gorbachev as the first president of the Soviet Union. The second president would be elected directly by the people. A few days after this momentous decision was made in Moscow, the people in East Germany held their first free general election. To the surprise of most observers, the big winners were the conservative parties allied with Kohl that had openly favored a rapid pursuit of reunification. Kohl's coalition of conservative parties, called the Alliance for Germany, won a strong plurality of the vote.

Two months later, the East and West German foreign ministers signed an agreement in Bonn outlining terms for reunification. Those terms were essentially a West German takeover of East Germany with the Deutsche Mark quickly becoming the currency for both. East German citizens became eligible for the benefits enjoyed by residents of West Germany. The roadmap for reunification of the two Germanys was now set. What remained were the decisions by the former allied powers on issues of European security.

FROM SUMMIT TO SUCCESS

When Gorbachev arrived in Washington for the June 1990 summit with President Bush, he had a long list of domestic and international concerns. German reunification was only one of them. Bush, after securing the dramatic concession that a reunited Germany could choose its own alliances, tried very hard to help Gorbachev achieve some substantive, or at least some symbolic, successes at the summit. One of Gorbachev's highest priorities was a trade agreement with the United States that had not been finalized when he arrived and was likely to be held up by a Congress alarmed at Gorbachev's actions against the Baltic republics in the aftermath of their declarations of independence. Bush agreed to sign a trade agreement, though he told Gorbachev he could not take it to Capitol Hill for formal approval until matters were resolved with Lithuania. The president went out of his way to celebrate the informal events of the summit that included Gorbachev's visit to Camp David. He also promised to introduce changes in NATO alliance strategy that would address the new circumstances emerging in Europe. This was something that would almost certainly have occurred in any case, but Bush promised to accelerate NATO reforms, in part, to help Gorbachev withstand the criticisms he would receive at home regarding German reunification and the other political changes in Eastern Europe.

Following the Washington meeting, the Bush team quickly put together a package of NATO reforms with very little direct or detailed consultation with America's allies or with the alliance's permanent institutions and representatives. There was no time for extensive consultation. Instead, Bush personally appealed to his counterparts in Britain, France, Canada and across the alliance to give the American proposals a rapid review. At a NATO meeting in London in July the American recommendations were largely approved as proposed. The "London Declaration" issued at the end of the NATO meeting included commitments to the reduction of front-line troops, proposed limitations on the size of the German army, a revision of NATO's strategy on first use of nuclear weapons and a pledge by the United States to remove nuclear artillery shells from the European theater if the Soviet Union followed suit. These were major changes in both NATO's military forces and war-fighting doctrines. More of the controversial short-range nuclear weapons would be removed from Central Europe, deployed troop numbers would come down and the old NATO plans to use tactical nuclear weapons in a Euro-

pean conventional war would be revised, adding new cautions against
the first use of such weapons.

Finally, there was another critically important trip by Kohl to Moscow. This was the negotiation that sealed the deal. Kohl offered Gorbachev roughly twenty-two billion dollars in loan guarantees, a sum large
enough to make a difference in the chaotic and challenging economic
transition that Gorbachev was trying to manage.[47] Bush was never able to
offer Gorbachev any significant foreign aid or financial assistance. He
couldn't because of US deficits and the constant struggles between the
president and Congress over budget priorities. And he couldn't because
of congressional sensitivity to the plight of the Baltic republics. Kohl was
freer to provide economic relief to Gorbachev and he did so at a time
when it was desperately needed. In addition, Kohl promised to pay the
costs related to the Soviet troops stationed in East Germany during their
final years of deployment and to pay for their eventual transportation
and relocation back to the Soviet Union. He reiterated promises that Germany would not pursue nuclear, biological or chemical weapons. On the
delicate question of how East German territory would be treated while
Soviet forces were still present, Kohl adopted a formula originally proposed by Hans-Dietrich Genscher. He promised that non-German NATO
forces would not be deployed to or operate in the territory of the former
GDR. He also promised a cap on the size of German military forces once
reunification took place. These German financial commitments and security guarantees, together with the NATO reforms, gave Gorbachev just
enough concessions to justify acceptance of the final agreements on German reunification.

One more important concession came from the United States. If a
reunited Germany remained as an active member of NATO, the US
would not push for any further eastward extension of NATO military
deployments. This was the American version of the commitments that
Kohl had made to Gorbachev. It was meant to reassure the Soviet leader
that the reunification of Germany was not intended to threaten the security of the Soviet Union. Baker used a broad version of the Genscher idea
in his discussions with Shevardnadze and Gorbachev during the winter
and spring of 1990. The Secretary of State famously promised that NATO
would not move "one inch eastward" as a consequence of German reunification. There would be no NATO forces placed in the territory of the
former GDR while Soviet troops remained stationed in East German
bases during a transitional period; and even after those Soviet forces left
East Germany and returned to the Soviet Union, the territory of the former GDR would not be used for the forward deployment of non-German
NATO defenses or US nuclear weapons. There is some controversy about
whether the United States also pledged to refrain from expanding NATO
membership to include other East European nations.[48] But members of
the Bush administration and scholars of the diplomacy during this period

argue that there was no such commitment, and not much discussion of long-term NATO membership in the hectic days of 1990 when the terms for German reunification were finalized.[49] In a 2014 interview, Gorbachev confirmed that the "not one inch eastward" promise only involved restraints on NATO deployments in the former GDR. "The topic of 'NATO expansion' was not discussed at all and it wasn't brought up in those years."[50]

The agreements about reunification between the two Germanys were signed in Berlin in August, and in the following month, at the last two-plus-four meeting in Moscow, the participants signed a Final Settlement with Respect to Germany. The existing border between Poland and Germany was confirmed and the promises to refrain from any precipitous deployments of "foreign" troops into the former territory of East Germany were put in writing. The deadline for the withdrawal of Soviet troops from German territory was set for 1994, and the stage was set for the formal reunification of the two Germanys in October.

It had been a whirlwind of diplomatic communications, meetings and agreements occurring in rapid succession.[51] The conclusion—a united Germany continuing to play a prominent role in the NATO alliance and the European Union—was a result that very few in 1989 anticipated or predicted. The American president who led this process is typically described as cautious and prudent. But those traits don't explain much of what happened in connection with German reunification. If there was presidential caution, it was caution accompanied by radical change. If there was prudence, it was prudence in the service of revolutionary results. Perhaps we need to look more carefully at the qualities that George Bush brought to bear on the complicated and consequential European developments at the end of the Cold War.

THE PRESIDENT'S INSIGHT

The rapid and peaceful reunification of Germany that occurred at the end of the Cold War, and occurred without any significant disruption of the post-war economic and political institutions that linked the democratic nations of the continent to each other and with the United States, is a remarkable example of what can be accomplished by skillful diplomacy. George Bush led his administration through a major set of policy deliberations that involved considerable internal debate and high levels of political risk. He led the Western allies toward an outcome that most European leaders initially resisted or declared to be unrealistic.[52]

Bush maintained a high level of communication and coordination between the United States and the Federal Republic of Germany at all the critical junctures in the reunification process. And he secured the acquiescence of the Soviet Union to a dramatic shift away from policy positions that were at the heart of Soviet security calculations. He left behind a Europe that may not have been entirely "whole and free," but was certainly more secure and more stable than many observers had predicted. Anticipated confrontations and conflicts inside the East European nations undergoing revolutionary change, or within the Western alliance, or with the Soviet Union were mostly avoided.[53] These are dramatic accomplishments for American diplomacy. The stakes were high, the risks were real, and the president of the United States followed a consistent path to a successful resolution of complicated and consequential questions about the future of democracy and security on the European continent.

Of course, it is essential to acknowledge that the circumstances Bush and his administration encountered were created by courageous East Europeans who stood up to brutal regimes, voted for dramatic change, emigrated in dangerous days and took personal risks of many kinds to bring about the revolutions that occurred. And throughout these events, Mikhail Gorbachev encouraged change in Eastern Europe and then refrained from using force to suppress or channel that change. There are good reasons why Gorbachev was awarded the Nobel Peace Prize.

But even if you make a full and fair accounting of the fact that America, and America's president, were not the makers of the East European revolutions that occurred at the end of the Cold War, it has to be said that Bush and his foreign policy team played the very unusual hand they were dealt with a level of skill and a degree of success that are impressive to any serious student of statecraft. Ironically, the president made his successes in connection with German reunification look so easy and seem so inevitable that he may not have received the broad public appreciation for his accomplishments that should have accompanied them. Two key participants in the foreign policy decisions of this period, Condoleezza Rice and Philip Zelikow, conclude that Bush's performance on German unification was carried out "so quietly and sometimes inarticulately" that it left "little public record of his impact."[54]

Some critics of Rice and Zelikow, and the other authors of Bush administration memoirs, argue that reunification of a Germany that stayed fully committed to the Western camp was a conservative victory — a status quo success. And because of that success opportunities may have been missed to shore up Gorbachev and seek more dramatic changes to the Soviet Union and the structures of European security. There was no actual new world order, just a holding on to Cold War ideas and institutions.[55] It is fair to say that Bush and his administration wanted stability and continuity in Europe in the midst of the revolutionary changes underway in 1989 and beyond. But securing that stability and continuity was no easy task given all the changes that took place before and after the fall of the Berlin Wall. If Bush was a conservative realist, he succeeded in pushing that objective against long odds and multiple obstacles.

How should we explain Bush's success? First and foremost, Bush was persistent in his pursuit of a clear objective. From a very early point in the developments in Eastern Europe, President Bush saw the opportunity for a reunification of Germany that would not involve German neutrality or a breakup of the NATO alliance. He welcomed the developments that were underway and, unlike other leaders he dealt with across the European continent, he did not have reservations about a reunited Germany. This was crucial. The president acted on the basis of a core insight. He was convinced that the German people, or at least the West German people he knew and worked with in his diplomatic career, had learned the lessons taught by their national experiences in the twentieth century. West Germans had fully embraced democratic practices and principles, and a larger and more powerful Germany would not pose a threat to her neighbors or to the world community.

This conclusion allowed Bush to gain and hold the trust and respect of Helmut Kohl, and it ensured that West Germany and the United States were in step with each other at most of the critical moments in the policy-making process. The president's confidence in contemporary German political culture allowed him to get ahead of Margaret Thatcher, François Mitterrand and other European leaders, and to be comfortable in that leadership position. It solidified his determination to press for a rapid reunification and helped him to calculate and calibrate the steps he was taking in a way that would not alienate Gorbachev or embolden his enemies within the Soviet Union. Knowing where you are trying to go, and having confidence in your destination, helps enormously in any diplomatic endeavor.

Many commentators describe George H. W. Bush as a leader who lacked vision. It is tempting to see his success on German reunification as evidence running counter to that commentary. But it might go too far to call Bush a visionary on the events that took place at the end of the Cold War. The president and his foreign policy advisers, like most people in the world, were initially surprised by the pace and magnitude of the changes taking place in East Germany and across Eastern Europe. As we have seen, the administration had been famously cautious about Gorbachev in the early months of 1989. In the weeks when the administration was gearing up for the first presidential meeting with the Soviet leader in Malta, the Berlin Wall suddenly collapsed and the scope of opportunities for fundamental change in Central Europe expanded in a way, and at a speed, that few, if any, leaders had foreseen. Bush was never the predictor of these East European events. And he made a conscious decision not to be the public spokesman for their significance.

The crucial quality that President Bush possessed was not the vision that German reunification was forthcoming. It was the disposition to accept it, and embrace it, when it emerged. Unlike many European leaders and foreign policy experts, Bush never felt conflicted about the prospects of a reunited Germany. According to Bush's assistant national security advisor, "Our European allies did not have the same kind of faith in Germany that Bush did. And he just flat believed that the Germans had changed."[56] The president had this insight and held this position from the outset of serious discussions about German reunification; and he made his position known. He announced it in Helena, Montana, in September of 1989. About a month later when Kohl called to express concern that newspaper articles in the West were suggesting that Germany would become a neutral nation to assuage concerns about Germany's historic nationalism and territorial expansion, Bush responded immediately. He called in a *New York Times* reporter and gave an interview in which he said, "I do not share the concern that some European countries have about a reunited Germany."[57] According to one observer of these events, after that date, Bush's position on German reunification, and his comfort with the prospect that it might be forthcoming, was clear to everyone inside and outside of Washington.[58]

The president was consistently confident that German reunification could be a good thing for the German people and for all of Europe. And he understood from the outset that the best version of a reunited Germany would be one that remained an active partner in existing Western economic and security organizations. This would be the best outcome for Germany, for the United States, and ironically for the Soviet Union as well. Bush did not waver from those convictions, and his confidence in the feasibility and desirability of a reunited Germany tied to the West made him the ideal leader of the diplomacy that followed the collapse of the Berlin Wall.[59]

Other factors were also crucial to the president's success. Knowing the players helped enormously. Bush may have been slow to initiate direct communication with Gorbachev, but after the Malta meetings he contacted the Soviet leader frequently and spoke freely. At the Washington Summit, he went out of his way to include relaxed activities and discussions at Camp David as well as more formal negotiations. Secretary of State Baker simultaneously established a close working relationship with Eduard Shevardnadze that played a large role in the unfolding events. Brent Scowcroft had excellent channels of communication to his peers in London, Paris and Bonn and used them to good effect. Dennis Ross, one of Secretary Baker's senior advisers, reports that across the administration experienced staff members established close relationships with counterparts in European capitals.[60] The staff work done, particularly in the Department of State and on the National Security Council, in support of German reunification was of a very high caliber. A special White House committee was established to facilitate prompt and substantive coordination during the critical months of negotiations, and its meetings and memos made a significant contribution to its eventual success.[61]

It is frequently observed that Bush put together an unusually talented and congenial team of foreign policy advisers and had a unique set of personal relationships with a long list of international leaders when he entered the White House.[62] During his early months in office, he actively cultivated those relationships—particularly the ones with Thatcher, Mitterrand and Kohl—at the same time he was preparing to initiate a new relationship with Gorbachev. He would, from time to time during his presidency and after, refer to all of these individuals as friends. Personal communications from the president, and from others at different levels in the administration, played a significant role in the ability of the team to move quickly, to do big things on relatively short notice and to expect that their ideas and initiatives would receive a fair reception in distant capitals.

The numbers of senior-level contacts and communications in the critical period of German reunification deliberations were unusually high. Bush met with Kohl on these issues privately, or at sessions with other European leaders, on nine occasions during the year when reunification was under active consideration. He met nearly as often with both Mitterrand and Thatcher. He talked on the phone with all of them on a regular basis. In the same period, Secretary Baker had close to thirty meetings with relevant foreign ministers and heads of state.[63] This was a full-out commitment to personal diplomacy. And it was necessary both before and after Gorbachev made his Washington Summit commitment to the full sovereignty of a reunited Germany.

According to Shevardnadze, the NATO meeting in London during the summer of 1990 when new strategies, military postures and alliance objectives were adopted was crucial to the ultimate success of German reunification.[64] Information about the forthcoming and finalized NATO changes was reportedly shared with Shevardnadze and helped him respond to internal critics during the important Party Congress taking place while NATO representatives met in London. The reforms adopted in London in July of 1990 were American led and could not have been reviewed or approved as quickly as they were without support at the very highest levels of the participating governments. Bush made personal appeals to his counterparts across the Atlantic, and those requests were respected. His willingness and ability to do this was crucial to securing the NATO reforms that were, in turn, decisive to Soviet acceptance of a united Germany remaining in the Western alliance.

Finally, strategic priorities guided the president and his administration in their pursuit of German reunification. When choices had to be made about the weight to be given to the plight of Lithuanians in their struggle for independence within the Union of Soviet Socialist Republics and the reforms and revolutions taking place in Eastern Europe and within the Soviet Union, the president and his advisers kept their eyes on what they judged to be the larger and more important prizes. They never abandoned or repudiated the Lithuanians seeking independence, or the revolutionaries in the other Baltic republics. But the administration did refrain from becoming the international champions of Baltic independence when they were urged, and pressured, to do so. And the president approved a trade agreement with Gorbachev at the conclusion of the Washington Summit when congressional pressure to punish the Soviet Union for its Baltic policies made his decision controversial and costly.

Successfully resolving a new set of international relationships in Central Europe was arguably more important than the short-term prospects for Baltic independence. Priorities had to be set. This never meant that if the Soviets went too far in the suppression of Baltic independence that any behavior on their part would have been accepted. There was always a danger that Gorbachev would use excessive force in Lithuania and bring all the issues in play in East-West relations, including German reunification, to a grinding halt. That could have occurred. What the administration's priorities did mean was that when judgments had to be made about immediate decisions, the long-term value of a peaceful and successful German reunification had to have its proper weight on the scales. Critics can say, and have said, that the president had the wrong priorities or failed to balance the scales correctly, but they cannot say that he lacked the ability, or the willingness, to make hard choices.

From the very beginning of the Bush presidency policymaking on the Cold War involved a combination of caution and boldness. The caution came from the suspicion that Gorbachev might not be willing or able to carry out his promised changes in policy or that he might be making those promises purely for public consumption in the West. The boldness came from the conviction that relations between the United States and the Soviet Union could move far beyond routine summits and tedious arms control negotiations to substantive shifts in the politics and security of Europe. Scowcroft reports that even before the inauguration he was floating the idea that maybe both superpowers could fully withdraw their ground forces from either side of the Iron Curtain and bring to a conclusion the military standoff that had been in existence throughout the Cold War.[65] That idea was considered far-fetched in the winter of 1988. The ideas that the Soviet Union would withdraw its forces from Central Europe, bless the transformation of the East European regimes into independent states, and endorse a reunited Germany with continued membership in the NATO alliance were inconceivable at the outset of the Bush presidency. When they happened, the Cold War came to an end.

Of course, there are many opinions about when the Cold War ended.[66] Margaret Thatcher thought it was over just as Bush was preparing to enter the White House.[67] Some observers said that the speech Gorbachev delivered to the United Nations in December of 1988 was the real end to the conflict and the rhetorical bookend to Churchill's description of an Iron Curtain descending in the center of Europe.[68] Others choose the collapse of the Berlin Wall as the seminal event marking the end of East-West conflict. Long after the tumultuous events of the late 1980s and early 1990s, Gorbachev observed that the phrase "Yalta to Malta" had a nice ring to it.[69] Brent Scowcroft, as we have seen, thought that the critical turning point took place at the June 1990 Washington Summit when Gorbachev made his concession that a reunited Germany could choose its own alliances. Jim Baker thought the Cold War ended a few months later when he and Shevardnadze issued a joint statement condemning Saddam Hussein's invasion of Kuwait.[70]

According to Curt Smith, one of the president's speechwriters, it was in October of 1990—when German reunification was finalized—that George Bush finally began to speak freely and frequently in public about the conclusion of the Cold War.[71] President Bush was late to make that declaration.[72] But his early insight that a rapid German reunification was both possible and desirable, and his persistent pursuit of it, together with the preservation and transformation of the NATO alliance, contributed to a significant diplomatic achievement.

NOTES

1. George Bush and Brent Scowcroft, *A World Transformed* (New York: Alfred A. Knopf, 1998), 130.

2. The president's question was not new to Gorbachev. Secretary of State James Baker had posed it at a meeting in Moscow just prior to the Washington Summit. See, James Baker, *The Politics of Diplomacy* (New York: G. P. Putnam, 1995), 251.

3. Bush and Scowcroft, *A World Transformed*, 282.

4. "Excerpt from Minutes No. 187 of CC CPSU Politburo Session from May 16, 1990," National Security Archive, accessed on March 15, 2019 at https://nsarchive2.gwu.edu/NSAEBB/NSAEBB320/04.pdf

5. Mary Elise Sarotte argues that the significance of the "Helsinki principle" concession at the Washington Summit has been exaggerated by members of the Bush team. See Mary Elise Sarotte, *1989: The Struggle to Create a Post-Cold War Europe* (Princeton, New Jersey: Princeton University Press, 2009), 166–169.

6. Bush and Scowcroft, *A World Transformed*, 299.

7. Brent Scowcroft Interview, November 12–13, 1999, George H. W. Bush Oral History Project, Miller Center, University of Virginia.

8. Ibid.

9. This observation is usually attributed to the French novelist François Mauriac; see for example, Walter Isaacson, "Is One Germany Better Than Two?" *Time Magazine*, November 20, 1989. Gorbachev's interpreter attributes a version of this observation to Italian leaders. Pavel Palazchenko, *My Years With Gorbachev and Shevardnadze* (University Park: Pennsylvania State University Press, 1997), 158–59.

10. Brent Scowcroft Interview, November 12–13, 1999.

11. Ridgeway in SNR-5 quoted in Phillip D. Zelikow and Condoleezza Rice, *Germany Unified and Europe Transformed: A Study in Statecraft* (Cambridge, MA: Harvard University Press, 1995), 26.

12. "Memorandum for the President on Dealing with the Germans," Robert L. Hutchings, through Robert D. Blackwill, to Brent Scowcroft, April 28, 1989. George H. W. Bush Presidential Records, National Security Council, Hutchings, Robert L., Files, Country File CFO1413, Folder Title: Federal Republic of Germany, General.

13. See the memorandums of conversation between George H. W. Bush and Helmut Kohl for October 23 and November 10, 1989. Between those two dates the estimated scale of the emigration grew from 150,000 to 230,000. These declassified documents are available at several locations including "German Reunification," Wilson Center, Digital Archive, accessed on April 17, 2019 at https://digitalarchive.wilsoncenter.org/collection/489/german-reunification

14. Zelikow and Rice, *Germany Unified and Europe Transformed*, 119.

15. Ibid., 74.

16. Baker, *The Politics of Diplomacy*, 150.

17. "Oct. 7, 1989: How 'Gorbi' Spoiled East Germany's 40th Birthday Party," *Spiegel Online International*, October 7, 2009.

18. Zelikow and Rice, *Germany Unified and Europe Transformed*, 105.

19. Baker, *The Politics of Diplomacy*, 162–63.

20. Bush and Scowcroft, *A World Transformed*, 165.

21. Ibid., 78.

22. Arnaud de Borchgrave, "Bush Would Love 'Reunited Germany,'" *Washington Times*, May 16, 1989.

23. "Speech at Mainz," May 31, 1989.

24. Robert Hutchings, *American Diplomacy and the End of the Cold War* (Washington, DC: The Woodrow Wilson Center Press, 1997), 94–98.

25. "The Thatcher-Gorbachev Conversations," National Security Archive, accessed on June 14, 2018 at http://nsarchive.gwu.edu/NSAEBB/NSAEBB422/

26. For a careful and nuanced analysis of Bush's attitudes toward West Germany and his conclusions about German transformation after the Second World War see, Jeffrey A. Engel, "A Better World . . . But Don't Get Carried Away: The Foreign Policy of George H. W. Bush Twenty Years On," *Diplomatic History*, 34, no. 1 (2010): 25–46.

27. "The President's News Conference in Helena, Montana," September 18, 1989.

28. Robert Gates Interview, July 23–24, 2000, George H. W. Bush Oral History Project, Miller Center, University of Virginia.

29. Barthlomew Sparrow, *The Strategist: Brent Scowcroft and the The Call of National Security* (New York: Public Affairs, 2015), 369–70.

30. Baker, *The Politics of Diplomacy*, 166.

31. "The President's News Conference in Brussels," December 4, 1989.

32. "A Strategy for German Unification," Memorandum for the President from Brent Scowcroft, dated January 20, 1990, George H. W. Bush Presidential Records, National Security Council, Blackwill, Robert D., Files, Subject File, Folder CF00182-020.

33. See for example, a memo written by Scowcroft prior to the February 1990 meeting between Bush and Kohl in which he writes that "the temptation for the Chancellor will be to assuage Gorbachev's difficulties and boost Kohl's domestic political prospects with concessions on Germany's membership in NATO." Memo from Brent Scowcroft, "Meetings With German Chancellor Helmut Kohl," George H. W. Bush Presidential Records, Brent Scowcroft Collection, German Unification Files, Folder ID Number 91116-003.

34. While deliberations about German reunification were underway, the Western Europeans were also negotiating changes to their economic and political ties. The European Community (previously called the Common Market) was on the cusp of yet another name change. It would soon be called the European Union.

35. Thomas Risse argues that the Bush success with Gorbachev on German reunification was primarily the result of "friendly persuasion" rather than coercion. Baker's litany of things that might go wrong with a neutral and independent Germany was a prime example of this persuasion. Thomas Risse, "The Cold War's Endgame and German Reunification: A Review Essay," *International Security*, 21, no. 4 (Spring 1997): 159–185.

36. Mikhail Gorbachev, *Memoirs* (New York: Doubleday, 1995), 529.

37. For the care taken to monitor internal issues in West Germany and the differences in public statements made by Kohl and Genscher see, Hutchings, *American Diplomacy at the End of the Cold War*, 120–121. Hutchings also observes that the US could "sometimes supply Bonn with the policy coordination it lacked," 114.

38. Pavel Palazchenko, *My Years With Gorbachev and Shevardnadze* (University Park: Pennsylvania State University Press, 1997), 171–72.

39. Zelikow and Rice, *Germany Unified and Europe Transformed*, 137.

40. Dennis Ross, *Statecraft: And How to Restore America's Standing in the World* (New York: Farrar, Straus and Giroux, 2007), 44.

41. Hutchings admits that Germany was the higher priority, while observing that in the end both German reunification and Baltic independence were eventually achieved. Hutchings, *American Diplomacy at the End of the Cold War*, 127–28.

42. Bush and Scowcroft, *A World Transformed*, 165.

43. Ibid., 167.

44. Kohl quoted in Jeffrey Engel, *When the World Seemed New* (Boston: Houghton Mifflin, 2017), 334.

45. Hutchings, *American Diplomacy at the End of the Cold War*, 114. The rush to get two-plus-four done led to some tensions within the Department of State and between various actors in the foreign policymaking process. See the National Security Council Project, Oral History Interviews, "The Bush Administration National Security Council," 4–15.

46. Bush and Scowcroft, *A World Transformed*, 257.

47. Some scholars argue that German "bribery" of Gorbachev at a time when the Soviet economy was in crisis offers the best explanation of why the Soviet leader accepted a reunified Germany in NATO. For an excellent summary of the scholarly debate see: Mary Elise Sarotte, "'His East European Allies Say They Want to be in NATO': U.S. foreign policy, German unification, and NATO's role in European security, 1989–1990," *German Reunification: A Multinational History*, Frederic Bozo, Andreas Rodder, and Mary Elise Sarotte, eds. (New York: Routledge, 2017), 82–103.

48. Svetlana Savranskaya and Tom Blanton, "NATO Expansion: What Gorbachev Heard," National Security Archive, December 12, 2017, accessed July 30, 2019 at: https://nsarchive.gwu.edu/briefing-book/russia-programs/2017-12-12/nato-expansion-what-gorbachev-heard-western-leaders-early

49. Mark Kramer, "The Myth of a No-NATO-Enlargement Pledge to Russia," *The Washington Quarterly*, 32, no. 2 (April 2009): 39–61.

50. Steven Pifer, "Did NATO Promise Not to Enlarge? Gorbachev Says 'No,'" Brookings, Up Front, accessed July 30, 2019 at: https://www.brookings.edu/blog/up-front/2014/11/06/did-nato-promise-not-to-enlarge-gorbachev-says-no/

51. The best accounts of these events are available in Zelikow and Rice, *Germany Unified and Europe Transformed*, and Engel, *When the World Seemed New*.

52. According to Bob Gates, "It was a very special achievement of George Bush in my view because every other leader, East and West, was against it. The French were against it, the British were against it, the Soviets were against it, the Poles . . . the Czechs . . . the Hungarians . . . the Italians were against it. We were totally isolated. And it was by sheer force of personality and determination that I think Bush finally got all those people on board." Robert M. Gates interview, July 23–24, 2000.

53. For fascinating speculations about what might have occurred in the complicated politics surrounding German reunification see: Robert L. Hutchings, "The US, German Unification and European Integration," in Frederic Bozo, Marie-Pierre Rey, N. Piers Ludlow and Leopoldo Nuti, eds., *Europe and the End of the Cold War: A Reappraisal* (New York: Routledge, 2008), 119–132.

54. Zelikow and Rice, *Germany Unified and Europe Transformed*, 368.

55. Sarotte, "'His East European Allies Say They Want to be in NATO': U.S. foreign policy, German unification and NATO's role in European Security, 1989–1990."

56. Robert Gates interview, July 23–24, 2000.

57. R. W. Apple, "Possibility of a Reunited Germany Is No Cause for Alarm, Bush Says," *New York Times*, October 25, 1989, A1.

58. Lothar Kettenacher, *Germany 1989: In the Aftermath of the Cold War* (New York: Routledge, 2009), 134.

59. For a thoughtful and thorough examination of where Bush's disposition toward German reunification came from see Jeffrey Engel, "Bush, Germany, and the Power of Time: How History Makes History," *Diplomatic History*, 37, no. 4 (2013).

60. Ross, *Statecraft*, 45.

61. Robert Gates reports that the importance of this special committee may be exaggerated. Robert Gates interview, July 23–24, 2000.

62. For an excellent description of the staff relations and capacities for strategic planning see Robert Hutchings, "American Diplomacy and the End of the Cold War in Europe," in Robert Hutchings and Jeremi Suri, eds., *Foreign Policy Breakthroughs: Cases of Successful Diplomacy* (London: Oxford University Press, 2015), 158–160.

63. These numbers of contacts are reported in Ross, *Statecraft*, 39.

64. Zelikow and Rice, *Germany Unified and Europe Transformed*, 349.

65. Brent Scowcroft interview, November 12–13, 1999.

66. For an interesting perspective on this topic see, John Mueller, "When Did the Cold War End?" *Political Science Quarterly*, 119, no. 4 (Winter 2004–2005): 609–631.

67. In November of 1988, during her last visit with President Reagan, Thatcher said, "We are not in a Cold War now." See Engel, *When the World Seemed New*, 20.

68. Senator Daniel Patrick Moynihan called the Gorbachev UN speech "the most astounding statement of surrender in the history of ideological struggle." For this and other reactions to the speech see, Thomas Blanton, "When Did the Cold War End?" *Cold War International History Project Bulletin* 10 (March 1998): 184.

69. In the transcript of a conversation recorded in February 1995 that brought together Bush, Gorbachev, Thatcher and Mitterrand, Gorbachev repeats his observation that the Cold War ended at the Malta summit. "Recalling the Fall of the Berlin Wall," *New Perspectives Quarterly*, 27, no. 1 (Spring 2009). The phrase "Yalta to Malta" was first used by a Soviet spokesman in the immediate buildup to the Malta meetings. See, Jim Hoagl, "From Malta to Yalta," *Washington Post*, November 9, 1989.

70. Interview with James Baker, October 1997, for the documentary "Cold War," Episode 23, "The Wall Comes Down," National Security Archive, accessed on June 12, 2018 at https://nsarchive2.gwu.edu/coldwar/interviews/episode-23/baker3.html

71. Curt Smith, *George H. W. Bush: Character at the Core* (Washington, DC: Potomac Books, 2014), 144.

72. In 1992, when he was running for reelection, Bush often used the words "the Cold War is over" and "freedom finished first." See for example, "Remarks at the National Affairs Briefing in Dallas, Texas," August 22, 1992; and "Remarks at Missouri Southern College in Joplin, Missouri," September 11, 1992.

FIVE

Audacity

Doubling Down on Desert Shield

The month of October 1990—when German reunification was finalized—should have been a triumphant one for George H. W. Bush. It wasn't. He remembers it as "one of the most frustrating periods of my presidency."[1]

In the weeks just before the mid-term congressional elections, long negotiations with Democratic congressional leaders over budgets, deficits and taxes came to a conclusion. The president, going against his popular campaign promise that there would be "no new taxes" in a Bush presidency, agreed to put everything on the table in the budget negotiations. And everything included taxes. When the start of the new fiscal year arrived on October 1 without a budget agreement, pressure to reach a compromise grew dramatically. Continuing resolutions kept the government temporarily funded while highly publicized talks took place. At the end of October, a final compromise, including concessions on taxation, was reached but it was a compromise that divided the Republican Party and ultimately weakened the president's prospects for reelection.

The other issues commanding presidential attention in October 1990 involved the Middle East. Late in the summer of 1990, Saddam Hussein had invaded Kuwait, the small oil-rich nation on his southern border. In the days that followed, the nation rallied round President Bush's condemnation of the Iraqi invasion, his movement of American troops to Saudi Arabia—in a mission called Desert Shield—and the imposition of sanctions on Saddam Hussein. Those responses to the Persian Gulf crisis were broadly popular and largely successful. But by October, support for them was beginning to fray. And the budget talks were connected to the Gulf crisis. If no deal could be reached between the president and Congress, mandatory cuts, including significant reductions in defense spending, would be triggered at precisely the time when the United States was struggling to hold together a broad international coalition against Iraq.

The biggest issue facing President Bush in October of 1990 did not make headlines or receive significant public attention. The president and his senior advisers spent the month considering what to do next in the Persian Gulf. At the beginning of the month, the Pentagon produced detailed plans for military operations against the Iraqi troops in Kuwait. American military commanders recommended a direct assault across the Saudi-Iraqi border. It was a conventional plan likely to succeed, but it was also likely to produce significant casualties. After it was rejected, Pentagon planners in Washington and Saudi Arabia went back to the drawing board and came up with bigger and bolder ways to conduct a war against Iraq. The new ideas, presented at the end of October, called for a massive armored attack across southern Iraq, outflanking and encircling Iraqi troops in Kuwait. These plans required a much larger American military deployment. At the very end of October, in support of the bolder Pentagon proposals, the president ordered a doubling of the size of US military forces in the Persian Gulf. The US commitment would rise from just under a quarter million to almost half a million. And, at least initially, the decision to increase the forces deployed to Saudi Arabia would be a secret. The double-down decision would be shared with Congress and the American people only after the mid-term elections were over.

The story of the first Gulf War is complicated; and it is possible to identify a number of critical decisions on the timeline between Saddam Hussein's invasion of Kuwait in August of 1990 and the expulsion of his forces from that country roughly six months later. The decision to double the number of American military personnel in the Persian Gulf in the fall of 1990 was among the most important of those decisions. It was also a decision that illustrates something significant—and perhaps something surprising—about George H. W. Bush.

THE CRISIS BEGINS

The Gulf War began as a surprise. Though intelligence agencies detected the buildup of Iraqi forces on the border with Kuwait in the summer of 1990, almost no one expected Saddam Hussein to invade his neighbor. The buildup was written off as flamboyant diplomacy. Iraq had borrowed heavily from Kuwait during its long war with Iran in the 1980s. In the aftermath of that war, when oil prices were relatively low, Saddam Hussein wanted debt relief and leverage in the Organization of Petroleum Exporting Countries (OPEC). Kuwait could provide him with both. Hosni Mubarak, the long-time ruler of Egypt, told President Bush that the Iraqi troops would never cross the Kuwaiti border; they were there

for intimidation while the two countries debated financial and oil production issues. Israeli and Saudi intelligence experts agreed with Mubarak's assessment.[2] Moving troops to a border was a tactic that Saddam
Hussein had used in the past. It was probably all that he was doing in the
summer of 1990.

When the US ambassador to Iraq, April Glaspie, was called to a meeting with Saddam Hussein late in July, she conveyed two messages: the
United States took no position in the disputes between Iraq and Kuwait,
and expected that those disputes would be resolved peacefully. The first
half of her communication was something Saddam Hussein was happy
to hear; the second half was something he thought he could ignore. In
Hussein's published version of what was said by the American ambassador, Glaspie's statement about a peaceful resolution of issues between
Iraq and Kuwait was downplayed.[3] That was unfair to the ambassador,
but even the full and accurate transcript was problematic. Dennis Ross, a
senior adviser to Secretary of State Baker was with the secretary on an
international flight when he read the official State Department account of
Glaspie's conversation with Hussein. He thought the words he was reading had the wrong tone and might have inadvertently conveyed a signal
to Saddam that the US would not care about an Iraqi invasion of Kuwait.
"It can't be that bad," Baker said. Ross handed Baker the transcript; he
read it and said, "Damn."[4]

The intelligence community conclusion that Hussein was moving
troops for diplomatic leverage could not be sustained when the supplies
necessary for an actual invasion began arriving at the border. The official
assessment changed and there was a last-minute effort to get President
Bush to give the Iraqi leader a serious warning, but the preparations for a
high-level phone call were still underway when Iraqi forces attacked Kuwait.[5]

The initial American reaction to the unexpected invasion was somewhat confusing. Talking to reporters just before the first meeting of the
National Security Council to take up the Kuwait crisis, the president said:
"We're not discussing intervention. One of the things I want to do at this
meeting is hear from our Secretary of Defense, our Chairman, and others."[6] What Bush meant to say, and clarified later, was that no decisions
had yet been made about any of the actions the United States might take.[7]
The use of force was not off the table. The table had not yet been set. The
participants in that first NSC meeting, on August 2, like the president in
his informal remarks to reporters, were cautious about what could be
done in a distant part of the world where a huge Iraqi army was rapidly
overwhelming the modest security forces of Kuwait. They were worried
about what was going to happen to the price of oil and unsure about
whether the unfolding events in the Middle East were historic or just "the
crisis *du jour*."[8]

The next day, after the president returned from a speaking engagement in Aspen, Colorado—and a meeting with Margaret Thatcher who was attending the same Aspen event—the NSC met again. This meeting was different.[9] Brent Scowcroft, with the president's permission, broke with customary procedures and began the deliberations with an emphatic statement. "My personal judgment is that the stakes in this for the United States are such that to accommodate Iraq should not be a policy option."[10] Allowing Saddam Hussein to get away with his conquest was unacceptable. By prior arrangement, Larry Eagleburger, the deputy secretary of state filling in for Baker while the secretary returned to Washington, and Secretary of Defense Dick Cheney endorsed Scowcroft's sentiments.[11] According to Richard Haass, the NSC expert on the Middle East, those three statements by senior members of the Bush national security team ended any possibility that an Iraqi acquisition of Kuwait would go unchallenged by the United States. There had not yet been much detailed discussion of specific courses of action, but "the future direction of U.S. policy was," for Haass, "there for all to see."[12]

In his memoir about the two American wars with Iraq, Haass goes on to observe that "the difference between the first and second NSC meetings," early in August of 1990, "highlights a fundamental truth. People matter."[13] It was never a foregone conclusion that the world, or the United States, would actively oppose Saddam Hussein's aggression. Kuwait was a small nation that few Americans had ever heard of or could find on a map. It was ruled by a wealthy royal family that showed little interest in democracy or human rights. Kuwaiti rulers were neither popular nor powerful in the Middle East and there was no bi-lateral or regional treaty obligating the United States to come to their defense. A different president with a different collection of foreign policy advisers might have reluctantly accepted the *fait accompli* that Saddam Hussein was busily creating. But a different president and a different group of foreign policy advisers were not in the White House situation room. George Bush, his senior staff and his cabinet officers were not prepared to accept an act of unprovoked aggression in the Persian Gulf. Their refusal to accept it shaped everything that would follow.

The next day, after a third NSC meeting, this time at Camp David, the president returned to the White House via helicopter. On the lawn of the executive mansion, in brief remarks, Bush made a declaration: "This will not stand. This will not stand, this aggression against Kuwait."[14] The message was short, simple and without rhetorical flare. But it was clear. The United States would not allow Iraqi aggression to succeed. Paul Wolfowitz, undersecretary of defense for policy, called the president's statement "a gutsy decision."[15] James Baker called it "the most famous—and courageous—line of his presidency."[16] President Bush, later reflecting on his "this will not stand" declaration, observed that "I never wavered from the position that I would do whatever it took to remove Iraq from Kuwait."[17]

In the early days of the crisis, the administration took a number of actions. At the United Nations, a resolution of condemnation was introduced and quickly passed by the Security Council. There was no Soviet veto, as might have been expected during the Cold War. Instead, Secretary of State Baker and Soviet Foreign Minister Eduard Shevardnadze held a joint press conference and together read a joint statement criticizing Iraqi aggression. In another early policy decision, the president issued executive orders to freeze American-held Iraqi and Kuwaiti assets. A more controversial and consequential response to the crisis involved Saudi Arabia. Kuwait was a small triangle wedged between Iraq and Saudi Arabia on the shores of the Persian Gulf. Once Saddam controlled Kuwait he would hold 20 percent of the known oil reserves in the Middle East.[18] If he moved into the northeastern provinces of Saudi Arabia, which were thinly populated and weakly defended, he could control much more. During the first weekend of the crisis the Bush administration decided to offer aircraft and ground forces to Saudi Arabia in order to prevent any Iraqi attempt to acquire additional territory and oil.

Making the offer was relatively easy, getting the Saudis to accept it was somewhat harder. The Saudis were American allies and major buyers of US arms but had never allowed the stationing of American military forces within their borders. The president spoke directly to the Saudi Crown Prince, and members of the administration worked closely with the Saudi ambassador to the United States in order to secure Saudi cooperation. A high-level delegation, led by Dick Cheney, traveled to Riyadh to speak in person with Saudi leaders, and shortly thereafter, American forces began arriving in Saudi Arabia. In 1990, Saddam Hussein had over 400,000 men under arms, the fourth-largest army in the world. During his invasion he moved nearly half that number into Kuwait and stationed additional forces in southern Iraq. The number of troops necessary to deter further aggression would also be large.

Throughout the remaining days in August, and well into September, a massive American deployment to the Persian Gulf was executed. Three aircraft carriers were moved to the region, squadrons of bombers and fighters were put on Saudi airfields and American combat units were assembled in locations close to the Saudi borders with Iraq and Kuwait. In the earliest weeks of the deployment, the American military forces were insufficient to stop an Iraqi invasion of Saudi Arabia. But the buildup grew, and the pipeline of new arrivals was kept full and flowing. By the end of September, General Norman Schwarzkopf, the US commander in the region, had a substantial military force ready to defend Saudi Arabia. More soldiers and equipment were on the way and December 1 was the official deadline for completion of the Desert Shield deployment. Of course, American forces arriving in the Middle East during November had to be prepared for that deployment, and put in transit, weeks before they were in a position to support General Schwarzkopf's mission. Colin Powell described the movement of troops and material as a funnel; a great deal could be poured into the top, but there was a bottleneck on the way to Saudi Arabia. Powell told Cheney and the president that a decision would have to be made in October about whether or not to continue pushing forces into the top of the funnel.[19]

In other words, the issue in October was whether the Pentagon would continue its ongoing deployment process or shift gears and begin planning for a long stay in Saudi Arabia and for the orderly rotation of units assigned to duty in the Persian Gulf. There was a tipping point involved. If the United States put 200,000 troops in Saudi Arabia, it would be possible to maintain that number for a long period of time with regular rotations between units training in the United States and those stationed overseas. If the deployment became much larger, rotation would be difficult, and the morale of the troops stationed in the Saudi desert without any anticipated relief could become a problem. There were already some indications that this was happening in the fall of 1990. Would the movement of US forces to the Persian Gulf end when we had a sufficient number to carry out the Desert Shield mission? Or would more forces be sent? That was a major national security agenda item in October 1990, a month that was already busy with other matters.

THE CRUCIAL MONTH

In the 1980 campaign for the Republican presidential nomination, George Bush famously called Ronald Reagan's plans to cut taxes, raise defense spending and balance the budget "voodoo economics." Reagan's economic promises did not add up, and after he chose Bush as his running mate, he delivered on only two of them. Taxes came down and defense spending soared. So, of course, did the annual deficit and the national debt. Congress responded to the growing debt late in the Reagan presidency by passing legislation (named for its Senate sponsors Phil Gramm and Warren Rudman) that set targets for deficit reduction and mandated across-the-board spending cuts if those targets were not met.

When Bush succeeded Reagan, having promised not to raise taxes, he found himself in a bind. Large Democratic majorities controlled the House and Senate—the largest opposition numbers ever faced by a newly elected modern president. Democrats wanted to cut defense spending, which seemed justified with the winding down of the Cold War; and they wanted to protect entitlements while finding new money for a variety of discretionary spending programs. They were willing to raise taxes, particularly on wealthy Americans, to fund worthy projects or reduce the deficit. Republicans also wanted deficit discipline and spending cuts but did not think that all, or even most, of the cuts should come from defense. Moreover, Republicans were adamant about keeping the popular Bush campaign commitment against new taxation. There was political controversy at nearly every stage in the making of national budgets and it was hard to imagine real progress in reducing the annual deficit unless both sides gave ground on core principles.

During President Bush's first year in office, the administration worked with Democrats on Capitol Hill to craft a budget that would not require new taxation. Instead, the first Bush budget used some one-time savings, some optimistic economic projections and other tricks of the trade to make things appear to be in compliance with the Gramm-Rudman requirements. Because the national economy slowed down in 1990, because special funding was needed to help depositors at failing savings and loan associations, and because oil prices were rising after the Iraqi invasion of Kuwait, there was no way to repeat the games that had been played in 1989. The budget prepared in 1990 (for the 1991 fiscal year) would have to address deficit pressures or run the risk of triggering automatic cutbacks. In the summer of 1990, Bush agreed to a crucial concession. In the ongoing budget deliberations with Democratic congressional leaders, new taxes could be considered if Democrats accepted some budget cuts to existing programs.

The 1991 fiscal year began on October 1, 1990, without congressional action on a budget agreement. A few days later, the president went on national television to express his support for a proposed deal that included both spending constraints and tax increases. The revenue proposals in the early October compromise did not involve any changes in the personal or corporate income tax rates, but tax increases of any kind were controversial with conservative Republicans. Newt Gingrich, then a member of the House Republican leadership and a participant in the budget negotiations, backed away from the proposed agreement. Gingrich and his supporters joined forces with liberal Democrats who did not like the spending reductions in the proposed budget and helped to defeat it on the floor of the House. This brought forth a flurry of new negotiations, temporary spending resolutions, proposed compromises and still more negotiations. At one point, the nation experienced a brief government shutdown when the president vetoed one of the congressional stopgap spending measures.

The final result, passed on October 24, included an increase in income taxes for the highest bracket from 28 to 31 percent, and was arguably less favorable to the president's preferences than the budget legislation proposed at the beginning of the month. Throughout October, the administration fought a complicated triangular battle with members of the president's own party as well as the Democratic opposition. The issues under negotiation were not limited to the budget decisions necessary for the new fiscal year. In a major innovation, congressional leaders agreed to reforms in budgeting procedures that would restrain all new spending that did not specify a source of funding from cuts in current expenditures or new sources of revenue. This was the origin of what came to be called "pay as you go" budgeting—no new spending without an identified source of funding. In this way, the budget agreement for 1991 addressed the long-term problems that had produced party conflict throughout the late 1980s and put the nation a few steps closer to fiscal responsibility. Neither side got exactly what they wanted in the complicated and confusing negotiations, and both sides made significant concessions. Years later, the John F. Kennedy Library Foundation would declare George Bush's role in the 1990 budget compromise to be a "profile in courage."[20] It didn't feel that way at the time.

During the month of October there were at least nineteen days on which the *New York Times* ran a major front-page story on budget-related issues. The on-again, off-again spending and revenue compromises occupied a significant amount of presidential time and attention, a reality that belies the common observation that President Bush was more concerned with foreign affairs than domestic policy. Throughout the month, Bush called members of Congress, gave public speeches and talked with journalists in a concerted effort to get an acceptable budget compromise. In the middle of the month, he did a five-state tour to build popular support for a resolution of the negotiations. He wanted the best budget possible, but he was also worried about the state of the economy, the price of oil and the need to avoid a sequestration of defense dollars that could complicate operations in the Persian Gulf. And he was fully committed to taking steps to fix the longer-term problems of debt and deficit. The Gingrich rebellion left the Bush administration more at the mercy of Democratic congressional leaders who pushed on revenue compromises the president felt forced to accept.

The other big generator of headline news in October 1990 was the Middle East. Most of the news was bad. On October 8, after violent demonstrations in Jerusalem near the Temple Mount, 21 Palestinians were killed and 150 injured in a confrontation with Israeli security forces. Twenty Israelis were also injured on the bloodiest day "in the twenty-three years of Israeli occupation of the West Bank."[21] Israel's critics accused the government of using excessive force and called for a UN Security Council resolution condemning their actions and mandating an international investigation. The United States worked to soften the UN resolution, and after doing so, joined the other permanent members of the council in criticizing the Israeli response to the demonstrations. Throughout these negotiations, there was an American concern that a reinvigorated Arab-Israeli conflict would strain the anti-Iraq coalition or, in the worst case, give Saddam Hussein a chance to present himself as the real Arab leader of the region—the one who stood up to Israel and to Israel's closest ally.

Elsewhere in the region, trouble came not from acts of violence but from proposals for peace. Officials in both Jordan (not a member of the American-led coalition against Saddam) and Saudi Arabia (a leading member of that coalition) put forward ideas to resolve the confrontation with Iraq by giving Saddam Hussein something he wanted in exchange for a full or partial withdrawal from Kuwait. These peace proposals followed an earlier one proposed by the Soviet Union in September and a suggestion from François Mitterrand that democratic reform in Kuwait should become a goal for the coalition. Throughout the month of October, Yevgeny Primakov, representing Gorbachev, traveled in the Middle East and in Europe trying to win support for some version of a negotiated settlement between Saddam Hussein and the coalition. The Bush administration stood firm in opposition to all of these proposals, insisting on unconditional Iraqi withdrawal from Kuwait and full restoration of the deposed Kuwaiti government. Any discussion of Iraq's future relations with Kuwait, or Kuwait's form of government, would come after a withdrawal, not before. On October 20, the president wrote a long and heartfelt letter to the king of Jordan bluntly criticizing him for his pro-Saddam public statements and his failure to condemn Iraqi atrocities in Kuwait.[22] Successfully opposing these peace plans was important for the Bush administration, but left American diplomats increasingly worried that world opinion, or opinion in the Middle East, might soon favor a resolution of the crisis that did not significantly punish or weaken Saddam Hussein.

President Bush has been properly praised for putting together a large and diverse coalition of nations opposed to the Iraqi invasion of Kuwait. In fact, it may have been easier to put the coalition together than it was to keep it together and moving toward a decisive resolution of the crisis. The events in Jerusalem, the subsequent controversies at the United Nations and the peace proposals provided clear confirmation that there were tensions in the coalition. So did the problem of foreign citizens held by Saddam in Iraq and Kuwait. Sometimes referred to as hostages, the coalition nationals unable to leave Iraq and Kuwait gave Saddam leverage in the crisis. Throughout the fall of 1990, he experimented with different ways to use it. In October, American and British citizens were held at strategic locations that might become coalition bombing targets. To mitigate the negative public relations related to hostage holding, women and children were allowed to go home in September. French citizens were released in October, presumably as a reward for some of the efforts by French officials to avoid war in the Persian Gulf. Would the European members of the coalition stay together in their opposition to Saddam? Would the volatile Middle East leaders do so? Or would coalition partners be drawn to compromises with Saddam that gave the Iraqi leader some reward for his invasion of Kuwait or some face-saving way to retreat from it? Would the early months of 1991, with the arrival of Rama-

dan and the annual pilgrimage to Mecca, make military action against
Iraq impossible? Would the hot weather that followed cause its own set
of operational problems? During the late fall of 1990, the Bush administration was looking ahead to how the Persian Gulf crisis might end and
beginning to worry that time was not on their side.

THE DECISIVE DEPLOYMENT DECISION

A reasonable assessment of US policy in the Persian Gulf early in October
would have called the policy highly successful. After the early commitment to "this will not stand," a great deal had been accomplished. The
Soviet Union had joined the United States in condemning Iraq's invasion
of Kuwait. Strongly worded UN resolutions against the invasion had
been passed. A broad coalition including nations in the Middle East,
Europe and Asia had agreed to join forces in opposition to Iraqi aggression. Saddam Hussein was isolated in the region and from much of the
world. Over 200,000 American military personnel were deployed to Saudi Arabia or to the waters of the Persian Gulf. The planes, ships, soldiers
and heavy equipment in place were enough to convince Saddam that any
attack on Saudi Arabia would be foolhardy and the Iraqis were taking
defensive positions in Kuwait, not preparing for new attacks. Stiff sanctions against Iraq had been approved at the United Nations and implemented by coalition partners. The most important of these was an embargo on the sale of Iraqi oil. Pipelines that carried Iraqi oil through Saudi
Arabia and Turkey were shut down. The southern ports of Iraq and
Kuwait were blockaded by American and coalition naval forces. According to an estimate made by Secretary Baker in congressional testimony in
mid-October, Iraq was losing 80 million dollars a day in lost oil revenue.[23] Without that money, Iraq could not purchase food and other essential imports. Rationing of scarce commodities was already taking
place; and although there was smuggling on the Iraqi borders with Jordan and Iran, there was never enough to offset the sting of the sanctions.

Of course, the sanctions hurt both Iraq and Iraq's trading partners, but
there was burden sharing and compensation for some of the sanction
consequences. The wealthier members of the coalition contributed to a
fund that would pay for costs associated with the coalition deployments
and sanction enforcement. During September, Jim Baker traveled the
globe in what came to be called "tin cup diplomacy" securing significant
financial commitments from Japan, Germany, Saudi Arabia and other
coalition partners. Controversial proposals to give Egypt debt relief and
Turkey greater access to American and European markets were passed
despite resistance in the US Congress and the European Union.

A great deal had been accomplished since the world community had
been caught off guard by the Iraqi invasion of Kuwait at the beginning of

August. Despite these accomplishments, the late fall of 1990 was a period of foreboding for George H. W. Bush. The administration was losing the high levels of public support it had achieved at the outset of the crisis. In mid-September, the president noted in his diary that 23 percent of Americans were opposed to his handling of the Gulf crisis. That was a minority of Americans, but Bush observed, it "used to be 7 percent opposed, and I worry, worry, worry about eroded support."[24]

The president also worried about the fate of Kuwaitis suffering at the hands of their Iraqi occupiers. Some widely reported human rights violations, like the claim that Iraqis removed Kuwaiti babies from incubators before shipping the confiscated hospital equipment to Baghdad, were exaggerated or invented. But there were also many reliably reported acts of brutality during the Iraqi occupation. There were civilian executions, rapes and thefts taking place on a massive scale. President Bush complained that there was insufficient media coverage of the abuses that had become routine in Kuwait and worked to publicize the reports he received. He worried that if it took much longer for Kuwait to be liberated, there might not be anything left of the nation to liberate.

If public and international support for the president's Persian Gulf policies was waning and fragile, and if Kuwaitis were suffering irreparable harm from their extended occupation, something would have to be done to bring the crisis to a conclusion sooner rather than later. Colin Powell had already alerted the Secretary of Defense and the president that October would be the month when American deployments to Saudi Arabia tapered off and the troops settled in for a long-term commitment to protect Saudi territory and contain Iraqi aggression. Or it would be the month when new deployments would have to be planned in order to build coalition forces beyond what was needed for containment. The president would have to tell the Pentagon which way he wanted to go. And if the pressure for ending the crisis was rising, there was a related question. Were the forces in place and in transit for Desert Shield sufficient to carry out the assignment of forcibly removing Iraqi troops from Kuwait? Or would more be needed?

On October 11, the senior foreign policy advisers in the administration heard from General Powell and Schwarzkopf's representative, Major General Robert Johnson, about the plans for a coalition military offensive in the Gulf using the Desert Shield assets.[25] It would begin with a huge air campaign of missile strikes and bombing runs. Iraq was described as a target-rich environment with major vulnerabilities that American airpower could exploit, but there was little confidence that air attacks alone would drive Iraqi forces out of Kuwait. A ground war would be needed, and the October 11 plans were simple and direct: "a corps-sized frontal assault through the heart of Kuwait, with an initial goal of seizing the major road intersection north of Kuwait City."[26] Schwarzkopf told Major General Johnson to end his briefing with clear statements that the ground war plans were preliminary and that current troop levels in Saudi Arabia were insuffficient to support an optimal offensive.[27]

The president's senior foreign policy team was not impressed. Brent Scowcroft found the briefing "unenthusiastic" and "delivered by people who did not want to do the job."[28] Dick Cheney shared Scowcroft's disappointment and promised new plans would be forthcoming. The next day the president wrote in his diary that he had had lunch with his chief of staff John Sununu, Scowcroft and Baker to discuss the next steps in the crisis. He wanted to be prepared to act if Saddam Hussein provided some new provocation that justified or required a military response. The October 11 briefing described the military response he would make if provoked by Saddam. But the frontal assault on defended Iraqi positions in Kuwait looked like it would produce significant coalition casualties. Bush worried "about sending kids into battle and the lives being lost," remembering his own combat experiences in the Pacific. But while those memories made him a cautious commander in chief, they also reminded him of "the importance of winning."[29]

Winning may have been on his mind again on the evening of October 17, when the president had dinner with Brent Scowcroft. According to his diary, they talked about "how we get things off center in the Middle East."[30] "Off center" was a somewhat vague and imprecise phrase, but probably referred to the president's growing concern that additional steps needed to be taken in the Persian Gulf. In the same diary entry, the president observed that "support is eroding in the Middle East, and the budget is a loser . . . I think this [the budget negotiations and the Persian Gulf crisis] is the biggest challenge of my life—by far."[31]

Among the president's professional foreign policy advisers, the month of October was filled with meetings and memo writing aimed at developing viable options for new steps in the Gulf crisis—the kind of things that would move the administration "off center." The so-called "small group" of foreign policy experts included Bob Gates and Richard Haass from the NSC, Bob Kimmitt from the Department of State, Paul Wolfowitz from Defense, Admiral David Jeremiah from the Joint Chiefs of Staff and Dick Kerr from the intelligence community. They met regularly throughout the month of October and outlined three options to present to the president: standing pat with sanctions; issuing an ultimatum to Saddam to leave Kuwait or be forced out; and waiting for a new Iraqi provocation that would trigger a coalition use of force against the occupation of Kuwait.[32] Though all three options were developed with pros and cons for the president's review, Haass preferred the ultimatum.[33] It gave Saddam a choice and an opportunity to avoid war. At the same time, it made clear that American patience was running out and that a final resolution, whether by diplomacy or force, would take place soon. In Haass' judgment, Scowcroft, Gates and Baker were coming around to the ultimatum option, but "the military seemed most wary."[34]

"Colin Powell," Haass writes, "was a reluctant warrior" who would only support a use of force against Saddam if it involved large commitments of manpower and firepower without any political micromanaging of operations in the field.[35] In the Pentagon, Powell's JCS staff developed a list of options not very different from the ones under consideration in the small group.[36] They included standing pat, ratcheting up sanctions, going to war, or building up a large enough force to make credible threats of war an effective diplomatic tool. Powell was careful not to tell his staff which option he preferred since he was not fully certain about what the president wanted, and which mission the military might be given.[37]

Towards the middle of the month, Powell and Baker got together for an important private conversation. On Saturday, October 19, Powell went to see Baker.[38] The Chairman of the Joint Chiefs expressed his concern that US policy in the Gulf crisis was "drifting." Though the administration had great success in its early policy initiatives against Saddam Hussein, thus far, Saddam had not budged. What would make him do so? Would we have to wait for the sanctions to so severely punish the Iraqi nation that Saddam would be compelled to take action? How long would that take? In the meantime, should we simply defend Saudi Arabia from attack or begin to prepare for the military action that would force the Iraqis to leave Kuwait. These were essentially the first two options under development by the "small group." It was also related to Powell's earlier concern about the deployment pipeline for Desert Shield. Was the administration going to turn off the tap in October, or keep it flowing? In his conversation with Baker, Powell boiled it all down to two words: "Defend or eject?"[39] Was the United States going to stop, stand pat, and defend Saudi Arabia? Or were we going to get ready for a war that would eject the Iraqi forces from Kuwait? At the beginning of the month, when Powell raised questions about the pipeline decisions for sending more troops and equipment to Saudi Arabia, the president did not give Powell a definitive answer. But Bush did express doubt that there was enough time "politically" for a sanction-driven policy to work.[40] Two weeks later, Powell was still not sure which way the president wanted to go. In his conversation with Baker on October 19, the two senior presidential advisers agreed that the best course of action would be to deploy additional forces to the Persian Gulf, enough to allow the United States and the coalition to confidently carry out the eject mission.

That decision would help in two ways. In the first instance, it would make an ultimatum to Saddam credible. If the United States and the coalition were obviously getting ready for war, Saddam might choose retreat as his best, or only, option. And if he did not, the United States would be properly prepared to carry out the war that would get the job done. There would be no more drift; one way or the other Saddam would leave Kuwait.

The next day Baker took time to write down his thoughts about the advantages of combining a military buildup with an ultimatum. He wanted the administration "to get ahead of [the] erosion of support" that might occur if Powell's drift was left unresolved.[41] Baker called the president and asked for an opportunity to speak with him in private; their conversation took place on Sunday, October 20. Bush listened attentively to his friend and secretary of state but said that he needed time to think about the arguments Baker was making. This, Baker observed in his memoirs, was the typical Bush response to an important issue: listen to advisers but take time to think about the matter before making a decision. Over the next four days, Baker reports that there were a number of discussions among the president, Baker, Cheney, Powell and Scowcroft in different combinations and at different times. The topic was always next steps for the Persian Gulf. According to Baker, on October 24, the president had reached a tentative conclusion.[42] He was leaning toward the approval of a major augmentation of the US deployment to the Persian Gulf and preparation for the use of force to remove Iraqi forces from Kuwait if an ultimatum was rejected.[43] Scowcroft puts the date of the presidential decision somewhat earlier. "It was my impression that somewhere in early to mid-October, President Bush came to the conclusion, consciously or unconsciously, that he had to do whatever was necessary to liberate Kuwait and the reality was that that meant using force."[44] The president does not dispute Scowcroft's claim.[45]

Powell, who traveled to Saudi Arabia for direct consultations with General Schwarzkopf on October 22, returned to Washington ready to present new plans for how military operations against Saddam Hussein could be conducted. Some confusion and bureaucratic competition arose when plans developed by senior policy advisers in the Pentagon conflicted with those that were proposed by Schwarzkopf's staff.[46] The Schwarzkopf preferences prevailed. They involved a feint against the Iraqi positions in Kuwait accompanied by a huge flanking maneuver by armored units moving across southern Iraq. That maneuver would surround the Iraqi forces in Kuwait and cut them off from easy escape and resupply. And it would forego the necessity of a dangerous frontal assault on fortified Iraqi positions. The sweep across southern Iraq could not be done with the equipment and personnel currently in Saudi Arabia and would require a force roughly twice as large as the one that had been authorized for Desert Shield. On October 30, Powell briefed the Secretary of Defense on the list of troops and equipment that would be necessary to carry out this large-scale offensive operation. It was a long list. Later that day, there was a two-hour meeting in the White House of the senior national security team.[47] Powell later called it "the most crucial" meeting the administration had "since Saddam had grabbed Kuwait."[48]

Robert Gates, the deputy national security advisor, speaking in an oral history interview some years later, paints a vivid portrait of what transpired at the crucial meeting. Gates may not have been fully aware of the emerging consensus at the highest level of Bush administration deliberations. By the end of October, Powell and Baker were on the same page in thinking that preparation for offensive action was wise. Cheney agreed. The president was leaning in the same direction and, according to Scowcroft, had already made up his mind that an active war against Saddam Hussein might soon be necessary. Gates thought "defend"—continuing sanctions and the defense of Saudi Arabia—was still a likely option and speculated that "I think the military strategy was in this [October 30] meeting with Bush, to put together a package that was so daunting he [the president] would say, 'Well, let's stand pat.'"[49]

In other words, Gates thought that he was hearing a list of military requests that were intentionally outlandish in order to force the president to back off from any plans to "eject" Saddam Hussein from Kuwait. Though Gates may have been a little out of step with what was actually taking place at the meeting, his perspective on this occasion is critically important. His recollections document just how big and just how bold the decision-making of the Bush administration was at this juncture of the Persian Gulf crisis. "So the [Pentagon] briefer starts out," Gates recalls,

> "First we'll need the Seventh Corps out of Germany." Okay, you're going to take the heart of NATO's defense, that had been in Germany since 1945 . . . and you're going to move it from Germany to Saudi Arabia, the two heaviest divisions in the American Army. Okay. "Then we'll need six carrier battle groups." We had never put six carrier battle groups in the same theater of action since there were aircraft carriers, and we're looking, that's sort of a hundred ships or something like that by the time you count all of the other stuff.[50]

And the Pentagon wish list was not yet complete. Gates continues,

> Remember, this is a week before the mid-year [mid-term] elections. And then the poison pill. If that hadn't gotten him, this one would. "Oh, and you'll have to activate both the National Guard and the Reserves." In other words, you're going to reach into every community in America and take people away from their homes and their jobs. To the day I die I'll never forget, Bush pushed his chair back, stood up, looked at Cheney and said, "You've got it, let me know if you need more," and walked out of the room.

According to Gates, "Cheney's jaw dropped. Powell's jaw dropped. Cheney looks at Scowcroft and says, 'Does he know what he just authorized?' And Brent smiled and he said, 'He knows perfectly well what he authorized.'"[51]

Bush was decisive and deliberate because for nearly a week, and maybe longer, he was committed to the ultimatum option, and the prospect of war if Saddam failed to respond. He knew what he was doing because for the better part of a month, he had been seeking advice on the next steps in the crisis. The advice had come in formal NSC memos and in a series of private conversations with the people he most trusted. The key decisions were to dramatically increase the Persian Gulf deployment, to seriously threaten the use of force and, if the Iraqis did not withdraw from Kuwait, to use the coalition's military power to bring the crisis to a conclusion. Once these decisions were made, the president was prepared to give the Pentagon whatever they needed to carry them out.

He was not, however, prepared to make his decision public. The fact that the United States was doubling its military deployments to the Persian Gulf was withheld from Congress and from the American people for more than a week. He could not withhold public acknowledgement of the new deployments much longer than that. Some of the actions that would be taken by the Pentagon to implement them would be noticed by alert news organizations. You can't hide, for very long, the movement of two hundred thousand people. Though secrecy would be hard to maintain for very long, there were reasons for it.

The first involved diplomacy. Secretary of State Baker, early in November, conducted extensive consultations with allies and diplomatic representatives of the permanent and temporary members of the UN Security Council. He was trying to assess the level of support for a new UN resolution giving Saddam Hussein a clear ultimatum and authorizing the use of force if he failed to comply. Having such a resolution would enhance the weight of an ultimatum against Saddam Hussein and give added international legitimacy to any conflict that might follow. Of course, seeking such a resolution, and failing to win the Security Council vote, would have had the opposite effect. So Baker needed a window for confidential conversations in order to measure the likelihood of success for a UN endorsement authorizing the use of force. He was furious when that window was closed by a public announcement of the new deployments on November 8.[52]

The second reason for secrecy almost certainly involved the mid-term elections. None of the memoir writers say that the politics of the approaching congressional elections led to the initial secrecy, but it must have been a factor under consideration. Did Bush want to put the administration one or two steps closer to war with Iraq on the eve of mid-term voting? Was that a good time to expect healthy debate about Persian Gulf policy? Would an announced expansion of the US deployment to the Middle East, and speculation that the US was gearing up for war with Iraq, be seen as a stunt to get more Americans to rally round the president, perhaps helping Republican candidates? Or would making the announcement in the heated buildup to a national election divide the parties and threaten the bipartisan foreign policy support the Bush administration had thus far enjoyed? By withholding information about the new deployments, President Bush prevented Iraq from becoming a controversial issue in the final days of the congressional campaign. Publicly announcing the plan to double down on Desert Shield at the end of October 1990 was a damned if you do, damned if you don't, decision. Bush chose the latter form of damnation.

Shortly before the public announcement, there were courtesy calls to members of Congress informing them about what was forthcoming. Congressional leaders were surprised by the president's decision and angry that they had not been informed sooner. According to a detailed account of these events provided by Bartholomew Sparrow, Sam Nunn, the powerful chair of the Senate Armed Services Committee, "went bananas" when he learned about the new deployment decision.[53] Les Aspin, Nunn's counterpart in the House of Representatives, had the same reaction. At a White House meeting with the Democratic congressional leadership, including Senator Nunn, a Baker aide describes the Democrats as "apoplectic," and observes that "it was the closest we came to losing these guys on this issue."[54]

Nunn fully understood that the new and larger deployment numbers would make rotation of forces impossible. He regarded the deployment enhancement as a backhanded way of declaring war against Saddam Hussein and deeply resented the lack of congressional consultation from the administration before the making of such a consequential commitment. In the weeks following the public announcement of the new deployment numbers, Nunn scheduled hearings with witnesses who warned the American public that the now more likely war with Iraq would be dangerous and painful. Former Chairman of the Joint Chiefs of Staff, Admiral William Crowe, was one of Nunn's prominent witnesses making the case for giving sanctions a chance to work before using force. He argued that punishing Saddam Hussein, or removing him from power, would not solve the underlying problems in the Middle East which had a long history and deep social, economic and cultural origins.[55] If war could be avoided, it should be. In the wake of the hearings and a growing public debate about the Persian Gulf crisis, congressional opposition to the administration grew.

Winning international endorsement for the ultimatum and authorization for the use of force was actually easier than winning domestic endorsement. Some members of the administration, especially Dick Cheney, urged the president to consider conducting military operations against Iraq without congressional approval. Saddam Hussein had clearly violated the UN Charter's prohibition against acts of aggression and the US was a signatory of the Charter—a treaty the Senate had ratified. That was all the authorization necessary. Moreover, seeking congressional support and failing to achieve it (like seeking a Security Council resolution and failing to achieve that) would do considerable harm. It was better, Cheney thought, to act on executive power under existing international law and treaty obligations than to seek congressional approval and risk a long-drawn-out debate that "could convey a sense to our allies and to Saddam Hussein that we weren't resolute in our commitment to liberate Kuwait."[56]

The president agreed with parts of Cheney's analysis and on more than one occasion publicly stated that he could authorize the use of force against Saddam Hussein without specific congressional approval. But he ultimately decided to seek a congressional endorsement because, like the UN resolution approving the use of force, a congressional resolution supporting the ultimatum would make Iraqi compliance with it more likely. The vote in Congress came after the UN resolution and was a close call. It won a particularly narrow margin in the Senate. Prominent Democrats, including Sam Nunn and John Kerry, voted against it.

In the final days before the expiration of the UN ultimatum deadline, there were multiple efforts to secure a last-minute diplomatic agreement. As with the earlier peace proposals, the administration stood firm against any suggested resolution of the crisis that did not include full Iraqi compliance with an unconditional withdrawal from Kuwait. A last-minute meeting between Baker and the Iraqi foreign minister, Tariq Aziz, in Geneva gave Saddam Hussein a final chance to avoid war. He did not take it. Aziz even refused to accept a letter President Bush had addressed to Hussein. The war came and the combination of superior airpower followed by the rapid armored assault across southern Iraq led to a decisive coalition victory with far fewer coalition casualties than anyone, including the Pentagon, had expected. As General Schwarzkopf famously observed, once the ground fighting began, Saddam Hussein quickly went from having the fourth-largest army in the world to having the second-largest army in Iraq.[57]

AUDACITY

"Prudence," pronounced in the exaggerated fashion used by Dana Carvey on *Saturday Night Live*, is the trait most commonly associated with America's 41st president. Audacity is rarely mentioned in connection with President Bush. But Richard Nixon once told Larry King that it was a mistake for anyone to underestimate George Bush. "Every time you tend to write off George Bush, he makes the big play."[58]

In the month of October 1990, George Bush made two big plays—one in public and one behind closed doors. The budget compromise, and the tax increases that it included, divided the Republican Party and arguably cost Bush his chance for reelection in 1992. It also moved the nation gradually and grudgingly toward a resolution of the fiscal problems created by the Reagan Revolution. It was arguably the right thing to do, but it was hard, and the president made sure that it was a big compromise and not a modest one that muddled through one more budget cycle.

The decision to double the Desert Shield deployment was audacious. It was not, as some claimed or feared, a decision to go to war with Saddam Hussein, though it was definitely a decision to bring the Gulf crisis to a conclusion. The US-led coalition would prepare to carry out a massive military operation against Saddam Hussein and combine those preparations with an ultimatum: withdraw from Kuwait or face the coalition's military might. It is one of the enduring mysteries of the first Gulf War that Saddam did not take the ultimatum seriously and withdraw from Kuwait. The humiliation of withdrawal could have led to a revolt against his leadership, but the humiliation of defeat at the hands of coalition forces involved the same risk, a risk that Saddam Hussein ultimately survived. Did the Iraqi dictator doubt that Bush would carry out an attack? Did he underestimate the superiority of the forces—air, sea and land—arrayed against him? Did he expect the coalition to come apart at the last moment before military action or at the first occasion of coalition casualties? Did he think that his rocket assaults on Israel would be enough to change the dynamics of the crisis in a way that favored him and his supporters in the Middle East? There are multiple questions about the decision making on the Iraqi side of the first Gulf War.

Bush's decision to ramp up American deployments to the Middle East is easier to explain. Doubling the deployment increased the chances for success and the chances for a rapid resolution of the conflict. Of course, no one, including the president, could have confidently predicted just how quick and just how successful the actual fighting would be. Coalition losses in the hundred hours of ground combat were extraordinarily low. According to the Department of Defense, the US suffered 148 deaths in combat; the United Kingdom 47 and all the other allies (excluding Kuwait) 46. These numbers were not what had been predicted. They were dramatically lower than the lowest estimate made by the Pentagon before actual fighting began.[59] This was a case where the "fog of war"— the unknowable things that happen in armed combat—disguised a favorable outcome rather than a disastrous one. It was fog all the same. And the boldness of the president's decision needs to be measured not against the actual outcome, but against the outcome that was prudently predicted and widely expected.

It was a big play. Why did Bush make it? As we have already seen, he was worried that support from the American public and from the international community would not last and that, despite the severe sanctions, the passage of time might actually have been helping Saddam more than it was helping the coalition. Those tactical and temporal considerations were accompanied by some broader lessons from history.

Bush was criticized on a number of occasions during the buildup to the Gulf War for his frequent comparisons of Saddam Hussein to Adolf Hitler. All comparisons to the twentieth-century dictator who gave us a world war and the Holocaust are problematic, but Bush made clear that he had two points of comparison in mind. One involved the failure of the international community to punish acts of aggression in the years before 1939. Dictators, Bush had learned in his youth, responded to perceived weakness by taking advantage it. That life lesson was probably reinforced by a history of the Second World War that the president was reading in the early days of the crisis.[60] There was another way in which the president saw Saddam as comparable to Adolf Hitler. Throughout the crisis, Bush was moved and motivated by the atrocities reported to him that were occurring during the Iraqi occupation of Kuwait. The killings, the confiscations, the harassment of hostages, the abuses of all kinds weighed heavily on his deliberations. When he met with an Anglican cleric who wanted war to be avoided, Bush responded by citing details from some of the reports by human rights organizations that he had recently read and making the classic just war argument that sometimes the evils of war were necessary and justified by the evils that might be averted or prevented.[61]

In some commentaries these arguments about responding to aggression and preventing atrocities were read as public relations tactics that were marshaled in order to build domestic and international support for a war that was actually about oil and the economic consequences of its greater concentration in the hands of an American enemy. Though there may be some justice in these observations, there is good reason to believe that the president's views on these subjects were personal and powerful. These were arguments he made in private as well as in public, and though he was advised to cut back on his comparisons of Saddam and Hitler, he never did.[62]

And there was another powerful point of historical comparison that Bush, Colin Powell and others clearly saw in the Gulf crisis. These were lessons learned from Vietnam. Like Powell, Bush believed that if military force was to be used, it should be used at levels that increased the likelihood of success, with public support and with political leaders who would not second-guess or micromanage the professional military decisions during actual operations. Like the lessons from World War II, these were not abstract lessons. They were things Bush learned from observation of international events in his long career of public service.

The justice in fighting a dictator and the logic of fighting with a robust military force are relatively easy to see, but they still don't, by themselves, fully explain the audacity of Bush's decision in October 1990. His decision involved multiple risks. The UN Security Council members might not have supported the resolution that justified the use of force against Saddam. The Congress came close to rejecting the ultimatum and the threatened use of force that was the key to its potential success. When the president sent Baker to a last-minute meeting with the Iraqi foreign minister, he was taking one more risk. Diplomacy in the final days of the ultimatum period might have worked, but it also involved the danger that a partial or finessed resolution of the crisis would avert war and give Saddam an opportunity to claim that his aggression had been successful.

Ultimately, the president got approval from the UN and from the Congress along with credit for going the extra mile in final diplomatic efforts. Saddam did not withdraw from Kuwait. The peace proposals supported by the Soviet Union, and other players, produced no halfway measures that might have broken the back of the coalition. The meeting between Baker and Aziz produced no awkward breakthrough. That left a war to be fought and fought without any guarantee of the kind of success that the United States and its coalition allies actually achieved. What made the supposedly prudent George H. W. Bush take all of those risks?

Nearly always prudent in speech, often prudent in action, Bush nevertheless led a life that was full of high-risk decisions. At seventeen, he elected to join the Navy when he could easily have done what his parents wanted him to do and delayed military service until after he had earned additional education. When he graduated from Yale, he could have followed a career path that had been paved and prepared for him on Wall Street. Instead, he took his young family halfway across the country in order to pursue new opportunities in business (admittedly with family assistance) in the Texas oil fields. When Bush was in his twenties and a recent founder of Zapata Petroleum Corporation, he and his partner each raised half a million dollars to fund their new endeavor. Then they bet it all, $850,000 of their newly raised capital, on a single oil field.[63] They did not sell percentages in their leases to other companies—the common way to hedge bets in the oil business. They did not spread their investments across multiple drilling sites. They put everything into one set of leases and drilled 127 wells in the Jameson field, eighty miles from Midland, Texas. All of the wells produced oil.[64] The beginning of George Bush's personal wealth and independence, his ability to eventually leave business behind and pursue a political career, was based on a huge gamble he took at a very young age in a line of work that was notorious for its risks.

George Bush could do, and often did, audacious things. His manner, his speech, his presentation of himself were almost always modest and famously unboastful. These things helped him to earn a reputation for prudence. But underneath there was a capacity for boldness, for making big plays. In the run-up to the war in Iraq, on the eve of off-year congressional elections, in the midst of intense controversy about the federal budget, President Bush decided to double US troop deployments to Saudi Arabia and the Persian Gulf. When he made that decision, he surprised and shocked many people in Washington and around the world, including some of his senior advisers. No doubt, he also surprised Saddam Hussein.

NOTES

1. George H. W. Bush and Brent Scowcroft, *A World Transformed* (New York: Alfred A. Knopf, 1999), 357.
2. James A. Baker, *The Politics of Diplomacy* (New York: G. P. Putnam's Press, 1995), 274.
3. For a discussion of the controversy surrounding the Glaspie/Hussein meeting see, Jeffrey Frank, "Twenty-Five Years After Another Gulf War," *The New Yorker,* July 16, 2017.
4. Dennis Ross Interview, August 2, 2001, George H. W. Bush Oral History Project, Miller Center, University of Virginia. For a brief review of the Glaspie controversy see: David Kenner, "Why one U.S. diplomat didn't cause the Gulf War," *Foreign Policy,* January 6, 2011.
5. Richard Haass, *War of Necessity, War of Choice* (New York: Simon & Schuster, 2009), 59.
6. Christian Alfonsi, *Circle in the Sand: Why We Went to War in Iraq* (New York: Doubleday, 2006), 53.
7. George H. W. Bush, "Remarks and an Exchange with Reporters on the Iraqi Invasion of Kuwait," August 2, 1990.
8. This is Scowcroft's reaction to the first NSC meeting. Bush and Scowcroft, *A World Transformed,* 317.
9. For a detailed discussion of NSC deliberations in the early days of the Gulf crisis see H. W. Brands, "George Bush and the Gulf War of 1991," *Presidential Studies Quarterly,* 34, no. 1 (March 2004): 113–131.
10. Haass, *War of Necessity, War of Choice,* 62–63.
11. Bush and Scowcroft, *A World Transformed,* 322.
12. Ibid., 63.
13. Ibid.
14. George H. W. Bush, "Remarks and an Exchange with Reporters on the Iraqi Invasion of Kuwait," August 5, 1990.
15. Alfonsi, *Circle in the Sand,* 73.
16. Baker, *The Politics of Diplomacy,* 276.
17. Bush and Scowcroft, *A World Transformed,* 333.
18. Richard Haass, "The Gulf War: Its Place in History," in *Into the Desert: Reflections on the Gulf War,* Jeffrey A. Engel, ed. (Oxford: Oxford University Press, 2013), 67.
19. Bob Woodward, *The Commanders* (New York: Simon & Schuster, 1991), 299.
20. The John F. Kennedy Library, accessed on January 15, 2019 at: https://www.jfklibrary.org/events-and-awards/profile-in-courage-award/award-recipients/george-hw-bush-2014
21. Dilip Hiro, *Desert Shield to Desert Storm* (New York: Routledge, 1992), 211.
22. George H. W. Bush, *All the Best* (New York: Scribner, 1999), 483–485.
23. Hiro, *Desert Shield to Desert Storm,* 226.
24. Bush and Scowcroft, *A World Transformed,* 372.
25. Schwarzkopf did not like the fact that he was not called to Washington to do the briefing and warned Powell that "as far as a ground offensive is concerned, we've still got nothing." H. Norman Schwarzkopf, *It Doesn't Take a Hero* (New York: Bantam Books, 1992), 358.
26. Bush and Scowcroft, *A World Transformed,* 381.
27. Schwarzkopf, *It Doesn't Take a Hero,* 360.
28. Ibid.
29. Bush and Scowcroft, *A World Transformed,* 382.
30. Bush, *All the Best,* 482.
31. Ibid., 483.
32. Haass, *War of Necessity, War of Choice,* 92–93.
33. Ibid., 94.
34. Ibid.

35. Ibid., 96–97.
36. Woodward, *The Commanders*, 308.
37. Ibid., 309.
38. Baker, *The Politics of Diplomacy*, 301–302.
39. Colin Powell, *My American Journey* (New York: Random House, 1995), 488.
40. Hiro, *Desert Shield to Desert Storm*, 225.
41. Baker, *The Politics of Diplomacy*, 303.
42. Ibid.
43. Richard Cheney, *In My Time* (Simon & Schuster: New York, 2011), 203.
44. Bush and Scowcroft, *A World Transformed*, 382.
45. Ibid.
46. Schwarzkopf, *It Doesn't Take a Hero*, 368–69.
47. This was the so-called gang of eight: the president, Baker, Scowcroft, Cheney, Powell, Quayle, Sununu and Gates. For the October 30, 1990 meeting Quayle was not present due to out-of-town travel. Powell, *My American Journey*, 487.
48. Ibid.
49. Robert Gates Interview, July 23–24, 2000, George H. W. Bush Oral History Project, Miller Center, University of Virginia.
50. Ibid.
51. The quotations in the last two paragraphs come from Robert Gates Interview, July 23–24, 2000.
52. Haass, *War of Necessity, War of Choice*, 97–98.
53. Bartholomew Sparrow, *The Strategist: Brent Scowcroft and the Call of National Security* (New York: Public Affairs, 2015), 394.
54. Ibid.
55. Micah L. Sifry and Christopher Cerf, eds., *The Gulf War Reader* (New York: Random House, 1991), 234–37.
56. Cheney, *In My Time*, 205.
57. Herbert Norman Schwarzkopf, Military Quotes, accessed on April 28, 2019 at: http://www.military-quotes.com/Schwarzkopf.htm
58. Quoted in Michael Duffy and Dan Goodgame, *Marching in Place: The Status Quo Presidency of George Bush* (New York: Simon & Schuster, 1992), 13.
59. Schwarzkopf, after the war, told a congressional committee that he had expected coalition casualties to be as high as 20,000. John M. Broder, "U.S. Was Ready for 20,000 Casualties," *Los Angeles Times*, June 13, 1991.
60. In the early weeks of the crisis, Bush was reading Martin Gilbert's *History of the Second World War*; Bush and Scowcroft, *A World Transformed*, 375.
61. Ibid., 427–28.
62. Bush made public references to Saddam Hussein and Hitler on October 23, October 31 and November 1. H. W. Brands, "George Bush and the Gulf War of 1991," *Presidential Studies Quarterly*, 34, no. 1 (February 2004): 129, fn 53.
63. Richard Ben Cramer, *Being Poppy* (New York: Simon & Schuster, 1992), 68.
64. According to Cramer, by the end of the year, the company was pumping 1,250 barrels of oil a day at a rate worth 1.3 million dollars a year. Ibid., 78.

SIX

Compassion

The American Military Intervention in Somalia

In the month after his defeat by Bill Clinton, George Bush ordered 28,000 American troops into the Horn of Africa to provide security for the humanitarian relief efforts then underway to feed the starving victims of Somalia's civil war. The operation was called "Restore Hope." It rather quickly restored enough order to the ports and roads of Somalia to allow efficient food distribution to those who desperately needed it. Whether the operation restored much hope in a failed and fractured state, or in a post–Cold War international community coming to terms with a variety of humanitarian disasters, is harder to judge.

Existing accounts of the Somalia intervention tend to deal with two aspects of the administration's decision. One involves the role of the media in generating demand for action—the so-called CNN effect—that is alleged to have gotten us into Somalia under Bush and out again under Clinton. The other is the connection between this intervention and the broader themes in the administration's thinking about a New World Order. To some, Somalia was the hopeful harbinger of things to come when a generous United States, working through the United Nations, would use its unchallenged power to address pressing problems around the world. The Somalia operation broke new ground in national and international politics. For the first time in its history, the United Nations authorized the deployment of military forces by a great power to deal with problems in the internal affairs of a member state. And for the first time in a much longer history, the United States committed substantial military resources to a humanitarian mission lacking even a remote connection to traditional definitions of the national interest. The fact that all of this took place in the aftermath of an electoral defeat and constituted a

123

controversial commitment initiated by a lame-duck president adds to its uniqueness. The subsequent events in the Clinton administration—when American forces were attacked and later withdrawn from Somalia—adds to the importance of any reexamination of the original commitment.

For students of President Bush's character, the questions of why and when the decision was made to use American military power to feed the hungry in Somalia returns us to the kind of speculation that we engaged in when considering the invasion of Panama. In both cases, strategic, political and personal motives are mixed in ways that are hard to parse. But the parsing is important. In the immediate aftermath of the Cold War, precedents were being set, and arguments were being made, about how the United States should use its uniquely powerful position in the world community. President Bush decided not to use military force in Bosnia but did deploy troops, under the auspices of the UN, to feed the famine victims in southern Somalia. Reexamining those decisions, and the distinction between them, should tell us something about the man who sat in the White House and the new world he was trying to create.

SENSELESS STARVATION

Somalia, a nation a bit smaller than Texas on the northeast coast of Africa, has a number of features that make it similar to other sub-Saharan states and a few that make it distinctive. Somalia has an agrarian economy that suffers from an unreliable climate. In the south, there are farmers who grow bananas for export and sorghum, corn, coconuts and rice for domestic consumption. In the north, where arable land is in short supply, the people are nomadic herders of cattle, camels, goats and sheep. Like many African countries, Somalia achieved independence in the early 1960s and, after a brief period of democratic rule, saw their newly created government fall to a military coup. Mohamed Siad Barre, the leader of the coup in 1969, ruled the country for over twenty years until he was deposed in 1991. Unlike most African states, the population of Somalia shares a common faith. The overwhelming majority are Sunni Muslim. They have a similar ethnic origin and a single spoken language, but despite this apparent homogeneity, there are deep divisions within Somali society. Most Somalis have strong connections and loyalties to extended families, or clans, that have long played a vital role in the social and political fabric of the society. Children in Somalia are expected to learn and recite the names of their ancestors for twenty generations.[1] In a land where drought and disease can easily threaten your survival, it is important to know that you have a family you can call on in an emergency. The clans connect those families. When the clans work together for a common cause, like reclaiming lost territory in Ethiopia or overthrowing the dictator Siad Barre, they bring the nation together. When they fight against each other, as they did once Barre was deposed, they add anarchy to the many challenges that already confront the Somali people.

During the Cold War, the regime of Siad Barre successfully sought arms and aid from the Soviet Union. In the late 1970s, after the Ethiopians overthrew their traditional monarchy and after Barre invaded the Ogaden region of Ethiopia, the Soviets saw an opportunity to recruit a larger and more important client in the Horn of Africa and shifted their support to the Ethiopians. The Carter administration reluctantly improved relations with a Somali regime that had a horrendous record on human rights but a geographic location of growing strategic importance. The revolution in Iran and the later Soviet invasion of Afghanistan led the United States to make tentative plans to develop the Somali port of Berbera on the Gulf of Aden as a possible base for the newly created Central Command. During the Reagan years, Somalia became the second-largest recipient of US aid in sub-Saharan Africa. But American patience with Siad Barre ran out in the late 1980s when it was clear that he repressed the clan-based insurgencies that opposed his rule. American military aid to Somalia was cut off in 1988; economic aid was suspended in the following year. Early in January of 1991, the United States evacuated its embassy in Mogadishu and urged all Americans to leave a country that was then engulfed in a violent civil war.

Barre also abandoned the capital city and eventually escaped to Kenya. But throughout 1991, he and his supporters fought the forces of General Mohamad Farrah Aidid, the leader of an armed faction of the Hawiye clan from south-central Somalia. The civil war ravaged the agricultural economy of the south. Crops were burned, wells poisoned and farms abandoned. Planting became nearly impossible. The last stages of the civil war produced massive numbers of refugees, estimated at 800,000 by one American official later in the crisis.[2] And the nation would face a predictable famine in the following year when the devastated agricultural economy failed to produce sufficient food.[3] The Bush administration ambassador to Kenya, the former conservative journalist Smith Hempstone, visited the border region of Kenya and Somalia in July of 1992 and sent a vivid account of what he saw back to Washington. President Bush reportedly read the ambassador's report, and wrote in the margin, "This is a terribly moving situation. Let's do everything we can to help." The ambassador's report was titled "A Day in Hell."[4]

The humanitarian crisis in northeast Africa was hellish, but it was not the only place in the world where starvation and refugee squalor were the by-products of political violence. There were many such places around the world and many international organizations standing by to provide assistance when situations of this kind arose. Somalia's humanitarian problems were uniquely challenging because of an inconclusive civil war. The revolt against Barre did not produce a clear successor and left the country without any functioning governing bodies. When international aid and food shipments began arriving, there were no Somali officials to coordinate a relief effort or to guarantee that aid workers would be protected. General Aidid, whose forces had played a leading role in the fighting against Barre in southern Somalia, thought he had earned a legitimate claim to lead the nation. Other clan leaders had their own claims to put forward. Armed militias from various clans terrorized the streets of Mogadishu and from November of 1991 to February of 1992 Aidid and Ali Mahdi Muhammad, the leader of another clan, battled for control of Mogadishu. According to reports in the *Washington Post*, the fighting in the nation's capital cost a thousand civilian lives each week as artillery shells and rockets were fired into densely populated sections of the city.[5] By the time the battle wound down the capital city and its government were in shambles.

The fighting in the south, the disruption of food production, an ill-timed drought that coincided with the political crisis and lawlessness in the capital city made it increasingly difficult for the international community to provide emergency services to the hundreds of thousands of refugees and potential famine victims. Throughout 1992, it was clear to knowledgeable observers that normal relief efforts would be insufficient to meet the growing crisis in Somalia. The appalling situation that Ambassador Hempstone saw in the border area refugee camps in the summer of 1992 was somewhere on the arc of a downward slope that had not yet reached its lowest point. At first, very few people in the Western world were watching these events unfold and, even those who were, may not have known a name for the state of affairs you enter when you take a step down from hell.

THE AUGUST INTERVENTION

In the spring of 1992, the United Nations tried to broker a ceasefire among the clan militias in Mogadishu and optimistically authorized a small group of international observers to see that the ceasefire was implemented. The UN was traditionally reluctant to take action in the internal affairs of its member states, particularly when there was no official government to request its services. Moreover, there were a large number of peacekeeping missions in the late 1980s and early 1990s and important member states, including the United States and Russia, objected to the rising costs of UN operations. Still, Somalia was a special case. Thousands of lives were at risk, if not tens of thousands. Mohamed Sahnoun, Secretary-General Boutros Boutros-Ghali's special representative, met with Aidid and other clan leaders, and had some success in local negotiations. He urged his UN superiors in New York to send international troops to Mogadishu, but when a small deployment of fifty peacekeepers arrived, they found very little peace to keep. The worst of the fighting in

Mogadishu was over, but the city had settled into anarchy. According to one observer, "The UN's little contingent in Mogadishu had just enough people to notice that everything was still getting worse, but nowhere near enough to do anything about it."[6]

As the drought reduced food supplies further, the growing dimensions of the humanitarian crisis eventually became discernible to a world community equipped with satellite broadcasting and twenty-four-hour news networks. CNN sent a reporting team to Somalia in May of 1992 where they provided sustained coverage of the emerging crisis when other television news outlets gave the issue only sporadic attention.[7] Official documents confirmed what the CNN cameras in Somalia were recording. A July report to the Secretary-General of the United Nations estimated that four and a half million Somalis, well over half the population of the country, needed food assistance and a million Somali children were at risk of starvation.[8] Most of the seventy functioning hospitals that existed in Somalia in 1988 had been destroyed or shut down by the civil war. Only fifteen were still open in 1992.[9] Food distribution in the northern portions of the country was reasonably effective, but the area around three southern Somali cities, Kismayo, Berbera and Baidoa, was now being called the "Triangle of Death." Visits to the refugee camps and war-torn areas of Somalia by Senator Nancy Kassebaum, and hearings called by her colleague on the Senate Subcommittee on African Affairs, Paul Simon, made the humanitarian crisis a political issue in the United States. The dramatic television coverage from CNN, and later from other television networks, brought the scenes of starvation to the American public and to the world at large.

In July, the president instructed Acting Secretary of State Lawrence Eagleburger to search for new policy options on Somalia.[10] In August, just before the Republican national convention, the United States, working with the United Nations, agreed to provide planes and logistical support, as well as increased food contributions, for an airlift to selected locations in the south. There was evidently some reluctance on the part of Pentagon officials for even this limited American involvement, but no other nation in the world had the capability to mount a substantial airlift operation on short notice.[11] In the fall of 1992, both before and after the presidential campaign, Operation Provide Relief flew hundreds of flights into Somalia and delivered over 12,000 metric tons of food and supplies to refugee camps in Kenya and to airfields and parachute drop points in the famine-stricken areas.[12] Lives were saved by this effort, but aircraft deliveries could not keep pace with the needs in many communities. Major roadways remained dangerous to relief workers and the chaos and lawlessness in much of Somalia continued to complicate the distribution of the relief aid that was arriving at a variety of locations.

In November, a merchant ship was fired on in the waters near Mogadishu and left without delivering the food it was carrying.[13] When food did get to the docks much of it was confiscated by armed Somali gangs, given to people who did not need it, horded in guarded warehouses where it did no good, or put on trucks that were vulnerable to capture on the roads heading south. Clan militias had to be hired, or bribed, to provide protection for supplies and aid workers and they were often unreliable. A twenty-five-truck convoy traveling from Mogadishu to Baidoa in November lost twenty-one of its trucks to hijackers and was unable to deliver sufficient food to the troubled southern city.[14] Five hundred Pakistani troops were ordered to Mogadishu by the United Nations but were slow to arrive and never managed to do more than secure a small area around the capital city's airport. Negotiations to bring in an even larger contingent of Pakistani troops were frustrated by delays and demands from a number of the clan leaders, especially General Aidid.

In the southern city of Baidoa the estimate in the fall of 1992 was that 40 percent of the population and 70 percent of the children were already dead from hunger and disease.[15] Late in the year the number of deaths per week in Baidoa and some other hard-hit areas began to decline, but the decline was not good news. It was just another measure of how dire the crisis had become. The diminished death rates meant that the most vulnerable portions of the population, those who succumb quickly to starvation, were already gone. A frustrated relief worker asked about the declining death toll reportedly observed that even in Somalia "people can only die once."[16] In the country as a whole, half a million Somalis were victims of the civil war and famine, many more had been forced from their homes, and 25 percent of the children under the age of five were counted among the dead.[17] The worst of the humanitarian disaster may have been stemmed by the airlift, or by the rapid attrition among the young, the old and the weak, but hunger and disease persisted.[18] And the starvation of anyone in a country awash with international food donations was hard to explain, hard to tolerate and hard to watch.

The heart-wrenching stories and pictures coming from reporters and camera crews in Somalia helped to generate pressure in August for the American decision to support an airlift. Media coverage of the disaster reached a second crescendo in November of 1992 just as the lame-duck administration of George H. W. Bush was getting ready to do something much more substantial for the starving citizens of Somalia.[19]

THE GATHERING CONSENSUS

Somalia was a minor issue in the 1992 presidential campaign. Clinton mentioned it in one of the candidate debates and from time to time criticized the administration for humanitarian failures in Haiti and Bosnia as well as Somalia. But those criticisms were never given much coverage or attention in an odd three-way race that focused primarily on domestic and economic issues. When Clinton became the president-elect, he was confronted with a crowded foreign policy agenda that involved difficult decisions about all of the issues he had mentioned in the campaign— refugees from Haiti, ethnic warfare in Bosnia, the pending creation of a North American Free Trade Agreement, economic problems in the nations that emerged from the former Soviet Union and the continuing humanitarian crisis in Somalia. All of those items were on the agenda when Clinton went to the White House on November 18 for a session with the president he had recently defeated. Though the meeting produced the usual comments about "useful discussion," there was no public hint that the Bush administration was getting ready to act on Somalia.

But it was. In the second week of November, and his first week as a lame-duck president, Bush met with his senior foreign policy advisers and asked for a review of Somalia policy.[20] The president wanted to know what the United States could do to stem the starvation. Even before the president called this meeting, an interagency planning group was developing a detailed analysis of the situation in Somalia for the benefit of senior policymakers. They produced an extensive Somalia status report on October 15, 1992.[21] The early staff work and the meeting of senior advisers set in motion a series of deliberations by the National Security Council. There were four meetings of the deputies committee of the NSC to discuss Somalia between November 20 and 24. At the second meeting, on November 21, Admiral David Jeremiah, the representative of the Joint Chiefs of Staff, surprised some of his colleagues with an announcement that "if you think US forces are needed, we can do the job."[22] Jeremiah's comment was reported in the press and accompanied by speculation that there was a major shift in the Pentagon's position on Somalia.[23] According to Jeremiah, it was nothing of the kind. It was merely an expression of his personal frustration with a policymaking process that was moving too slowly. It was obvious to him that a US military intervention for the purpose of improving food distribution was, in fact, possible. Jeremiah had recently visited Somalia and knew that the airlift was inadequate. He also knew that hundreds of thousands of lives could be saved by a modest restoration of order by American or international military forces. He was pleading with his colleagues to reach a decision on whether or not that option was seriously under consideration.[24]

It was. A number of people in the administration were exploring military action in a serious fashion shortly after the election.[25] This activity may have reflected the president's preferences as well.[26] In the State Department, the new secretary, Lawrence Eagleburger, was reportedly committed to greater American involvement in Somalia shortly after he received a vigorous appeal for action from his senior assistant for politico-military affairs, Robert Gallucci, on November 12.[27] Powell and Eagleburger, along with other senior members of the administration, may have been willing to entertain a greater role for the United States in the Somali disaster, in part, because they simultaneously opposed American military action in Bosnia.[28] Both cases involved political violence that generated humanitarian disasters for Muslim populations. The international community was not dealing well with either situation, but appeared to care more about Bosnian Muslims on the outskirts of Europe than about the African Muslims living in Somalia, a point that UN Secretary-General Boutros-Ghali made in conversations with President Bush.[29]

The difference between the two situations had very little to do with American national interests, which were arguably modest in both cases. It was feasibility. The relative weakness of the clan-based militias in Somalia meant that US forces could easily overwhelm and intimidate local opposition to an American intervention. This would not be true in Bosnia where Serbian forces had heavy equipment, rugged mountainous terrain, well-organized military units and conflicting political objectives that went well beyond the lawless theft of food supplies that bedeviled Somalia. As the administration moved toward more decisive action in the Horn of Africa speculation would continue that the decision to take action in Somalia was related to the administration's agonizing inaction in the Balkans.[30] Members of the administration would later justify the Somalia intervention with the simplified explanation that something needed to be done and that the US could easily do it.[31] Something needed to be done in Bosnia as well, but there was never much confidence that doing anything in that part of the world would be easy.[32]

The deliberations about doing something in Somalia within the NSC deputies committee coincided with a variety of political pressures from other players in Washington. Senator Kassebaum publicly called for an enhanced UN deployment to Somalia. Frederick Cuny, an expert on humanitarian missions who helped organize the relief efforts for the Kurds in northern Iraq, promoted the idea of bypassing Mogadishu and establishing internationally guarded safe zones for food distribution. These ideas were given national publicity by prominent newspaper columnists.[33] Representative John Lewis, a Democrat from Georgia with a record of leadership on civil rights issues, led a delegation making another visit to Somalia in November. His delegation gave a Washington press conference on November 18 calling for greater American and United Nations action. Network television stories carrying statements by Lewis and scenes of starvation from Somalia were broadcast throughout this period.

The November 24 NBC evening news broadcast contained a particularly powerful and emotionally charged segment. Tom Brokaw told his television viewers, "In Somalia, children under the age of five have all but disappeared. Hundreds die each week. It's a place where a thousand die today, and a thousand will die tomorrow, and the day after that, and the day after that." While Brokaw spoke, black and white pictures taken by a famous photographer filled the screen. They showed the distended bellies, skeletal limbs and fly-covered faces of those on the brink of star-vation in Somalia.[34] By the time their pictures appeared on American network news, many of the people being shown were almost certainly already among the victims of the disaster. They could not be saved, but others might be.

The next day, November 25, just before the Thanksgiving holiday and just after the president returned to Washington from attending his moth-er's funeral, the National Security Council met to formally consider the options on Somalia that had been developed by the deputies during the previous week. The president began the deliberations with a simple state-ment: "We want to do something about Somalia."[35] He then heard the three options that the deputies had been working on—continuing the airlift operation while awaiting the deployment of 3,500 UN peacekeep-ers; providing transportation and logistics for an even larger internation-al military deployment (with no American ground forces) that would establish sufficient order to allow for the distribution of food; or using US troops as the vanguard of that multinational military intervention.[36] After listening to a broad-ranging discussion, President Bush chose the third option. Of the three, it had the best prospects for producing results in the shortest period of time. The United States was the only country in the world with the ability to deploy thousands of troops to a distant land on short notice. We could share our logistical capabilities with other countries, as was envisioned in the second option, but that would have delayed the arrival of effective relief to many communities in Somalia. The president reportedly expressed a preference for an American deploy-ment that could end before Clinton's inauguration in late January but was told that such a date for ending the American participation in the mission was unrealistic. Even with American military mobility, it was going to take weeks to send troops and equipment to Somalia and to fully secure the ports, the airfields and the roads that would have to be re-opened. Turning the operation over to UN forces would take even longer.

According to the *Washington Post*, Colin Powell took no formal posi-tion on the three available options at the November 25 NSC meeting. Instead, he expressed general reservations about the introduction of American troops into Somalia.[37] Powell had not objected to the detailed development of Pentagon plans for military action in Somalia earlier in November and had on one occasion reminded other policymakers of the ease with which they tolerated African deaths.[38] Officially neutral but ready to carry out the president's decision, the JCS chairman expressed reservations at the November 25 meeting. Powell was worried that we would have a hard time bringing the mission to a conclusion. He had recently met with General Frank Libutti, the commander of the Somalia airlift operation, who returned to the United States and briefed a number of Pentagon officials before the NSC meeting.[39] For Powell, and for Libut-ti, the problem was going to be getting out of Somalia once we were in.

American troops could easily deal with the lightly armed Somali forces that might resist a freer flow of food and supplies. But what would happen after the ports and roadways were reopened? If American troops left Somalia after successfully feeding the starving villagers in the south, what would stop the militias from reasserting their territorial claims, disrupting future humanitarian shipments and returning the country to chaos? Who would maintain order after the GIs left?

Obviously, if the militias were disarmed and a stable national government were established, it would be easy to imagine an orderly withdrawal of both the American and international forces from Somalia. But creating a stable regime in Mogadishu was not the mission that American troops were preparing to carry out in the final weeks of 1992. It was not a mission that could be accomplished in a matter of weeks or months. Libutti estimated that outside military forces might be needed in Somalia for ten or fifteen years.[40] Ambassador Smith Hempstone, who had written passionately about the humanitarian crisis over the summer, was just as passionate in his opposition to sending US troops into Somalia. In a memorandum written shortly after the decision was announced, Hempstone guessed that it would take five years to get Somalia back on its knees; he refused to venture a judgment as to how long it would take to get the country back on its feet. "If you liked Beirut, you'll love Mogadishu," wrote the provocative ambassador who incorrectly predicted significant Somali guerrilla resistance to the initial intervention as well as difficulty in producing a permanent political settlement.[41] No one at the senior-level deliberations within the Bush administration, before or after the Hempstone memo, expressed confidence about the long-term prospects for Somali political stability. None of them, except perhaps Powell, who would remain as chairman of the JCS, would be in office when those issues would have to be confronted.

For the departing Bush advisers, a clear exit strategy was not essential. They had a lateral strategy. The UN would authorize the mission and take it over sometime after the United States had accomplished the restoration of reliable delivery of food to the starving and medicine to the sick. The United States would save lives; the United Nations could then deal with whatever peacekeeping and nation-building might be needed thereafter. The difficulty of the later mission, and the murkiness about when a multilateral UN force would take it on, set the stage for the problems that the Clinton administration would later confront.

Shortly after the November 25 meeting, Secretary Eagleburger was dispatched to New York to inform a surprised Boutros-Ghali that the United States was prepared to take decisive action in Somalia. The secretary-general was already convinced that drastic action was needed in Somalia and quickly agreed to the proposal.[42] Boutros-Ghali also indicated that he hoped that the United States would play a role in disarming the clans, which would be essential to the long-term stabilization of the country. Differences between what the US was willing to do and what the UN wanted done were evident from the outset. On December 3, the United Nations Security Council passed a resolution authorizing the initial American intervention. It was the first time the United Nations authorized a purely humanitarian mission without an explicit invitation from one of the parties to a conflict. [43]

On December 9, US marines landed on the beaches of Somalia where many observers noted that the only resistance they encountered was from the bright lights of the camera crews broadcasting their arrival. General Aidid and Ali Mahdi Muhammad, the two most powerful Somali warlords in Mogadishu, had met with Robert Oakley, the president's newly appointed representative to Somalia, and agreed to withdraw their forces from areas where they might come in contact with arriving Americans. [44] The clan leaders had no particular desire to generate or perpetuate massive starvation. There was more indifference than intention in the political dynamics of the humanitarian crisis. As a result, there was very little initial opposition to reopening transportation facilities. Shortly after their arrival, American troops established enough order to allow for the reliable delivery of relief supplies. [45] The media coverage at Christmas, when President Bush made a short trip to Somalia, showed American soldiers holding Somali children who were finally receiving food and medicine.

President Bush left office with Somalia counted, by most commentators, as one of his foreign policy successes. The humanitarian mission was popular with the American public who saw on television the need for doing something about starvation in Somalia. Senior Bush administration officials understood the difficulties that would arise in turning things over to the United Nations and addressing the underlying political instability in the country. The CIA reportedly warned the president that "the anarchy in Somalia is so sweeping and the warring factions so deeply entrenched that the country will require long-term international involvement, such as a United Nations protectorate or even a formal trusteeship." [46] But those difficulties had not yet come to the fore when George Bush watched Bill Clinton take the oath of office.

Along with the more important events connected to the liberation of Kuwait and the resolution of humanitarian disasters in Iraq following the Gulf War, Somalia was sometimes seen as evidence that a new era, "a new world order" as the president repeatedly called it, had arrived. Now that the Cold War was over, many (though not all) international problems could be dealt with by a reinvigorated United Nations under American leadership sometimes using American military power.

In a speech he delivered at West Point in the final month of his presidency, George Bush considered his own foreign policy legacy and the difficulties in deciding when to use military force. He freely admitted that the United States could not send troops everywhere in the world that suffered from political and humanitarian disasters. Sometimes using force would be essential, sometimes counterproductive. There could be no set formula or hard-and-fast rules for the difficult case-by-case judgments that a commander in chief is required to make. However, where we could make a difference in the alleviation of suffering and where we could make that difference "without excessive levels of risk and cost," we should do so.[47]

After the Vietnam War a number of senior American foreign policymakers had tried to define or describe the legitimate circumstances for the deployment and use of American troops abroad. Richard Nixon and later Caspar Weinberger and Colin Powell had famously set out guidelines or doctrines. The Weinberger and Powell doctrines involved lists of criteria that should be met before American troops were committed to dangerous overseas missions: a clear mission, sufficient military forces to accomplish the mission, popular support and an exit strategy that would bring successful, or unsuccessful, missions to a conclusion. If the principles were fully and faithfully applied, there would be very few American military operations overseas. President Bush at West Point provided his own ideas for justifying the use of military force. They were less precise than the Powell/Weinberger doctrines. According to President Bush, "Using military force makes sense as a policy where the stakes warrant, where and when force can be effective, where no other policies are likely to prove effective, where its application can be limited in scope and time, and where the potential benefits justify the potential costs and sacrifice."[48] The short version of this position, as applied to Somalia by the president's senior advisers, reduced the argument to two or three propositions. If the humanitarian need is great, and if the United States (and only the United States) can do something about it and if the costs and risks are acceptable, then we should act.

In Somalia the administration did. In Bosnia they did not. Many of the commentators who applauded the decision to send troops to Somalia continued to complain about the failure to address human suffering in the Balkans. Charles Krauthammer defended the distinction by pointing out that the suffering in Somalia was greater than in Bosnia, if you measure suffering by the number of lives lost. He argued that the death rates in Somalia justified a robust international response and went on to make the conventional observation that it would be harder for the US to send troops to Bosnia than to Somalia. "We don't do mountains," Krauthammer wrote, quoting an unnamed Washington wit.[49]

The Clinton team, who entered office hoping to do more for the Bosnians, found that to be a frustrating objective and ended up doing less in Somalia after a disaster in Mogadishu caught the president and others off guard. The early cooperation of the clan leaders in Somalia broke down when it became clear that the United States and the UN were not going to declare Aidid, or any of his rivals, the new ruler of the country. Aidid's forces attacked Pakistani troops who were trying to interfere with his control of local radio stations, an important source of power in a nation without high levels of literacy or an established written language. The US, on behalf of the UN, mounted a major operation to punish Aidid. That mission produced a tragic encounter when US Blackhawk helicopters were shot down and the body of a dead American was dragged through the streets of Mogadishu. Once again media coverage of events in Somalia is alleged to have turned American public opinion, this time against the deployment of military personnel in the Horn of Africa. A few months after the Blackhawk attack, the United States withdrew its forces from Somalia leaving UN troops to deal with the difficult long-term political problems in a failed state.

To some observers, the problem in Somalia was rooted in a fundamental dilemma. By the time American troops arrived, the only effective power in the country belonged to the separate clan militias. There were only two choices in dealing with Somalia—accommodate the clan leaders or crush them.[50] In the end, both the United States and the United Nations tried to do a bit of both with understandably inconclusive results.

THE MEDIA AND THE MAN

Somalia is frequently cited as a prime example of how the power of modern communications moves public opinion and foreign policy decisions. Pictures of starving children in Somalia led the United States to send in its military forces. When the humanitarian deployment became a longer and more complicated mission than was originally envisioned, media coverage of violence against American troops in Mogadishu contributed to a shift in public opinion in the opposite direction. Commentators call this "the CNN effect." Emotionally powerful news reports elicit strong popular reactions that then have a big impact on decisions in American foreign policy.[51]

There is some truth in the observation that media mattered in Somalia, but there are also some problems with taking this analysis too far. Jonathan Mermin argues persuasively that the role of the media in the Somalia intervention deliberations has been exaggerated.[52] No one in a network news office invented or hyped the story in Somalia. It was there, and it deserved to be covered. An international humanitarian crisis of huge proportions belongs on the evening news and on the front page of major newspapers. Moreover, as Mermin points out, most of the news stories about Somalia were initiated by, or tied to, the actions of prominent political actors. Officials at the United Nations would pass a resolution or issue a report. A presidential candidate would make a statement. A senator or members of the House of Representatives would travel to Somalia, give press conferences, hold hearings or make speeches. A celebrity would visit a refugee camp. An aid worker would be killed, a ship fired upon, an impassioned Red Cross official would issue a dire warning. All of this was news. Coverage of such events is routine and though there is editorial judgment exercised on any given day about what to put on the air, or on the front page, there is little reason to suspect that news executives were pushing their own agenda on Somalia coverage. They were following an unfolding disaster that many political actors and organizations were urging them to follow. Many of those actors and organizations thought the media were late in giving the disaster the attention it deserved.[53] The single largest exception to this observation may have been the spring 1992 CNN coverage of events in Somalia before other networks were giving the story comparable attention. But that coverage did not lead, by itself, to political action. Action came in August when many news outlets were giving coverage to a growing disaster that was being documented in UN reports, ambassadorial telegrams and public pleadings from a variety of prominent politicians. There is a classic chicken-and-egg question about the relationship between media coverage and political action in Somalia. The evidence does not provide a clear or simple conclusion that one was driving the other. It looks much more like the chaotic interaction of news organizations and political forces that characterizes Washington policymaking on a regular basis.

But perhaps the CNN effect lies less in the volume or timing of news coverage and more in its emotional nature. The pictures from Somalia were heart-wrenching. No one could look at them and not wish that something be done to save the lives of the innocent children who were disproportionately among the earliest victims of the famine. The later pictures following the helicopter attack had a very different, but equally powerful, emotional impact. George Kennan, in one of his last commentaries on foreign policy decisions, said that America's Somalia policy was "controlled by popular emotional impulses," that were produced or provoked "by the commercial television industry."[54] Of course, that industry did not invent the Somalia problems, but it may have amplified them with compelling visual images that moved public opinion and tugged at the hearts of policymakers. President Bush, speaking to a group of scholars gathered at his presidential library to consider military interventions in the post–Cold War world, admitted as much when he recalled sitting in the White House with Barbara watching those "awful pictures" from Somalia and deciding that something should be done.[55] The president did not say whether he was remembering the awful pictures from August or November or some other time in 1992. Nor did he say exactly when he decided to do something about them. But when he made his intervention decision matters and is often presumed to have followed the most powerful media coverage of the crisis.

Arguably, the most highly charged emotional broadcast involving starvation in Somalia was the NBC evening news segment on November

24 with its compelling black and white photographs and anchor commentary. Somalia is "a place where a thousand die today, and a thousand will die tomorrow, and the day after that." That Tom Brokaw broadcast was televised the night before the formal meeting of the National Security Council that took up the issue of Somalia and ended with the decision to send a large contingent of American troops. But the wheels of the Bush administration had been in motion on this issue prior to the NBC broadcast. Some observers date the decision to do something serious about Somalia from the November 21 deputies meeting when the JCS representative expressed a willingness to consider American military action.[56] Others put the date of decision even earlier when the Pentagon began to develop its plans and the schedule of deputies meetings was set.[57] Arguably, the United States was committed to using military resources to feed the hungry in Somalia from August of 1992 on and the November decision was a logical extension of an American airlift that was clearly failing to fully accomplish its objective. Formal points of decision are well documented and easily found in the public record; actual points of decision are harder to locate. President Bush decided to do something about Somalia in the summer of 1992 and again in the fall, almost immediately after the presidential campaign ended. He may have done so as a result of the awful pictures from Somalia, but his decisions were almost certainly made well before the media coverage of starvation reached its emotional peak on the eve of the crucial NSC meeting.

And, of course, the decision to do something in Somalia, whenever it was made, was not an isolated decision. It was clearly related to the inability of the administration to devise any effective course of action for the fighting in Bosnia. It was also related to the president's and the administration's broader thinking about a new world order. The United Nations was painfully slow to respond to the disasters in the Balkans and the Horn of Africa. The UN decisions to send 50, then 500, and finally a total of 3,500 Pakistani troops to Mogadishu were late in being made and later still in being implemented. United Nations responses to Bosnia were equally weak and slow in coming. In Bosnia, the UN tried to carve out identifiable humanitarian missions without directly confronting the ethnic warfare that was engulfing the region. The same caution was practiced in Somalia where it should have been possible to accomplish more. The fighting in Somalia was among people who shared the same religion, the same language, the same culture and a history of living together on the edge of poverty in an unforgiving land. There was clan warfare, a separatist movement in the north, chaos and anarchy in the aftermath of a civil war, but there was no ethnic cleansing and no intentional plan to starve the population. Yet tens of thousands were dying. The Somali people were experiencing famine by neglect, aided and abetted by anarchy. If a recently triumphant post–Gulf War United Nations could not save lives in Somalia, there wouldn't be much to be said on behalf of a new world order. There would instead be a painful admission that the only incidents that brought the international community together for effective action were the ones that occurred in places with oil.

There were big ideas at stake in the response to the Somali disaster and there were the "awful pictures" of starvation that cried out for action. Which of the two had the greater impact on President Bush? We do not know for sure, but we can guess. Bush was a deeply sentimental and caring man who, at least in public, tried very hard not to show those qualities. But they were there. Admiral Jeremiah, who played a key role in the Somalia deliberations, describes Bush as "one of the kindest, softest hearted guys in the world. . . . He is a real humanitarian. . . . With someone like President Bush it was just not possible, I don't think, for him to stand back and see people die when we could do something about it."[58] As between the idea of a New World Order and the repeated reports of dying children, it is not too hard to imagine which had the greater impact on George Bush.

Additional evidence for a simple, sentimental and humanitarian explanation of President Bush's decision to send US troops to Somalia comes from Andrew Natsios, an international relief administrator in the Bush administration who accompanied the president on his trip to Somalia in December of 1992—his final trip overseas as president of the United States. Natsios remembers the president talking with Phil Johnson, the president of CARE (a major international relief organization) about a visit he and Barbara had made to a CARE facility during the 1985 famine in Sudan. Memories of that visit and the victims of starvation he had personally seen were on his mind, President Bush said, when he decided to send troops to Somalia.[59] According to Natsios, the explanation for the American intervention was obvious. It was compassion. The president wanted starvation to stop.

NOTES

1. Noted in Miles Hudson and John Stanier, *War and the Media: A Random Searchlight*, (Phoenix Mill: Sutton Publishing, 1997), 247.

2. James Kunder, Director of the Office of Foreign Disaster Assistance, quoted in Herman J. Cohen, "Intervention in Somalia," in Allan Goodman, ed., *The Diplomatic Record, 1992–1993* (Boulder, CO: Westview Press, 1995), 58.

3. There tends to be a delay between the disruption of an agricultural economy and the worst stages of famine and disease. In the early months of a complex humanitarian crisis livestock is sold, seed stocks are eaten, and relatives assist each other. When food runs out and people begin to migrate to cities and relief camps the crisis rapidly escalates. Andrew Natsios, *U.S. Foreign Policy and the Four Horsemen of the Apocalypse: Humanitarian Relief in Complex Emergencies* (Westport, CT: Praeger, 1997), 13.

4. Don Oberdorfer, "U.S. Took Slow Approach to Somali Crisis," *The Washington Post*, August 24, 1992. Oberdorfer reports that Bush wrote a similar note in the margin of a July 19 *New York Times* story by Jane Perlez about death and starvation in Somalia.

5. Reports by Jennifer Parmelee cited in Cohen, "Intervention in Somalia," 53.

6. Daniel P. Bolger, *Savage Peace: Americans at War in the 1990s* (Novato: Presidio, 1995), 275.

7. Jonathan Mermin, "Television News and American Intervention in Somalia: The Myth of a Media-Driven Foreign Policy," *Political Science Quarterly*, 112, no. 3 (Autumn, 1997): 385–403.

8. Similar numbers were contained in an estimate produced by the International Committee of the Red Cross. Noted in Jonathan Stevenson, "Hope Restored in Somalia?" *Foreign Policy*, no. 91 (Summer, 1993): 138.

9. John L. Hirsch and Robert B. Oakley, *Somalia and Operation Restore Hope* (Washington, DC: United States Institute of Peace, 1995), 23–24.

10. Herman Cohen remembers Eagleburger saying the State Department was instructed by the president to be "forward leaning" on Somalia; Cohen, "Intervention in Somalia," 60.

11. Oberdorfer, "U.S. Took Slow Approach to Somali Crisis."

12. Cohen, "Intervention in Somalia," 63. Some of the dropped food was confiscated by armed Somali clansmen without effective distribution to those who needed it most.

13. Ibid.

14. Hirsch and Oakley, *Somalia and Operation Restore Hope*, 32.

15. The estimate of the number of deaths among children under five in Baidoa can be found at George H. W. Bush Presidential Library and Museum, Memorandum of Conversation, "Meeting with Philip Johnston, President of CARE," December 18, 1992, accessed on April 23, 2019 at https://bush41library.tamu.edu/files/memcons-telcons/1992-12-18—Johnston.pdf

16. Aid worker quoted in Maryann Cusimano, "Operation Restore Hope: The Bush Administration's Decision to Intervene in Somalia," Case 463, Pew Case Studies in International Affairs, Institute for the Study of Diplomacy, Georgetown University, 1995, 6.

17. Ibid., 31–32.

18. There is some controversy about the exact number of victims and the timeline of the crisis. One survey of death rates in Baidoa finds the peak of starvation in September of 1992 with significant improvements by mid-November when the administration would be considering further action. Hudson and Spanier quote from Centers for Disease Control, "Population-Based Mortality Assessment—Baidoa and Afgoi, Somalia, 1992," Morbidity and Mortality Weekly Report 41.49, December 1992, 913–917. Hudson and Spanier, *War and the Media*, 256. Hirsch and Oakley paint a grimmer picture. They note that while international food deliveries grew in September of 1992, the percentage of food reaching those most in need actually fell. Hirsch and Oakley, *Somalia and Operation Restore Hope*, 25.

19. For an excellent review of media coverage given to Somalia see, Mermin, "Television News and American Intervention in Somalia."

20. Robert C. DiPrizio, *Armed Humanitarians: U.S. Interventions from Northern Iraq to Kosovo* (Baltimore: Johns Hopkins University Press, 2002), 51.

21. "Somalia Planning Group Status Report," October 15, 1992, George H. W. Bush Presidential Records, National Security Council, Howe, Rear Admiral Jonathan, Files, Folder 21359-013, Folder Title: DC [Deputies Committee] Meeting, re: Somalia—October 21, 1992.

22. Quoted in Don Oberdorfer, "The Path to Intervention," *Washington Post*, December 6, 1992.

23. Ibid.

24. David Jeremiah Interview, November 15, 2010, George H. W. Bush Oral History Project, Miller Center, University of Virginia.

25. According to two knowledgeable authors, Powell was a leading figure in proposing a large-scale US intervention in the fall of 1992, even though he would raise

reservations about such a mission in the final stages of presidential deliberations. Hirsch and Oakley, *Somalia and Operation Restore Hope*, 42.

26. Alberto Coll, who worked in the Bush administration Pentagon, dates the president's interest in doing something about Somalia from mid-November. Alberto R. Coll, "The Problems of Doing Good: Somalia as a Case Study in Humanitarian Intervention," Case 518, Pew Case Studies in International Affairs, Institute for the Study of Diplomacy, Georgetown University, 1997, 4.

27. Oberdorfer, "The Path to Intervention."

28. For this argument see Jon Western, "Sources of Humanitarian Intervention," *International Security*, 26, no. 4 (Spring 2002): 112–142.

29. The conversation between Boutros-Ghali and President Bush took place in May of 1992. The Secretary-General reportedly said he was under pressure from Muslims complaining about UN inaction in Bosnia and Somalia and pleaded with the president, "Can't we do something about Somalia?" Oberdorfer, "The Path to Intervention."

30. Robert Oakley reportedly said about the November deliberations that "the inability to do anything meaningful for Muslims in Bosnia, together with a perception that we could actually help in Muslim Somalia, added to the media-driven desire for a fresh look at options." Quoted in Bolger, *Savage Peace*, 280.

31. Warren Strobel quotes both Eagleburger and Scowcroft about the importance of Somalia being "doable." Warren Strobel, *Late-Breaking Foreign Policy: The News Media's Influence on Peace Negotiations* (Washington, DC: United States Institute of Peace Press, 1997), 140.

32. For an excellent discussion of the administration's inaction on Bosnia see, the National Security Council Project, Oral History Roundtables, "The Bush Administration National Security Council," 26–31.

33. Leslie Gelb, "Shoot to Feed Somalia," *New York Times*, November 19, 1992; and Anthony Lewis, "Action or Death," *New York Times*, November 20, 1992. Gelb actually refers to the forthcoming meeting of the deputies in his column.

34. The quote from the NBC broadcast and other details of the media coverage come from Mermin, "Television News and American Intervention in Somalia," 399–401.

35. Quoted in Oberdorfer, "The Path to Intervention."

36. Cohen, "Intervention in Somalia," 64. See also, Memo from Brent Scowcroft, "Meeting on Somalia," November 25, 1992. George H. W. Bush Presidential Records, National Security Council, Rostow, Nicholas, Files, Folder 20424-005, Folder Title: Somalia #1 [4].

37. Cusimano, "Operation Restore Hope," 10.

38. "If these were not poor black folks in Africa, you guys would have done something by now," Powell reportedly told his NSC colleagues. Parmet, *George Bush*, 509.

39. Oberdorfer, "The Path to Intervention."

40. Ibid.

41. The Associated Press, "U.S. Envoy Urged Superiors Not to Send in American Troops," December 5, 1992.

42. Cohen, "Intervention in Somalia," 65.

43. Ioan Lewis and James Mayall, "Somalia," in James Mayall, ed. *The New Internationalism 1991–1994* (Cambridge: Cambridge University Press, 1996), 111.

44. "First U.S. Forces Arrive in Somali Capital in Operation Restore Hope," *Facts on File News Digest*, December 10, 1992.

45. Jonathan Stevenson, "Hope Restored in Somalia?" *Foreign Policy*, no. 91 (Summer 1993): 138–154.

46. Steven Hurst, *The Foreign Policy of the Bush Administration: In Search of a New World Order* (London: Cassell, 1999), 226.

47. "Remarks at the United States Military Academy in West Point," New York, January 5, 1993.

48. Ibid.

49. Charles Krauthammer, "Drawing the Line at Genocide: Two Principles of Humanitarian Intervention," *Washington Post*, December 11, 1992.

50. Mayall and Lewis, "Somalia," 109.

51. See for example, Warren Strobel, "The CNN Effect," *American Journalism Review*, 18, no. 4 (May 1996): 32–38.

52. Mermin, "Television News and American Intervention in Somalia."

53. Piers Robinson points out that media coverage of Somalia was much higher after the president made his decision to intervene than it was before. Piers Robinson, "Operation Restore Hope and the Illusion of a Media Driven Intervention," *Political Studies*, 49, no. 5 (December 2001): 941–56.

54. George F. Kennan, "Somalia, Through a Glass Darkly," *New York Times*, September 30, 1993.

55. George Bush, "Reflections on Presidential Decisions Regarding Intervention," luncheon address to a conference sponsored by The Center for the Study of the Presidency at the George Bush Presidential Center, October 23, 1999.

56. Oberdorfer, "The Path to Intervention."

57. Alberto Coll, "The Problems of Doing Good." Cohen reports that there were serious discussions of additional steps that might be taken in Somalia in early November, Cohen, "Intervention in Somalia," 64.

58. David Jeremiah Interview, November 15, 2010.

59. Andrew Natsios, *U.S. Foreign Policy and the Four Horsemen of the Apocalypse* (Westport, CT: Praeger, 1997), 134–35 and 178.

Conclusion

Character and Consequence

The most common observation made about the character of George H. W. Bush is that he was prudent. Jeffrey Engel, in an important book on the end of the Cold War, argues that the success George H. W. Bush had on the world stage was a product of his cautious nature. Bush, in Engel's phrase, was a practitioner of "Hippocratic diplomacy": he tried to do no harm. "He was neither creative nor innovative, neither a radical nor a revolutionary, but was instead content to follow 'what worked.'"[1] What worked in the late 1980s and early 1990s was preserving American military and diplomatic power, using it effectively, supporting allies and sustaining international institutions. The Bush administration avoided unnecessary confrontations with rising or falling great powers and managed, as best it could be managed, the chaotic collapse of the Soviet empire. Prudence may well have been the personal quality, and the diplomatic disposition, that made George Bush a successful statesman.

A different president—one more ideological, or more egotistical, or more nationalist or more flamboyant—might have made serious mistakes that Bush avoided. But Bush's caution, as important as it clearly was, needs to be seen alongside another aspect of his character. President Bush could, from time to time, be surprisingly bold. As we noted earlier, he signed up to fight in World War II before he was subject to the draft, and against his parents' advice. After graduating from Yale, he took his young family to Texas and the oil business when privilege and personal connections gave him a safer, and more conventional, path to success. In Texas, he gambled on the prospects of a single oil field, and the gamble paid off. When he entered politics, he started near the top and ran for the Senate as a Republican in a state with a century-long tradition of electing Democrats. He lost that race and lost a second run for the same Texas Senate seat six years later. In his subsequent career as a presidential appointee he twice took highly controversial positions—as Republican Party Chairman during Watergate and as CIA Director after congressional investigations of CIA scandals. Those jobs could easily have ended his political career. They didn't. He ran for the presidency in 1980 when the only elections he had previously won were two terms in the House of Representatives. He was briefly the front-runner in the 1980 primary season and eventually the vice-presidential candidate on the popular Reagan ticket.

Once he got to the White House on his own in 1989, Bush was exceedingly cautious in his public rhetoric. He avoided both boastful and controversial language and took a very long time before he was willing to speak directly to Mikhail Gorbachev or freely to anyone about the end of the Cold War. The speech that Bush gave at Texas A&M in the spring of 1989 is filled with the prudent rhetoric that the president preferred. His speechwriters sometimes proposed provocative language that might have grabbed headlines or made history, but a careful NSC staff reviewed those passages, toned them down or crossed them out. As Engel correctly notes, Bush was not innovative or radical in his thinking about world affairs. He did not generate the ideas from which memorable slogans might be crafted. The popular phrase he is most often associated with—the New World Order—was actually an old one, borrowed from Woodrow Wilson, and revived to describe the kind of international community that had been hoped for at the end of the Second World War. In Bush's New World Order, a reinvigorated United Nations, led by a powerful United States, free from Cold War Security Council vetoes, would respond effectively to blatant acts of aggression, as it did in Iraq, or major humanitarian emergencies, as it did in Somalia. The New World Order was not particularly new and the order it created was imperfect and incomplete. At the end of the Bush presidency, the Balkans had a very old-world ethnic war that the administration willfully ignored. For the most part, when Bush talked about foreign affairs, citizens and commentators heard more platitudes from the past than visions for the future.

But if Bush was unusually careful—and prudent—in his thinking and in his public speech, he was often deliberate and decisive in action. Pushing for a rapid German reunification, with a united Germany anchored in NATO, was an audacious move in the days after the collapse of the Berlin Wall. It was a goal that faced substantial opposition from both allies and adversaries. Even those world leaders or international commentators who thought reunification was possible did not expect it to come quickly and peacefully. Sticking with that objective, during months of complicated negotiations, involved its own form of decisiveness. So did the president's decisions in conducting the Persian Gulf War. The decision to double the deployment to the region and threaten the use of military force against Saddam Hussein was a major step in the policymaking process that eventually led to victory. The president took big chances in the fall of 1990. No one knew then that the coalition war against Iraq would be as successful, or as short, as it turned out to be. Triumph can't erase the risks that were taken on the road to its achievement. George Bush could sometimes do big things in a big way.

On three occasions George H. W. Bush approved the use of American military power: in Panama, in the Persian Gulf and in Somalia. In each instance he was given policy options by the Pentagon, and in all three cases he chose the largest recommended deployment proposed by his military advisers. Those choices might be counted as evidence of caution. After all, if you have to use force, it is usually a good idea to use plenty of it. Larger commitments raise the chances for success and reduce the risks to the troops involved. It is wise to use ample military might when there are real dangers in a prospective operation. But the choices Bush made in these three cases were more than the prudent protection of the military personnel involved. Asked if he wanted to approve smaller-scale and safer options, Bush declined. He wanted larger military actions in order to accomplish bigger objectives.

In Panama, he wanted more than the arrest of Manuel Noriega. He wanted a regime change that would end the stranglehold that the national guard, and Noriega's henchmen, held over the country and create an opportunity for democratic governance in Panama. In the Persian Gulf, there was substantial domestic and international support for allowing sanctions, and the embargo on the sale of Iraqi oil, to put pressure on Saddam Hussein and force him to withdraw from Kuwait. A case could be made that the sanctions were working. When Bush chose to double the forces in Desert Shield, he was not taking a cautious step to defend American and allied troops on the borders with Iraq; he was authorizing a massive military deployment that would either intimidate Saddam or take the coalition to war against him. Bush rejected the easier, the popular—and perhaps the more prudent—path of letting sanctions slowly crush the Iraqi economy.

The same observations might be made about the intervention in Somalia. Most lame-duck presidents would have avoided a major military intervention in the weeks after losing a bid for reelection. Smaller steps could have been taken in November of 1992 and the Pentagon provided detailed plans for how to execute them. The United States could have increased the airlift activities that were at least delivering some food and medicine to southern Somalia. Alternatively, the US could have offered rapid transportation to the Pakistani forces already approved for deployment to the Horn of Africa. Neither of those decisions would have been particularly controversial; neither would have tied the hands of the incoming administration. There was no prudent reason to send a large American military force to Somalia. There was a compassionate reason for doing it and a surprising willingness on the part of the president to make a major humanitarian commitment during his final days in the White House.

George H. W. Bush was consistently cautious in speech and sometimes awkward in the way he presented himself on the public stage. He was, as Engel noted, neither a broad thinker nor an original strategist. He was not ideological. He was a keen observer and an experienced player in both national politics and foreign affairs, and he was sometimes willing to take substantial risks and go for big accomplishments in his personal life and public career. He was both modest and ambitious, gracious and competitive, deferential and determined. These are not opposite traits, but they do not commonly go together or manifest themselves as seamlessly as they did for George H. W. Bush. It may not be surprising that our forty-first president was often misunderstood or underestimated.

Peggy Noonan, reflecting on the significant differences between the two presidents for whom she wrote speeches, observes that Ronald Reagan was often indifferent to the people around him, but displayed an emotional reaction to the major events and concepts in human history. George Bush was different. He "lacked a deep responsiveness and connection to history, and yet when he spoke to those he loved, his children and friends and family, his eyes filled with real tears."[2] Bush sincerely cared about the people who were close to him and the many friends he had made across the country and around the world. He could be sentimental, generous and empathetic to a degree that may sometimes have led him to make imprudent or incautious decisions.

He could be fiercely loyal. That loyalty earned him devotion, but it also had costs. John Tower was Bush's mentor and the victim of false and exaggerated accusations. He was not treated fairly in either his congressional confirmation hearings or in the sensationalized media coverage that accompanied his nomination. But there were also real questions about his history with alcohol and his personal conduct. There were reasons why he had two divorces and very few friends on Capitol Hill. Given the controversy the nomination generated and the mixture of fair and unfair criticisms that arose, it would have been easy to withdraw Tower's name, end the news media frenzy that was damaging Tower's reputation—and by association the president's—and move on to another nominee. Plenty of close aides and experienced Washington observers advised Bush to do exactly that. He dismissed their advice and stuck with his friend until the very bitter end.

George Bush, as Peggy Noonan observes, may have cared more about people than he cared about ideas. John Tower aside, he assembled a remarkable team of foreign policy players in the White House and in vital cabinet positions. Brent Scowcroft could provide the strategic thinking that the president needed. Jim Baker was an accomplished Washington hand and a superb negotiator who was strengthened in his negotiations by his long friendship and close association with the president. Dick Cheney was confident and competent, and always willing to offer candid advice. If that advice was considered and not taken, he reliably implemented the president's final decisions. Colin Powell brought broad political and national security experience to the newly enhanced role of Chairman of the Joint Chiefs of Staff and deeply appreciated working for a president who listened carefully before making his decisions about the use of military force. Bob Gates was a consummate bureaucrat with extensive experience in government that helped him bring disparate departments together for serious deliberations. The quality of the Bush administration's senior advisers on foreign policy, and of the staff members who served them, was unusually high. Many of the people who worked for the first Bush administration report that it was the best experience they ever had in public service.[3] Bush collected skilled people and then got them to work effectively together. They had vigorous policy disagreements and disputes, but did very little backstabbing, leaking or foot-dragging in the implementation of policy. This is what all presidents want, but what very few are able to achieve.

How did Bush assemble and keep this very effective foreign policy team? This is one of the most important questions about the first Bush presidency. The most common answer is that it was the product of long and uniquely varied experience in government. Bush had spent many years, in different roles, working with international issues and foreign policy professionals. He knew the players in the Nixon, Ford and Reagan administrations. Unlike many modern presidents who move into the White House after success in a governor's mansion or a congressional career, Bush had limited experience in elective office. Instead he worked at the United Nations, at the CIA and as a diplomat in China. His eight years in the vice presidency gave him an insider's view of the Reagan White House even if he had limited responsibility for important decisions. Experience matters, and Bush had a famously robust résumé before his successful run for the presidency in 1988.

But it is hard to believe that the cohesion and success of his foreign policy team was merely a matter of the president's prior experience. Both Lyndon Johnson and Richard Nixon had extensive experience in Washington, including service as vice president, before assuming the presidency. They did not organize or use their foreign policy advisers in the way that Bush did. In fact, Nixon was the model for what Bush wanted to avoid. Bush had seen the epic, and sometimes public, struggles among senior foreign policy advisers in the Nixon administration and disliked that kind of division. He sometimes found himself in the middle of disputes between the NSC and the State Department during his time in China and at the UN. He didn't like it, and he didn't like it any better when he saw a similar dynamic of dysfunctional disputes between the secretary of defense and secretary of state in the Reagan administration.

Bush did not create a highly successful foreign policy team simply by having years of experience and knowledge of the people involved. He did not do it by inspiration. He wasn't—and knew he wasn't—an inspirational leader. Bush built his team through personal relationships: friendship and acts of kindness. He set an example for hard work, shared credit for success, showed a ready sense of humor and treated people with respect. He earned the good work and support of his advisers by modeling the behavior he wished to see from them and creating a comradery that is rarely seen in modern presidential administrations. Bush worked hard at getting the best from those around him. And he applied many of the same qualities to the personal diplomacy that he practiced with American allies and with some of our former adversaries. Long after leaving office, Mikhail Gorbachev, reflecting on the world leaders he had known and worked with, said, "Bush was the best. He was a reliable partner; he had balanced judgment, and he had decency. He had the qualities that were and are critical to trust, and trust is what makes it possible to solve any international problem."[4]

At the beginning of this book we considered the commonplace observation that character counts in the understanding and evaluation of presidential behavior. It is not the only factor, or even the most important factor, in explaining foreign policy outcomes. But it matters. Deliberations about national security will always need to be carried out carefully, with the best available information, serious consideration of alternative courses of action and strategic frameworks that shed light on how the world works and what can be accomplished in a given set of circumstances. Policymaking is primarily an intellectual exercise. But there is more to it than that. There is a personal dimension to the processes by which deliberations are conducted and to the decisions that are ultimately made. That dimension often makes a difference. It probably made a bigger difference for a president who worked hard throughout his public life to support and appreciate the people around him and who received in response an unusual level of loyal and collaborative service. Bush combined a modest personal manner and cautious public rhetoric with constant attention to friends and friendship. He brought to the White House a high level of ambition and an underappreciated willingness to take big risks in pursuit of worthy goals. His character had consequences.

NOTES

1. Jeffrey A. Engel, *When the World Seemed New* (Boston: Houghton Mifflin Harcourt, 2017), 484.

2. Peggy Noonan quoted in Kitty Kelly, *The Family: The Real Story of the Bush Dynasty* (New York: Doubleday, 2004), 487.

3. As just one example, Bob Gates writes the following: "Through my entire career, I never had more fun or enjoyed as much personal and professional satisfaction as during the nearly three years I spent in the Bush White House as Deputy National Security Advisor." Robert M. Gates, *From the Shadows* (New York: Simon & Schuster, 1996), 453.

4. Gorbachev quoted in Roman Popadiuk, *The Leadership of George Bush: An Insider's View of the Forty-First President* (College Station: Texas A&M University Press, 2009), 145.

Bibliography

Alfonsi, Christian. *Circle in the Sand: Why We Went to War in Iraq*. New York: Doubleday, 2006.

Baker, James A., III. *The Politics of Diplomacy: Revolution, War, and Peace 1989–1992*. New York: G. P. Putnam's Press, 1995.

Barber, James David. *Presidential Character: Predicting Performance in the White House*. 4th edition. New York: Routledge, 2017.

Barnes, Fred. "Tottering Tower," *The New Republic*. December 19, 1988.

Beschloss, Michael R. and Strobe Talbott. *At the Highest Levels: The Inside Story of the End of the Cold War*. Boston: Little, Brown and Company, 1993.

Bolger, Daniel P. *Savage Peace: Americans at War in the 1990s*. Novato: Presidio Press, 1995.

Bose, Meena and Rosanna Perotti, eds. *From Cold War to New World Order*. Greenwood, CT: Greenwood Press, 2002.

Brands, H. W. "George Bush and the Gulf War of 1991." *Presidential Studies Quarterly* 34, no. 1 (March 2004).

Brune, Lester H. *The United States and Post-Cold War Interventions: Bush and Clinton in Somalia, Haiti, and Bosnia 1992–1998*. Claremont, CA: Regina Books, 1998.

Buckley, Kevin. *Panama: The Whole Story*. New York: Simon and Schuster, 1991.

Bush, Barbara. *A Memoir*. New York: Scribner, 2003.

Bush, George H. W. *Looking Forward*. New York: Doubleday, 1987.

———. *All the Best: My Life in Letters and Other Writings*. New York: Scribner, 1999.

———. *Speaking of Freedom: The Collected Speeches*. New York: Scribner, 2009.

———, and Brent Scowcroft. *A World Transformed*. New York: Alfred A. Knopf, 1998.

Bush, George W. *41: A Portrait of My Father*. New York: Crown Publishers, 2014.

Campbell, Colin and Bert Rockman, eds. *The Bush Presidency: First Appraisals*. Chatham, NJ: Chatham House, 1991.

Cheney, Dick. *In My Times*. New York: Threshold Editions, 2011.

Chernus, Ira. *Eisenhower's Atoms for Peace*. College Station: Texas A&M Press, 2002.

Cohen, Herman J. "Intervention in Somalia." Allan Goodman, ed. *The Diplomatic Record, 1992–1993*. Boulder, CO: Westview Press, 1995.

Coll, Alberto. "The Problems of doing Good: Somalia as a Case Study in Humanitarian Intervention," Case 518, Pew Case Studies in International Affairs, Institute for the Study of Diplomacy, Georgetown University, 1997.

Cramer, Richard Ben. *What It Takes*. New York: Random House, 1992.

———. *Being Poppy*. New York: Simon & Schuster, 1992.

Diebel, Terry. "Bush's Foreign Policy: Mastery and Inaction." *Foreign Policy*, no. 84, (Fall 1991): 3–23.

Dinges, John. *Our Man in Panama*. New York: Random House, 1990.

DiPrizio, Robert C. *Armed Humanitarians: U.S. Interventions from Northern Iraq to Kosovo*. Baltimore: The Johns Hopkins University Press, 2002.

Duffy, Michael and Dan Goodgame. *Marching in Place: The Status Quo Presidency of George Bush*. New York: Simon & Schuster, 1992.

Elvin, John. "Investigators Couldn't Catch Tower With Pants Down." *Insight*. March 27, 1995.

Encyclopedia of U.S. Foreign Relations. Vol. III. Bruce Jentleson and Thomas Paterson, eds. Oxford: Oxford University Press, 1997.

Engel, Jeffrey A., ed. *Into the Desert*. Oxford: Oxford University Press, 2013.

———. "Bush, Germany, and the Power of Time: How History Makes History." *Diplomatic History* 37, no. 4. (2013).

———. *When the World Seemed New: George H. W. Bush and the End of the Cold War*. New York: Houghton Mifflin, 2017.

Feldman, Leslie D. and Rosanna Perotti, eds. *Honor and Loyalty: Inside the Politics of the George H.W. Bush White House*. Westport, CT: Greenwood Press, 2002.

Frank, Jeffrey. "Twenty-Five Years After Another Gulf War." *The New Yorker*. July 16, 2017.

Garment, Suzanne. *Scandal: The Culture of Mistrust in American Politics*. New York: Random House, 1991.

———. "The Tower Precedent." *Commentary*. May 1989.

Garthoff, Raymond L. *The Great Transition: American-Soviet Relations and the End of the Cold War*. Washington, DC: The Brookings Institution, 1994.

Gates, Robert. *From the Shadows: The Ultimate Insider's Story of Five Presidents and How They Won the Cold War*. New York: Simon & Schuster, 1996.

Gilboa, Eytan. "The Panama Invasion Revisited." *Political Science Quarterly* 110, no. 4 (Winter 1995–1996).

Glennon, Michael. "The Gulf War and the Constitution." *Foreign Affairs* 70 (Spring 1991): 84–101.

Gorbachev, Mikhail. *Memoirs*. New York: Doubleday, 1995.

Graubard, Steven. *Mr. Bush's War: Adventures in the Politics of Illusion*. New York: I.B. Tauris, 1992.

Greene, John Robert. *The Presidency of George Bush*. Lawrence: University Press of Kansas, 2000.

Haass, Richard H. *War of Necessity, War of Choice: A Memoir of Two Iraq Wars*. New York: Simon & Schuster, 2009.

Hess, Gary R. *Presidential Decisions For War: Korea, Vietnam, and the Persian Gulf*. Baltimore: Johns Hopkins University Press, 2001.

Hersh, Seymour. "Our Man in Panama." *Life*. March 1990.

Hiro, Dilip. *Desert Shield to Desert Storm: The Second Gulf War*. New York: Routledge, 1992.

Hirsch, John L. and Robert B. Oakley. *Somalia and Operation Restore Hope: Reflections on Peacemaking and Peacekeeping*. Washington, DC: United States Institute of Peace Press, 1995.

Hudson, Miles and John Stanier. *War and the Media: A Random Searchlight*. New York: New York University Press, 1998.

Hurst, Steven. *The Foreign Policy of the Bush Administration: In Search of a New World Order*. London: Cassell, 1999.

Hutchings, Robert L. *American Diplomacy and the End of the Cold War: An Insider's Account of the U.S. Policy in Europe, 1989–1992*. Washington, DC: The Woodrow Wilson Center Press, 1997.

———. "The US, German Unification and European Integration," in Frederic Bozo, Marie-Pierre Rey, N. Piers Ludlow and Leopoldo Nuti, eds. *Europe and the End of the Cold War: A Reappraisal*. New York: Routledge, 2008.

Hybel, Alex Roberto. *Power Over Rationality: The Bush Administration and the Gulf Crisis*. Albany: State University of New York Press, 1993.

Isaacson, Walter. "Is One Germany Better Than Two?" *Time Magazine*. November 20, 1989.

Isikoff, Michael. "Psst: Inside Washington's Rumor Mill," *The New Republic*. January 2, 1989.

Jentleson, Bruce and Thomas Paterson, eds. *Encyclopedia of U. S. Foreign Relations, Vol. III*. Oxford: Oxford University Press, 1997.

Johnstone, Andrew and Andrew Priest, eds. *US Presidential Elections and Foreign Policy*. Lexington: University Press of Kentucky, 2017.

Kelly, Kitty. *The Family: The Real Story of the Bush Dynasty*. New York: Doubleday, 2004.

Kempe, Frederick. *Divorcing the Dictator*. New York: Putnam's, 1990.

King, James D. and James W. Riddlesperger, "The Rejection of a Cabinet Nomination: The Senate and John Tower." Meena Bose and Rosanna Perotti, eds. *From Cold War to New World Order*. Greenwood, CT: Greenwood Press, 2002.

Kolb, Charles. *White House Daze: The Unmaking of Domestic Policy in the Bush Years*. New York: The Free Press, 1994.

Kramer, Mark. "The Myth of a No-NATO-Enlargement Pledge to Russia." *The Washington Quarterly* 32, no. 2 (April 2009).

Lewis, Ioan and James Mayall. "Somalia." James Mayall, ed. *The New Internationalism 1991–1994*. Cambridge: Cambridge University Press, 1996.

Maier, Charles S. *Dissolution: The Critis of Communism and the End of East Germany*. Princeton, NJ: Princeton University Press, 1997.

Matlock, Jack F., Jr. *Autopsy on An Empire: The American Ambassador's Account of the Collapse of the Soviet Union*. New York: Random House, 1995.

McCain, John. *Worth the Fighting For*. New York: Random House, 2002.

McEvoy-Levy, Siobhan. *American Exceptionalism and US Foreign Policy: Public Diplomacy at the End of the Cold War*. New York: Palgrave, 2001.

Meacham, Jon. *Destiny and Power: The American Odyssey of George Herbert Walker Bush*. New York: Random House, 2015.

Medhurst, Martin J., ed. *The Rhetorical Presidency of George H. W. Bush*. College Station: Texas A&M University Press, 2006.

Mermin, Jonathan. "Television News and American Intervention in Somalia: The Myth of a Media-Driven Foreign Policy," *Political Science Quarterly* 112, no. 3 (Autumn 1997): 39–61.

Mervin, David. *George Bush and the Guardianship Presidency*. New York: St. Martin's Press, 1996.

Mullins, Kerry and Aaron Wildavsky. "The Procedural Presidency of George Bush." *Political Science Quarterly* 107, no. 1 (1992): 31–62.

Naftali, Timothy. *George H. W. Bush*. New York: Times Books, 2007.

Natsios, Andrew. *U.S. Foreign Policy and the Four Horsemen of the Apocalypse: Humanitarian Relief in Complex Emergencies*. Westport, CT: Praeger, 1997.

Nelson, Michael. "James David Barber and the Psychological Presidency." *Virginia Quarterly Review* 56, no. 4 (Autum 1980).

———, and Barbara Perry, eds. *41: Inside the Presidency of George H. W. Bush*. Ithaca, NY: Cornell University Press, 2014.

Oberdorfer, Don. *The Turn: From the Cold War to a New Era*. New York: Poseidon Press, 1991.

Palazchenko, Pavel. *My Years With Gorbachev and Shevardnadze: Memoirs of a Soviet Interpreter*. University Park: Pennsylvania State University Press, 1997.

Parmet, Herbert S. *George Bush: The Life of a Lone Star Yankee*. New York: Scribner, 1997.

Pfiffner, James P. "Presidential Policy Making and the Gulf War." In *The Presidency and the Persian Gulf War*. Edited by Marcia Lynn Whicker, James P. Pfiffner, and Raymond A. Moore. Westport, CT: Praeger, 1993.

———. *The Character Factor*. College Station: Texas A&M University Press, 2004.

Podhoretz, John. *Hell of a Ride: Backstage at the White House Follies 1989–1993*. New York: Simon & Schuster, 1994.

Popadiuk, Roman. *The Leadership of George Bush: An Insider's View of the Forty-First President*. College Station: Texas A&M Press, 2009.

Powell, Colin. *My American Journey*. New York: Random House, 1995.

Pytte, Alyson. "Questions of Conduct Delay Vote on Tower." *CQ Weekly*. February 4, 1989.

Risse, Thomas. "The Cold War's Endgame and German Reunification: A Review Essay." *International Security* 21, no. 4 (Spring 1997).

Robinson, Linda. "Dwindling Options in Panama." *Foreign Affairs* 68, no. 5 (Winter 1989).

Robinson, Piers. "Operation Restore Hope and the Illusion of a Media Driven Intervention." *Political Studies*, 49, no. 5 (December 2001): 941–956.

Ropp, Steve C. "Panama's Defiant Noriega." *Current History* 87, no. 533 (December 1988): 417–420.

Rose, Richard. *The Postmodern President*, 2nd ed. Chatham, NJ: Chatham House, 1991.

Ross, Dennis. *Statecraft*. New York: Farrar, Straus and Giroux, 2007.

Rostow, W.W. *Open Skies: Eisenhower's Proposal of July 21, 1954*. Austin: University of Texas Press, 1983.

Roth, David. *Sacred Honor: Colin Powell*. New York: Harper Collins, 1993.

Rottman, Gordon. *Panama 1989–1990*. Elite Series 37. London: Osprey Publishing, 1991.

Rozell, Mark J. *The Press and the Bush Presidency*. Westport, CT: Praeger, 1996.

Sabato, Larry. *Feeding Frenzy: How Attack Journalism Has Transformed American Politics*. New York: Free Press, 1991.

Sarotte, Mary Elise. *1989: The Struggle to Create Post-Cold War Europe*. Princeton, NJ: Princeton University Press, 2009.

———. "'His East European Allies Say They Want to be in NATO': U.S. foreign policy, German unification, and NATO's role in European security, 1989–1990." *German Reunification: A Multinational History*. Frederic Bozo, Andreas Rodder, and Mary Elise Sarotte, eds. New York: Routledge, 2017.

Schweizer, Peter and Rochelle Schweizer. *The Bushes: Portrait of a Dynasty*. New York: Doubleday, 2004.

Sebestyen, Victor. *Revolution 1989: The Fall of the Soviet Empire*. New York: Random House, 2009.

Sheehy, Gail. *Character: America's Search for Leadership*. New York: William Morrow and Company, 1988.

Shevardnadze, Eduard. *The Future Belongs to Freedom*. New York: The Free Press, 1991.

Sifry, Micah L. and Christorpher Cerf, eds. *The Gulf War Reader*. New York: Random House, 1991.

Smith, Curt. *George H. W. Bush: Character at the Core*. Lincoln, NE: Potomac Books, 2014.

Smith, Jean Edward. *George Bush's War*. New York: Henry Holt, 1992.

Solomon, Burt. "Being a Good Manager Isn't Enough If You Can't Deliver a Good Speech." *National Journal*. May 27, 1989.

Sosa, Juan. *In Defiance*. Washington, DC: The Francis Press, 1999.

Sparrow, Bartholomew. *The Strategist: Brent Scowcroft and the Call of National Security*. New York: Public Affairs, 2015.

Stevenson, Jonathan. "Hope Restored in Somalia?" *Foreign Policy*, no. 91 (Summer, 1993).

Strobel, Warren. *Late-Breaking Foreign Policy: The News Media's Influence on Peace Negotiations*. Washington, DC: United States Institute of Peace Press, 1997.

———. "The CNN Effect," *American Journalism Review* 18, no. 4 (May 1996): 32–38.

Strong, Robert A. *Decisions and Dilemmas*. New York: M. E. Sharpe, 2005.

Sununu, John. *The Quiet Man: The Indispensible Presidency of George H. W. Bush*. New York: Broadside Books, 2017.

Szabo, Stephen F. *The Diplomacy of German Unification*. New York: St. Martin's Press, 1992.

Tiefer, Charles. *The Semi-Sovereign Presidency: The Bush Administration's Strategy for Governing Without Congress*. Boulder, CO: Westview Press, 1994.

Thompson, Kenneth W., ed. *The Bush Presidency, Part Two: Ten Intimate Perspective of George Bush*. Lanham, MD: University Press of America, 1998.

Tower, John. *Consequences*. Boston: Little, Brown, 1991.

Tucker, Robert W. and David C. Hendrickson. *The Imperial Temptation: The New World Order and America's Purpose*. New York: Council on Foreign Relations Press, 1992.

Turner, Stansfield. *Burn Before Reading: Presidents, CIA Directors, and Secret Intelligence*. New York: Hyperion, 2006.

Watson, Richard. *Presidential Vetoes and Public Policy*. Lawrence: University of Kansas Press, 1993.

Western, Jon. "Sources of Humanitarian Intervention." *International Security* 26, no. 4 (Spring 2002): 112–142.

Woodward, Bob. *The Commanders*. New York: Simon & Schuster, 1991.

———. *Shadow: Five Presidents and the Legacy of Watergate*. New York: Simon & Schuster, 1999.

Zelikow, Philip and Condoleezza Rice. *Germany Unified and Europe Transformed*. Cambridge, MA: Harvard University Press, 1995.

Index

abortion, 9, 19, 45
Abrams, Elliot, 55
Adelman, Kenneth, 22
Afghanistan, 29, 125
Africa, 35, 123, 124, 125, 127, 130, 131;
    Horn of Africa, 135, 137, 145
Air Force, US, 17
Air Force One, 42, 44
Ali Mahdi, Muhammad, 126, 133
Alliance for Germany, 86
Arab-Israeli conflict, 106
Arias, Arnulfo, 53
Armenia, 38
Armitage, Richard, 54
arms control, 7, 10, 11, 27, 28, 30–31,
    38–39, 41, 94
Arab-Israeli conflict, 106
Asia, 18, 108
Aspen, Colorado, 102
Aspin, Les, 115
The Atlanta Constitution, 11
The Atlantic Charter, 32
"Atoms for Peace," 38
atrocities, 107, 118
Austria, 41, 73
Aziz, Tariq, 116, 119

Baidoa (Somalia), 127, 128
Baker, Jim (James A. III), 10, 12, 23, 32,
    58, 62, 70, 74, 75, 79, 80, 81, 83, 86,
    88, 92, 93, 95, 101, 102, 103, 108, 110,
    111, 112, 113, 114, 115, 116, 118, 119,
    146; and "four principles," 79, 80
balance of power, 70
Balkans, 130, 134, 137, 144
Baltic republics, 84, 85, 87, 88, 94
Barber, James David, 2, 4
Barletta, Nicholas, 53, 54
Barr, Dan (Lieutenant Colonel), 44
Bartlett, Charles, 18

Beijing (China), 18
Beirut (Lebanon), 132
Bentsen, Lloyd, 9, 17
Berbera (Somalia), 125
Berlin (Germany), 72, 75, 76, 81, 89
Berlin Wall, 38, 45, 74, 75, 76, 77, 78, 79,
    85, 90, 91, 92, 95, 144
"beyond containment," 27, 28, 29, 33,
    36, 39, 41
bipartisanship, 12, 114
Blackwill, Robert, 33
Blakley, William, 9
Bonn (Germany), 82, 86, 92
Bosnia, 124, 128–129, 130, 134, 137
Boston University, 28
Boston, Massachusetts, 42
Boutros-Ghali, Boutros (Secretary
    General of the UN), 126, 130, 132
Brady, Nicholas, 10, 12
Brezhnev Doctrine, 31
Broder, David, 42
Brokaw, Tom, 7, 130, 137
Brussels (Belgium), 40, 41
budget and taxation, 7, 11, 12, 20, 43,
    88, 99, 104–106, 110, 116, 119
Bundestag, 79
Buren, Martin van, 43
Bush Presidential Library, 1, 28, 29, 136
Bush, Barbara, 136, 138
Bush, George H. W., 1; ambition, 3,
    146, 148; audacity, 116, 117, 118, 119,
    144; boldness, 28, 33, 34, 39, 40, 43,
    44, 55, 94, 113, 117, 119, 143; caution,
    3, 28, 36, 37, 42, 43, 44, 85, 89, 91, 94,
    101, 110, 143–144, 145, 146, 148;
    compassion, 4, 138, 145; courage,
    102, 106; decision making style, 94,
    103, 112, 113, 114, 117, 119, 144, 146,
    148; decisive, 60, 78, 108, 113, 144;
    deliberate, 75, 113, 144;

155

determination, 18, 19, 91, 145; early career, 9, 10, 50, 119, 143, 147; elections of, 2, 3, 9, 10, 43, 45, 55, 61, 99, 104, 116, 143, 145, 147; family, 8, 38, 45, 119, 131, 136, 138, 143; friends and friendship, 3, 4, 7, 10, 18, 19, 20, 23, 24, 44, 93, 112, 146, 147, 148; gentility, 63, 64; insight, 78, 91, 92, 95; kindness, 45, 138, 147; loyalty, 3, 4, 8, 18, 20, 22, 23–24, 45, 55, 146, 148; military service, 119, 143; moderation, 28, 29, 42, 43, 45, 46, 75; modesty, 1, 119, 146, 148; persistence, 42, 72, 91, 95; prudence, 3, 28, 32, 75, 76, 89, 116, 119, 143–144, 145, 146; reluctance, 43, 46; restraint, 76; reticence, 4, 29, 45, 46; rhetoric of, 27–29, 33, 34, 35, 36, 37, 41, 43–44, 45, 75, 76, 85, 102, 119, 144, 145, 146, 148; vice presidency, 10, 20, 43, 45, 53, 55, 58, 144, 147; vision, 29, 39, 42, 91, 144; youth and education, 45, 119, 143
Bush, George W., 45
Bush, Prescott, 38, 45

Camp David, 86, 87, 92, 102
Canada, 39, 87
Capitol Hill, 8, 11, 21, 43, 87, 105, 146
CARE, 138
Carter, Jimmy, 1, 8, 23, 51, 56, 125
Carvey, Dana, 116
Castro, 51, 53
Ceauşescu, Nicolae, 61, 84
Central America, 52, 53, 64
Central Command, 125
Central Europe, 30, 32, 38, 39, 40, 41, 42, 77, 80, 84, 87, 91, 94
Central Intelligence Agency (CIA), 50, 51, 53, 54, 55, 60, 133, 143; director of, 8, 143
"Chance for Peace," 38
Cheney, Dick (Richard), 18, 36, 37, 59, 60, 62, 102, 103, 104, 110, 112, 113, 115, 116, 146
China, 18, 19, 64, 147
Churchill, Winston, 30, 31, 32, 94
civil rights, 9, 10, 130
Civil Rights Act of 1964, 9

Clinton, Bill (William Jefferson), 3, 8, 18, 123, 124, 128, 129, 131, 132, 133, 134
CNN, 123, 127, 136
"CNN effect," 123, 135, 136
Coast Guard Academy, 28
Cold War, 29, 30, 31, 33, 34, 37, 38, 39, 41, 43, 64, 69, 71, 73, 78, 83, 90, 94, 95, 103, 104, 124, 125, 133; end of, 4, 24, 30, 33, 35, 45, 76, 89, 90, 91, 95, 143, 144; post–Cold War, 29, 123, 136; reconciliation, as term describing end of Cold War, 35, 36, 37, 76, 77
College Station, Texas, 27, 29, 37, 44
Columbia, 51, 53, 54
Combest, Larry, 13–14
"common European home," 31, 32, 38, 41
communism, 28, 33, 34, 35, 36, 37, 45, 53, 61, 70, 84, 86; Central Committee of the Communist Party, 70
Conference on Security and Cooperation in Europe (CSCE), 80
Congress, 4, 8, 11, 13, 15, 18, 21, 22, 31, 43, 52, 55, 58, 62, 87, 88, 99, 100, 104, 106, 108, 114, 115, 116, 118; midterm elections, 99, 100, 113, 114, 119
Connally, John, 9
Connecticut, 17, 28, 40
containment, 28, 33, 34, 36, 37, 109
Contras, 52, 53
Costa Rica, 53
Council of the Americas, 56
Cramer, Richard Ben, 43
Crowe, William (Admiral), 40, 59, 64, 115
Cuba, 51, 53, 55
Cuny, Frederick, 130
Curtis, Adam (Navy Lieutenant), 49, 59, 60, 63, 64
Curtis, Bonnie, 49, 59, 60, 63, 64
Czechoslovakia, 73, 84

Davis, Mark, 33, 42
de Gaulle, Charles, 86
Defense Department, 41, 117
Delvalle, Eric, 54, 55, 57
Demarest, David, 42

Democratic Party, 9, 114
Department of State, 54, 73, 75, 78, 81, 92, 101, 110, 129, 147
Desert Shield, 103, 104, 109, 111, 112, 115, 117, 145
détente, 33, 36, 38, 69
Deutsche Mark, 86
Diaz Herrera, Roberto, 54
Dinges, John, 53
Dodd, Christopher, 17
Dowd, Maureen, 50
drugs, 34, 49, 51, 52, 53, 54, 57, 61, 62, 64
Dukakis, Michael, 2, 3, 19

Eagleburger, Larry, 102, 127, 129, 132
East Germany (German Democratic Republic), 70, 72, 73–75, 77, 78, 80, 81, 84, 86, 88–89, 91
East-West Relations, 27, 28, 32, 39, 42, 43, 94, 95
Eastern Europe, 27, 28, 29, 31, 34, 35, 36, 38, 39, 42, 45, 69, 70, 71, 73, 76, 78, 79, 83, 84, 87, 90, 91, 93
Egypt, 100, 108
Eisenhower, Dwight, 27, 38, 40
El Salvador, 53, 56
embargo, 108, 145
Endara, Guillermo, 56, 57, 61
Engel, Jeffrey, 143, 144, 145
Estonia, 84
Ethiopia, 124, 125
Europe, 27, 28, 29–31, 32, 34, 35, 36, 38, 39, 40, 41, 42, 44, 45, 69–70, 71, 72, 73, 74, 75, 76–77, 78, 79–81, 82–83, 84, 85, 86, 87–88, 89, 90–92, 93–94, 107, 108, 130; European Community (EC) and European Union (EU), 72, 79, 83, 89, 108. *See also* Central Europe; Eastern Europe; Western Europe
"Europe whole and free," 41, 90

Farrah Aidid, Mohamed, 125, 126, 128, 133, 134, 135
FBI, 11, 12, 13, 14–16, 17, 21–22, 51
Final Settlement with Respect to Germany, 82, 89
First World War (WWI), 71, 83

Fitzwater, Marlin, 60
Florida, 54–55, 57, 61, 64
Ford, Gerald, 9, 24, 147
France, 72, 76, 80, 81, 82, 86, 87, 107
Friedman, Tom, 42
Fuller, Greg, 12, 20

Gallucci, Robert, 129
Gates, Robert, 24, 58, 62, 63, 78, 110, 112, 113
Geneva, 7, 11, 36, 38–39, 116
Genscher, Hans-Dietrich, 83, 88
Georgia, 19, 130
Germany, 32, 41, 43, 45, 69–71, 72–78, 78–79, 80–84, 85–89, 90–92, 93–94, 95, 99, 108, 113, 144; "the German question," 77; neutrality of, 82, 83, 91, 92; unification of, 45, 69–70, 71, 72, 73, 74, 75, 76, 77–78, 79, 80–82, 83–84, 85, 86–87, 88–89, 90–92, 93–94, 95, 99, 144. *See also* East Germany; West Germany
Gingrich, Newt, 105, 106
Giroldi, Moises (Major), 57, 58, 59, 63
Glaspie, April, 101
Goldwater-Nichols Act, 59
Goldwater, Barry, 9
Goodpaster, Andrew, 40
Gorbachev, Mikhail, 3, 27, 28, 29, 30, 31, 32, 34, 35, 36, 37, 38, 39, 40, 41, 44, 45, 69, 70, 71, 73, 74, 75, 76, 77, 78, 79, 83, 84, 85, 86, 87, 88–89, 90, 91, 92, 93, 94–95, 107, 148; and end of Cold War, 144; at Malta meeting, 79, 84, 85; reforms of, 29, 31, 32, 34, 35, 36, 39, 43, 76, 90; at Washington Summit, 70, 87, 93
Gore, Al, 10
Graham, Daniel, 22
Gramm-Rudman Act, 105
Gramm, Phil, 44, 104
Gray, C. Boyden, 12, 18
Great Britain, 72, 73, 76, 80, 81, 82, 86, 87, 113
Great Society, 9
Greene, John, 50
Gulf of Aden, 125
Gulf War,. *See* Persian Gulf War

158 *Index*

Gulf War ultimatum, 110, 111, 112, 113, 114, 115–116, 117, 118

Haass, Richard, 43, 102, 110–111
Haiti, 128, 129
Hamtramck, Michigan, 28, 42, 73
Havel, Vaclav, 84
Heflin, Howard, 17
Helena, Montana, 78, 92
Helms, Jesse, 54, 58
Helsinki Accords, 69, 70, 79, 80
Hempstone, Smith, 125, 126, 132
Hendrickson, David, 50
Hersh, Seymour, 54
Hirohito, 18, 20, 77
Hitler, Adolf, 117, 118
Holocaust, 117
Honecker, Erich, 73, 75, 79
Horton, Willie, 2, 3
House of Representatives, 9, 56, 104, 105, 115, 135, 143; House Intelligence Committee, 56; Speaker of, 21
Houston, Texas, 9, 10
human rights, 34, 102, 109, 118, 125
humanitarian, 123, 125, 127, 128, 129, 130, 132, 133, 134, 135, 137–138, 144, 145
Hungary, 40, 41, 43, 73, 84
Hurst, Steven, 50
Hussein, Saddam, 95, 99, 100–101, 102, 103, 106–107, 108, 110–111, 112, 113, 114, 115–116, 117–118, 119, 144, 145

INF Agreement, 30, 31, 40
Iran, 100, 108, 125
Iran-Contra scandal, 7, 10, 24
Iraq, 99, 100–103, 105, 106–110, 111, 112, 114, 115–116, 117, 118, 119, 130, 133, 144, 145
Iron Curtain, 27, 40, 64, 76, 94

Jackson-Vanik amendment, 37, 43, 44
Jackson, Bob, 17
Japan, 18, 20, 77, 108
Jeremiah, David (Admiral), 110, 129, 138
Jerusalem, 106, 107

John F. Kennedy Library Foundation, 106
Johnson, Lyndon, 1, 9, 147
Johnson, Phil, 138
Johnson, Robert (Major General), 109
Joint Chiefs of Staff (JCS), 40, 58, 59, 110, 111, 115, 129, 131, 132, 137, 146; Chairman of, 58, 59, 111, 115, 132, 146
Jordan, 107, 108
Justice Department, 8

Kassebaum, Nancy, 17, 22, 127, 130
Kelly, Tom (Lt. General), 60, 63
Kennan, George, 31, 136
Kennebunkport, Maine, 40
Kennedy, John F. (Jack), 1, 106
Kennedy, Ted, 12
Kenya, 125, 127
Kerr, Dick, 110
Kerry, John, 54, 116
Khrushchev, 33, 39
Kimmitt, Bob, 110
King, Larry, 116
Kismayo (Somalia), 127
Kohl, Helmut, 44, 74, 79, 80, 82, 83, 85–86, 88, 91, 92, 93
Krauthammer, Charles, 134
Kremlin, 73
Krentz, Egon, 75
Kurds, 130
Kuwait, 95, 99–100, 100–103, 105, 107, 108–110, 110–112, 113, 114, 116, 117, 118, 119, 133, 145

Lance, Bert, 23
Latin America, 35, 50, 55, 56, 64
Latvia, 84
Leipzig (East Germany), 74
Lewis, John, 130
Libutti, Frank (General), 131, 132
Libya, 53, 55
Lithuania, 84, 87, 93, 94
London (Great Britain), 32, 79, 87, 92, 93
London Declaration, 87
Los Angeles Times, 11
Lugar, Richard, 56

Mainz (Germany), 41, 42, 43, 76–77
Malta, 69, 76, 79, 85, 91, 92, 95
Marcos, Ferdinand, 54
Marxism, 35, 37, 53
McCain, John, 7, 13, 15, 17, 22
McClure, Fred, 19, 44
McGovern, George, 2
Mecca (Saudi Arabia), 108
Medellin cartel, 54
Mermin, Johnathan, 135
Miami, Florida, 54
Middle East, 43, 99, 101–102, 103,
    106–107, 108, 110, 114, 115, 117
Midland, Texas, 119
Miller Center, 1
Missouri, 23
MIT (Massachusetts Institute of
    Technology), 76
Mitchell, George, 19
Mitterrand, François , 20, 28, 40, 45, 76,
    77, 84, 91, 93, 107
Modrow, Hans, 75
Mogadishu (Somalia), 125, 126, 127,
    128, 130, 132, 133, 134, 135, 137
Mosbacher, Robert, 10
Moscow (USSR), 29, 32, 70, 71, 82, 84,
    85, 86, 88, 89
Mubarak, Hosni, 100, 101
Muhammad, Ali Mahdi, 126, 133
Mulroney, Brian, 39
Muse, Kurt, 55, 60

National Ethics Week, 12
National Guard, 113
National Journal, 28
National Security Council (NSC), 10,
    24, 58, 63, 69, 78, 86, 92, 101–102,
    110, 114, 129, 130, 131, 136, 137,
    147; deputy national security
    advisor, 92, 112; national security
    advisor, 27, 60, 71, 82
nationalism, 77, 92, 143
NATO (North Atlantic Treaty
    Organization), 28, 30, 31, 32, 38,
    40–42, 45, 69–70, 71, 72, 73, 76, 77,
    79, 80, 81, 82–83, 84, 85, 86, 87–89,
    91, 94, 113, 144; reform of, 87–88, 93,
    95
Natsios, Andrew, 138

Navy, US, 49, 119
NBC, 7, 15, 130, 136, 137
Nelson, Michael, 2
New Frontier, 9
New London, Connecticut, 28, 42
"New World Order," 90, 123, 133, 137,
    138, 144
New York, 126, 132
The New York Post, 11
The New York Times, 28, 32, 40, 42, 54,
    92, 106
Newsweek , 13
Nicaragua, 53, 56, 62
Nixon, Richard, 1, 2, 116, 134, 147
Nobel Peace Prize, 90
Noonan, Peggy (and "Noonanism"),
    37, 38, 41, 44, 146
Noriega, Manuel, 49–50, 51–53, 53–55,
    55–58, 59–61, 63, 64, 145
North American Free Trade Area, 129
North, Oliver, 53
Nunn, Sam, 10, 13–15, 15–16, 19, 20,
    115, 116

Oakley, Robert, 133
Ogaden region (Ethiopia), 125
Oder-Neisse Line, 79
Open Skies, 27, 38, 39, 40, 41, 85
Operation Provide Relief, 127
Operation Restore Hope, 123
Organization of Petroleum Exporting
    Countries (OPEC), 100
The Organization of American States,
    61
Ottawa (Canada), 85, 86

Palestine, 106
Panama, 42, 49, 50, 51–52, 53–55, 55–57,
    58–64, 124, 144, 145; 1903 Treaty,
    Panama and US, 51; elections in, 2,
    43, 53, 54, 55, 56, 57, 63; Panama
    Canal, 49, 50, 51, 52, 55, 56, 57, 61,
    62, 64; Panama Canal Treaties
    (1977), 51, 61; Panama City, 49, 58,
    59, 61; Panama Defense Forces
    (PDF), 49, 51, 52, 53, 54, 55, 57–58,
    59, 60, 62, 63, 64; Vatican embassy,
    in, 61
Paris (France), 79, 92

partisanship, 2, 3, 19, 21, 43
Paz, Robert (Lieutenant), 49, 59, 60, 63, 64
Pendergast, Tom, 23
Pentagon, 7, 10, 11, 16, 44, 55, 60, 100, 104, 109, 111, 112, 113, 114, 116, 117, 127, 129, 131, 137, 145
Persian Gulf, 62, 99–100, 102, 103, 104, 106, 107–108, 109, 110, 111, 112, 113, 114, 115, 119, 144, 145
Persian Gulf War (First Gulf War), 18, 24, 62, 100, 117, 133, 137, 144
Pfiffner, James, 3
Philippines, 54, 56
Poland, 28, 40, 43, 73, 80, 84, 86, 89
Powell doctrine (or Weinberger doctrine), 134
Powell, Colin, 58, 59–60, 62, 104, 109, 111, 112, 113, 118, 129, 131, 132, 134, 146
Primakov, Yevgeny, 107
Profile in Courage, 106

Quinn, Sally, 11

race, 45
Ramadan, 107, 108
Reagan, Ronald, 3, 7, 9, 10, 24, 27, 30–31, 37, 43, 45, 49, 52, 53, 54, 55, 58, 60, 104, 116, 125, 144, 146, 147
The Red Cross, 136
religious right, 13
Republican Party, 9, 13, 19, 45, 99, 116, 143; Republican National Convention, 114, 127; Republican Senate Campaign Committee, 9
reserves, US Army, 113
Reykjavik (Iceland), 31
Rice, Condoleezza, 32, 33, 35
Riyadh (Saudi Arabia), 103
Robb, Charles, 10
Robertson, Pat, 22
Romania, 61, 84
Roosevelt, Franklin, 1, 3, 32, 84, 90
Ross, Dennis, 92, 101
Rudman, Warren, 104, 105
Russia, 15, 126. *See also* Soviet Union

Sahnoun, Mohamed, 126

sanctions, 54, 55, 57, 61, 64, 99, 108, 110, 111, 113, 115, 117, 145
Sandinistas, 52
Saturday Night Live, 116
Saudi Arabia, 99, 100, 101, 103–104, 107, 108, 109, 110, 111, 112, 113, 119
Schlafly, Phyllis, 22
Schwarzkopf, Norman (General), 103, 104, 109, 112, 116
Scowcroft, Brent, 10, 32, 33, 35, 36, 39, 40, 62–63, 71, 73, 75, 78, 82, 92, 94, 95, 102, 110, 112, 113, 146
SDI (Strategic Defense Initiative or "Star Wars"), 10, 22
Second World War (World War II), 28, 32, 37, 38, 51, 71, 72, 77, 78, 79–81, 82, 83, 117, 118, 143, 144
Secretary of Defense, 7, 8, 10, 11, 12, 16, 18, 19, 20, 36, 54, 60, 101, 102, 109, 112, 147
Secretary of State, 10, 12, 32, 55, 62, 71, 81, 88, 92, 101, 103, 112, 114, 127, 147
Senate, 7–8, 9–10, 11–12, 13, 14, 15, 17, 19–20, 21–23, 43, 44, 104, 116, 143; Senate Intelligence Committee, 56; Senate Armed Services Committee, 7, 10, 13, 15–16, 17, 18, 19, 20, 21, 115; Senate Select Committee on Intelligence, 55; Senate Subcommittee on African Affairs, 127
Serbia, 130
Seventh Corps, 113
Shelby, Richard, 12
Shevardnadze, Eduard, 70, 74, 83–84, 88, 92, 93, 95, 103
Siad Barre, Mohammed, 124–126
Simon, Paul, 127
Smith, Curt, 95
socialism, 51, 93
solidarity, 28, 73
Somalia, 123–124, 124–126, 126–127, 128–132, 132–133, 134–135, 135–138, 144, 145
Sorenson, Ted, 8
Soviet Union (USSR), 27–28, 30, 31, 32, 33–34, 35, 36, 37, 38–39, 41, 43, 45, 69, 70, 71, 72, 73, 74, 75–76, 78, 79, 81–82, 83, 84, 86, 87–89, 90, 91, 92,

93–94, 103, 107, 108, 119, 125, 129, 143; Third Soviet Congress of People's Deputies, 86; US-Soviet Relations, 28–29, 33, 34, 80, 85. *See also* Russia

Spadafora, Hugo, 53, 54

Sparrow, Bartholomew, 115

Special Forces, 60

"Spirit of Geneva," 36

Stalin, 38, 84

Sub-Saharan Africa, 124, 125

Sununu, John, 11, 22, 60, 110

Supreme Court, 8

Tampa, Florida, 54

Teeter, Robert, 12

Temple Mount, 106

Texas, 8–10, 14, 15, 17, 19, 21, 27, 29, 33, 35, 37, 40, 42, 44, 119, 124, 143

Texas A&M University, 27, 29, 33, 34, 35, 36, 38, 39, 40, 41, 44, 85, 144

Tiananmen Square, 79

Thatcher, Margaret, 41, 45, 77, 91, 93, 94, 102

"this will not stand," 102, 108

Thomas, Clarence, 8

Thurman, Maxwell (General), 56, 58, 59, 60, 64

Torrijos, Omar, 51, 52

Tower, John, 7–8, 8–11, 12, 13–17, 18–22, 23, 24, 146; Tower Report, 10

Truman, Harry, 1, 23, 31

Trump, Donald, 1

Tucker, Robert, 50

Turkey, 108

Two-Plus-Four, 81, 82, 84, 86, 89

U-2, 39

U.S. News and World Report, 42

United Nations (UN), 29, 31, 32, 39, 61, 94, 103, 106, 107, 108, 114, 115–116, 118, 119, 123, 124, 126–127, 128, 130, 131, 132, 133, 134, 135, 136, 137, 144, 147; resolutions on Iraq, 103, 108, 116, 118; Security Council, of, 103, 106, 114, 115, 118, 133; and Somalia,

123, 126–127, 128, 130, 131, 132, 133, 134, 135, 137

University of Virginia, 1

Van Buren, Martin, 43

Versailles, 80

Vietnam War, 118, 134

Voting Rights Act of 1965, 9

Wall Street, 119

Warner, John, 13–14

Warsaw Pact, 30, 31, 70, 73

Warsaw (Poland), 73

The Washington Post, 17, 55, 126

Washington, DC, 9, 11, 18, 19, 20, 29, 50, 51, 59, 69, 79, 84, 87, 92, 100, 102, 112, 119, 125, 130, 131, 134, 136, 146, 147

Washington, George, 1

Washington Summit (May–June 1990), 69–70, 71, 72, 84, 87, 92, 93, 94, 95

Watergate, 143

Weinberger, Casper, 134

West Bank, the, 106

West Germany (Federal Republic of Germany), 30, 32, 41, 70, 72, 73–74, 75, 76–77, 78, 79, 80, 82, 83, 86, 89, 91

West Point, 133, 134

Western Europe, 27, 28, 30, 40, 76, 77, 78, 82, 83

Weyrich, Paul, 13, 14, 19, 22

Will, George, 42, 58

Wilson, Woodrow, 32, 144

Woerner, Frederick (General), 56

Wolfowitz, Paul, 102, 110

Woodward, Bob, 17, 21, 63

Worth, Tim, 16

Wright, Jim, 21

Yale University, 119, 143

Yalta, 80, 95

Yerevan, Armenia, 38

Zapata Petroleum Corporation, 119

Zelikow, Philip, 90

About the Author

Robert A. Strong is the William Lyne Wilson Professor of Political Economy at Washington and Lee University and was a Fulbright Scholar at University College Dublin for the 2013–2014 academic year. In 2005 he was a visiting scholar at the Rothermere American Institute at Oxford University. He earned his PhD at the University of Virginia and before W&L taught at Tulane University and the University College of Wales. In 1988–1989 he was an American Political Science Association Congressional Fellow and worked in the offices of Congressman Lee Hamilton and Senator Richard Lugar. His book publications include *Working in the World: Jimmy Carter and the Making of American Foreign Policy* and a second edition of *Decisions and Dilemmas: Case Studies in Presidential Foreign Policy Making Since 1945*. From 2008 to 2013 he served in senior administrative positions at Washington and Lee. He has published essays in a variety of regional and national newspapers. Many of those essays can be found at: http://strong.academic.wlu.edu.